x, y, z, t: Dimensions of Science Fiction

BOOKS BY DAMIEN BRODERICK

Critical Reference

THE ARCHITECTURE OF BABEL: Discourses of Literature and Science

READING BY STARLIGHT: Postmodern Science Fiction

THEORY AND ITS DISCONTENTS

TRANSREALIST FICTION: Writing in the Slipstream of Science

Fiction

THE DREAMING DRAGONS

THE JUDAS MANDALA

VALENCIES (with Rory Barnes)

TRANSMITTERS

THE BLACK GRAIL

STRIPED HOLES

THE DARK BETWEEN THE STARS (ss coll)

THE SEA'S FURTHEST END

THE WHITE ABACUS

ZONES (with Rory Barnes)

STUCK IN FAST FORWARD (with Rory Barnes)

THE BOOK OF REVELATION (with Rory Barnes)

TRANSCENSION

THE HUNGER OF TIME (with Rory Barnes)

x, y, z, t: Dimensions of Science Fiction

DAMIEN BRODERICK

I.O. Evans Studies
in the Philosophy and Criticism of Literature
ISSN 0271-9061
Number Twenty 20

x, y, z, t: dimensions of science fiction
Copyright © 2004 by **Damien Broderick**
Cover design copyright © 2004 by **Sean Wallace**

Published in the United States by **Borgo Press / Wildside Press**
PO Box 301, Holicong, PA 18928-0301
www.wildsidepress.com

**I.O. Evans Studies in the
Philosophy and Criticism of Literature series: 20**
(ISSN 0271-9061)

HARDCOVER ISBN: 0-8095-0928-8
PAPERBACK ISBN: 0-8095-0927-X

For Barbara, with love

ACKNOWLEDGMENTS

For four decades, I have been a public reviewer and critic of science fiction, starting recklessly as a teenager in the Monash University newspaper *Chaos* (subsequently, under my co-editorship, *Lot's Wife*), moving on to professional reviewing in the Melbourne *Age*, the *Sydney Morning Herald*, the *National Times*, the *Age* again for a decade, *24 Hours*, *Australian Book Review*, and the Australian Broadcasting Corporation. Those were conversations with a general readership; I honed my critical skills among my sf friends and peers in samizdat journals such as *SF Commentary*, *Thyme*, *Australian SF News*, *The Notional* and the fabled second series of *Australian Science Fiction Review*. More recently, I've been fortunate to publish in such journals as the British *Foundation* and especially *The New York Review of Science Fiction*, the premier monthly magazine of commentary in the field. I am grateful to the editors of all these venues for supporting my critical work since 1963 or so, and for allowing me to draw upon some of that writing in this book. I am also happy to thank, for their continuing support, the Department of English and Cultural Studies at the University of Melbourne in Australia, where I have the good fortune to be a Senior Fellow, a post with no pay but no teaching duties. Thanks to Damien Sullivan, at Caltech, for reading the text and finding more than one horrid slip, and to Dave Langford and Phil Stephensen-Payne for turning up a misplaced citation. And of course I thank above all my delightful wife Barbara Lamar, for her love and encouragement, and for her generosity in creating (before we met) and maintaining (even afterwards) a website about my work at www.thespike.us.

PART I: THE SPACE OF VOLUPTUOUS CHOICE

0: LENGTH, BREADTH, DEPTH, DURATION

Real life, life at last laid bare and illuminated—the only life in consequence which can be said to be really lived—is literature, and life thus defined is in a sense all the time immanent in ordinary men no less than in the artist . . . Through art alone are we able to emerge from ourselves, to know what another person sees of a universe which is not the same as our own and of which, without art, the landscapes would remain as unknown to us as those that may exist in the moon. Thanks to art, instead of seeing one world only, our own, we see that world multiply itself and we have at our disposal as many worlds as there are original artists, worlds more different one from the other than those which revolve in infinite space . . .

Marcel Proust, *Time Regained* (931-2)

i

Science fiction—speculative fiction, syncretic fantasy—is the extreme narrative of difference, of *variation*.

That, at any rate, is its ambition. In commercial truth, it is largely a consumer literature—a telling—of audacious invention followed by ingenious variation followed by safe repetition, unto the fourth generation. At its best, the telling it tells is a tolling: the repetitive clang that alerts us, fires our nerves, steadies our gaze, with the message that something new and different has sprung upon us. At its worse, it is a machine for churning novelty into the comforting consolations of the familiar and impossibly gratifying.

Its best imaginative stories are told in full unblinking awareness of the true open dimensionality of space and time, by contrast with the provisional and largely contingent character of our own locality, our parochial epoch. At least those appear to be its possibilities. If the reality often falls short, it is hardly surprising. When our canvas is the entire cosmos across all of history past and future, stretched infinitely outward along the x, y and z dimensions of space, and up and down the long t of time, nobody should be distressed when poor human artists fail to do the text justice. Sometimes, though, the attempts are (to choose a word at once paradoxical and appropriate) *magical*. Science fiction, told right, can make your head and heart ring like a bell.

This is the narrative form that insists above all: new spaces and times, new ways of being, await us. These are the exotic places and states humans might enter, even if we begin by paving the earth over and remaking ourselves into posthumans.

Consider this raw poetry of the scientific imagination, penned by the late Carl Sagan decades ago for his book *The Cosmic Connection* (1975):

> There is a place with four suns in the sky—red, white, blue, and yellow; two of them are so close together that they touch, and star-stuff flows between them.
>
> I know of a world with a million moons.
>
> I know of a sun the size of the Earth—and made of diamond.
>
> There are atomic nuclei a mile across that rotate thirty times a second . . .
>
> There are stars leaving the Milky Way. There are immense gas clouds falling into the Milky Way . . .
>
> There are, perhaps, places outside our universe. (51)

That is not fiction, but simple reality—a kind of reality we have known only for a century, indeed perhaps only for half a century. Tomorrow's deathless humans will go there, into that extreme void, to gaze upon the diamond stars and the million moons. Here and now, long before that wonderful era opens, we can go with them in imagination.

And what we find there might not be all gushing astonishment and awe. Reality bites, even in science fiction—*especially*, perhaps, in sf. There is an underside to the human soul that finds its shadow in strange places. It will walk with us as we step from the airlock of the starship, through the portal of the time machine, exploring all the dimensions of spacetime's relativistic chart: the x and the y and the z of space, the t of time.

Readers who love traditional or mainstream or literary fiction, with its warm, desperate, always complicated characters, sometimes regard science fiction tales with suspicion. Can we actually relate to these odd, oddly imagined people and their futuristic worlds, their impossible powers over space and time, their silver jumpsuits and alien predators? Luckily, that's an erroneous and outdated impression. Like all compelling fiction, the best sf is about people. Unless you can be seized imaginatively by the characters (even if they are robots, or intelligent heart-broken squids), unless you can share a measure of empathy or loathing for them, no story can be successful. Human nature, however twisted by difference and technology it might become, can be the vital touchstone in an alien world.

Science fiction is the mystique of the outlandish, the dizzying, the variant, the large unknown region of search space. And that is everywhere around us in a time like this, an era of unprecedented change. No wonder science fiction is enjoying such a surge of popularity even as its best work is often lost to memory. Disorientation is itself part of the thrill, the addictive zing. Discomfort, exhaustion, sheer *foreignness* are a large part of what makes us tingle with anticipation at the prospect of heading out into the unknown, into the exotic, where we find ourselves energized, imagination and joy rekindled. And the stifling heat and freezing chills, the unappealing smells, the dismal waiting, the loneliness and anxiety of strange places without anything familiar to grab on to for solace . . . Like the best art, it is exactly what makes life piercingly poetic, if we're to believe that wise old Russian formalist, Viktor Shklovsky: `art exists to make us recover the sensations of life; it exists to make us feel things, to make the stone *stony*' (cited Scholes, 1974, 83).

Nothing makes a stone more stony than having one stuck in your shoe in the middle of nowhere.

In the last few decades, alas, huge industries have emerged to smooth the stones, in reality and fiction alike. The world stands in risk of being homogenized. Blanded into an episode of *Big Brother* or *Survivor.* Luckily, imagination isn't so easily trapped. Even if the whole earth sometimes seems doomed to a future of global uniformity, other places—Carl Sagan's astonishing planets and stars among them—lie in wait to bite. Some of them hang over our heads, in the deeps of space where we and our machines have just begun to step. Think of Sojourner, crawling years ago in the red dust of Mars, as we watched at home on TV over its solar-cell shoulder! Other places, no less peculiar, quiver in the long-lost past and the far future, or peer at us sideways from the shadows of worlds that might have been.

And even this apparently familiar world of ours isn't so easily subdued, for that matter. Away from the secure pathways, strange and slightly twisted locales wait to seize us, to make us tremble or sigh. We know too much today to take anything for granted. Think of the deep desert's profound solitude which increasingly evades us, snug in our cities. Even in our happiest garden moments, we deny ourselves (unless we go searching, travelers in the last wildness) the sight, say, of a remote Australian desert in flood, an ice mountain calving into the Greenhouse ocean. Today we may venture into such silence, stand under the awesome monolith of Uluru or enter the cold wastes of Antarctica. If we do go there, though, in reality or in prompted imagination, we voyage differently today, for we *know* even as we *feel*, as we gasp. To the city-dweller, those deserts are not merely alien and terrifying vacancy—they hold a history measurelessly deeper and more mysterious than any sacred writing has glimpsed. Floods appalling, thousands of years in duration. Landscapes broken into fire by comets smashing down from frigid space. Animals we know today only from their bones and scraps of their DNA.

But science fiction's imagination allows us even greater liberties: travel to all the worlds of the solar system and far beyond, all times from Big Bang to the exhaustion of unending time, and perhaps outside time itself. Sf uses a blend of romantic palette and gritty science, of whimsy and satire, of unchecked *possibility*. Such stories unfold themselves as they build their skewed worlds, and each carries its special frisson: of startlement, or laughter, or rueful irony, or hard political realism.

ii

Not everyone acknowledges this exhilarating perspective. Hard at work on her award winning novel *Reaching Tin River* (1990), the distinguished Australian novelist Thea Astley was afflicted most painfully: `I was terrified,' she told a journalist, `that it would turn into scifi.' In the event she was spared this gruesome fate, though it was about as likely as a landscape artist finding her paintbrush pouring forth a sestina, or a tensor equation. Late science fiction is a narrative form so sophisticated you can't stumble into it by mistake—only into its *derrière-garde* parody. True, most sf or fantasy on news-stand displays is neither artistic nor scientific. It is commercial white bread, grainless and starch-filled, equivalent to the busty romance or made-for-TV thriller. I doubt Ms. Astley, even in the darkest night of the soul, suspected her book might turn into that sort of *product*.

Science fiction, the pure quill and sometimes its smudged counterfeit, is our topic: speculative fiction, sf, even `sci fi', a term generally abominated by science fiction devotees even as it has become the default consumer term for everything gaudy and preposterous from *Stars Wars* mega-movies to unstoppable franchise lines. Back in 1978, Isaac Asimov—the very embodiment of the mode—observed: `We can define "sci-fi" as trashy material sometimes confused, by ignorant people, with s.f. Thus, *Star Trek* is s.f. while *Godzilla Meets Mothra* is sci-fi' (*Asimov on Science Fiction*, 28). More austere than Dr. Asimov, I would include *Star Trek* as well under that rubric, which doesn't mean that I don't enjoy it some-times. Enthusiasts steeped in traditional sf have now adopted `sci fi' (sometimes pronouncing it `skiffy') in self-defense—as shorthand for *pseudo*-sf kludged together by, and for, the placid grazers: exactly the sort of pap *product* that artists such as Ms. Astley deplore. Is the prevalence of *sci fi* necessarily a bad thing? Decades ago, the brilliant sf innovator Alfred Bester remarked with terrifying kindliness: `As for second-rate, commer-cial writing—ass-licking writing, as it were—what's the harm in that? Good god, people who read books in subways don't want to be startled too much, they like nice convenient stories . . . Good for them, good for all of them, that's great' (in Platt, 1983, 244).

Rather inconsistently, as often as I praise its x, y, z and t possibilities, I intend also to sink my boot into the genre. As the years unfurl along my personal t dimension—as the *decades* lumber past—I find myself increas-ingly in the role of a disillusioned priest or witch doctor, now turning his inside knowledge to use as a participatory anthropologist, trying to defend some barbarous piece of idiocy while knowing with a sinking heart that the faith is altogether lost. This assessment is incomplete, luckily, though you can catch yourself thinking that way on gloomy days. Sf is not just a childhood virus that kids catch and throw off after a brief temperature. Nor is it the logomachy of the academic seminar conducted by other means. It is an entire spectrum of narrative choices, an imaginative palette ranging from *X-Men* and Douglas Adams to Philip K. Dick and Olaf Stapledon, Joanna Russ and Ursula Le Guin and John Crowley. Any stark skeptical dichotomy catches the ultraviolet and infrared, but loses the rainbow.

In any case, the very best sf does not repudiate extremes; it appeals to something eager and open within the crustiest adult heart even as it dazzles the mind with the riches of abstract knowledge and the hard, constrained ambitions of scientific practice.

And that is true even when it falsifies our current view of the universe, because science itself insists that we know very little, and will know a great deal better by and by.

`We are the Smart Alecks,' encyclopedist Peter Nicholls stated more than two decades ago, in a feisty lecture at London's Institute of Contemporary Arts. `We take our metaphors from all over, from geology, dress design, traditional literature or relativity physics. We feel free to mix our fundamentally academic observations with an ironic raciness of manner' (*Explorations of the Marvellous,* 165-6). To the haughty academic world of criticism and theory, sf smacked of acne cures and lonely Saturday nights. That estimate was not altogether wrong then, and has become more apt since the triumph of *Star Wars, Total Recall* and groaning bookshelves of lucrative consumer fantasy fodder. `Academic readers dislike us for our vulgarity,' Nicholls the wry scholar observed, drawing deeply on an experience of exclusion known keenly by sf fans everywhere, but most sharply, perhaps, in Australia, `while ordinary readers dislike us for our constant display of our own cleverness' (166).

Wishing to advance the prospects of his chosen genre, Nicholls sought ways to cut through prejudice and self-erected hazard alike. Everyone would benefit, he decided, if he and his Smart Aleck mates made their judgements `in a level, friendly tone, veering neither towards condescension on the one hand nor obscurantism on the other' (166). He had in mind especially his Anglo-Canadian colleague John Clute, who had written previously, with resigned contempt, of genre sf's `mild ignorant readership'. The genre remained a problem for many sophisticated adult readers. Sf continues to be ignored or disliked by readers trained to enjoy literary or `canonical' texts while detesting anything else. I am inclined to view this disdain as a sort of learned incompetence, a bigotry that wounds its practitioners as much as its victims. More than one literary Australian journalist has asked me, in genuine puzzlement, `Why do you like science fiction when everyone else hates it?' This strange claim flies in the face of solid sales of sf and fantasy in a time when literary fiction struggles to survive. Worse, it ignores the striking realities of popular culture. Of the top-earning movies of all time, the majority are science fiction or fantasy. True, this is largely `product' tailored for unreflecting and sentimental teen consumers and, as we shall see, *real* sf is now in peril. But it can hardly be said that everyone hates sf when there's scarcely anything that viewers love more.

Sf's delight in sheer imagination blends magical escapism with an all-too-realistic awareness of the impact on our world of incessant techno-logical upheaval. Mass media versions of sf inevitably debase any subtle play with either component, so it is not surprising that huge success at the box-office fails to translate into fame, fortune or even critical esteem for sf's best artists. After all, periods when the whole family routinely settled down to watch the latest western did not produce a surge of nuanced novels about existential cowboys. With sf, it is more complicated. Despite spectacular epiphanies of shaped light, no Spielberg movie or TV series about UFOs or dinosaurs can approach the cognitive delights of print sf, from A. E. van Vogt's baffling super-intelligent protagonists to William Gibson's cyberspace and today's venturing into technocalypse.

iii

More than forty years back, I smuggled sf magazines with their lurid covers under my childhood mattress and later in my junior seminary cell, the better to preserve their delights from the salvatory clutches of parents and priestly supervisors who knew it rotted your brain. Of course it *did* rot your brain. Here I am all these decades later, still snorting the stuff up my nostrils, although with a seasoned connoisseur's diffidence. Apparently, habituation set in long ago, and by some process which gives hope for our recuperative powers generally, I have developed a considerable measure of resistance. The stuff that set my brains and emotions on the boil when I was a child and adolescent (A. E. van Vogt, Wilmar Shiras, Zenna Henderson) makes me seethe instead today with impatience and despon-dency. And yet—

Something indelible was marked on my soul: a coiled galaxy viewed from the dark remoteness of eternity, a dinky silver spaceship smoothed and gleaming under the light of an alien sun, a batch of comic strip cartoons where misunderstood supermen strove to subdue an ungrateful world, or at least to preserve inviolate all those secondhand copies of *Science Fantasy* and *Galaxy* hidden under their mattresses.

Finally at 17 I reached university, sat at the feet of philosophers and literary scholars, and learned the error of my ways. Still, although my improving taste severed me from the pure infantile joy of primitive science fiction, there remained a sense of large possibility in sf's tropes. They were undeniably metaphors peculiarly relevant to an age of unprecedented change. Indeed, their central iconography summoned unfashionable sentiments—hope and awe, a certain access to what I had learned to recognize as the technological sublime—and at the same time a roguish anarchist spirit not quite like anything in even the hard-boiled school of popular writing.

So there is quite often something joyfully exuberant and romantic in sf, fatally kitschy to the cultivated. Like those heightened screen epics that star Charlton Heston or Kirk Douglas—Anthony Mann's *El Cid*, say, or Kubrick's *Spartacus*—sf may play with the consequences of huge change through the rhetoric of melodrama. But so does Wagner, and I do not find our cultural arbiters complaining about arrested adolescence as they pay through the nose for their opera tickets.

Long before Vietnam and Richard Nixon, Iraq and George Bush *pere* and *fils,* sf fans nosed out the specters of conspiracy, bureaucracy and bitter farce which is the post-industrial community.

What I find quite incredible to contemplate is how near I was, in those lost days of childhood and adolescence, to the very font of it all. It is like having been present at the birth of hieroglyphics or agriculture. If not the birth, its ripening. Arguably, 1953 was the greatest year in sf history. Or maybe it was 1952. A spectacular number of pivotal sf stories appeared in 1953, presumably written in the year before. Half a century later, the situation is otherwise. For a start, the objective circumstances of commercial sf were very different: in the middle of the twentieth century; an abundance of small specialized sf magazines with dedicated readers and writers blended for the first time the grand ideas of the 1930s and after with the comparative realism of editor John W. Campbell's Golden Age, together with a dawning ability to *write* with some of the skills of literature. These small outlets faced no powerful competition from special effects movies or routine TV space opera, although there were radio serials and flamboyant comics. Out of that vortex in 1953 came such stuff as dreams are made on: Theodore Sturgeon's *More than Human*, Arthur C. Clarke's *Against the Fall of Night* and *Childhood's End*, Ward Moore's *Bring the Jubilee*, Clifford Simak's *Ring Around the Sun*, Hal Clement's *Mission of Gravity*, Frederik Pohl and Cyril Kornbluth's *The Space Merchants*, Ray Bradbury's *Fahrenheit 451*, Alfred Bester's *The Demolished Man*, Isaac Asimov's *The Caves of Steel* . . . Short story writers bloomed: James Blish's sublime novella `A Case of Conscience' appeared and Clarke's `The Nine Billion Names of God'. One could go on and on. The mind genuinely boggles at the fecundity of the period. Almost all of it was the strange fruit of American pulp sf magazines. Perhaps the most unsettling explorer of anxiety in the whole genre was Philip Kindred Dick (names to satisfy any Lacanian), whose oeuvre is notoriously a colossal testimonial to ontological insecurity. In the miraculous year 1953, Dick produced 33 pieces, few of them brief. His theme, increasingly, and long before Jean Baudrillard, became the dialectic of reality and illusion, the insistence of the simulacrum, the denial of stability. At the end, Dick's fictive paranoia teetered on actual breakdown. His demented images, always anchored in utmost mundane stolidity, stare at us through the surfaces of our ordinary lives with a terrible ferocity. Only the skimpiest sense of this scarifying vision is conveyed through the dumbing-down lens of the movie makers who turned his name into a synonym for big budget sci fi extravaganzas: *Total Recall, Minority Report*.

Today, fifty years on, sophisticated print sf teeters, perhaps, on the edge of extinction. In 2001, *Asimov's* editor and writer Gardner Dozois recalled his 1995 trip to a World SF Convention in Glasgow:

> the British science fiction industry is in ruins . . . One well-known middle-level British writer says that the only way he can get a science fiction book into print in Britain any more is by disguising it as fantasy, changing what otherwise would have been aliens into vampires and werewolves. (2001, 74)

Yet the book traders, Dozois notes, told him that customers complain that they are sick of Celtic trilogies and horror, and crave sf instead. `Something is wrong here somewhere. But if the perception of the publishers that no one wants to read science fiction *is* wrong, there seems no way to convince the publishers of it' (74). *Can* publishers get it so wrong? Apparently so, due to their reliance on marketing tools appropriate to selling soap and peanuts and gasoline. Computer systems now routinely track book sales, effectively in real time, across chain outlets. Any item that sells less than the mean is pulled quickly and pulped. New authors and others trying something fresh and disconcerting vanish like the dew; their names are poisoned for their next submission. Mega-corporations seek certified bestsellers; authors strive to become safe brand names. Brian Stableford, premier sociologist of sf, observed some years ago:

> In the busiest outlets—like those in airports, which are browsed by hundreds of people per hour—the rates of sale can be measured so quickly that many titles need only be displayed for a matter of hours before it becomes clear that the rational decision is to replace them with something else . . . Given the tendency of paperback publishers to overproduce and the existence of the sale-or-return convention, it was inevitable that publishers would find their returns coming back much more quickly and much more prolifically . . . [W]hile the print-runs of paperbacks remained fairly steady the sales of all but a tiny fraction—almost certainly less than 10%—suffered a precipitous collapse. By 1990 . . . almost all of these low-advance titles were failing to earn out those advances or make any profit at all for their publishers. (Stableford, 2000, 47-8).

This fall into nescience by the marketing conglomerates has only accelerated, and afflicts all publishing, but marginal modes such as science fiction are especially at risk. It is possible that sf published beyond the borders of the United States Homeland, with its distinctive contribution to the expansive and liberating dimensions of the mode, might soon perish entirely.

iv

But British sf stories were what I found closest to hand in the 1950s and 1960s and even 1970s—Wells, of course, even in school, perhaps Conan Doyle and Rudyard Kipling; and then the cream of the often tawdry stuff found in the Nova magazines (*New Worlds, Science Fantasy, SF Adventures*), John Brunner, J. G. Ballard, Brian W. Aldiss, James White, John Wyndham. The most canny of the adapted men wrote straight for the new homeland of this genre or mode created by Shelley and Verne and Wells and, it must be granted, Poe: Eric Frank Russell, with his wise-ass pseudo-American anarcho-capitalists snidely but firmly muttering `myob' (`mind your own business') to interfering gummint busybodies, J. T. McIntosh (or sometimes, mysteriously, M'Intosh) who also knew how to make John Campbell's toes curl up, Arthur C. Clarke whose finest stories even more mysteriously seem to have been rejected by Campbell (surely not for their technophilia! surely not for their crypto-mysticism!) but found a home in, say, *Infinity Science Fiction* which took `The Star', arguably the most perfect short sf tale ever written.

Later, as the decades ground away, the writing sharpened and at the same time relaxed, the ideas grew a little more subtle, the terrain to be explored moved behind the eyes. M. John Harrison showed how the mode could harbor true art, but seemed until *Light* (2003) to have left it long behind, as perhaps was inevitable. No preposterous cardboard for him, not any longer. Aldiss, always nimble, grew older and his craft stranger, enigmatic, detestable, perhaps, to the taste buds of most American consumers. Christopher Priest abandoned accountancy for literature, taking a byway through the skiffy archipelago. Bob Shaw, with his bracing meat-and-potatoes name and wry but direct narrative growl, fetched out one solid invention after another, if rarely anything as, well, transparent and long-lasting as slow glass, his great preposterous lamination.

In the fullness of time the UK bore scholarly and whimsical children forth: Ian Watson, a brain fuming on the stove with bursting bubbles, Brian Stableford with unexpected sexual chemistry amid musty scholarship and prodigious productivity, Mike Moorcock the large Ur-Father of everything New and Wavy and now Old and Forgotten (but assimilated, yes, fertilizing the land even in places where his name and seed are held anathema), and finally the British women: Josephine Saxton, blending Gurdjieff and other kinds of fancy in her capacious stockpot, Tanith Lee moving like a silver and black ghost amid landscape of horror and fantasy and science. And more: David I. Masson, the linguistic librarian like some Borges-upon-Avon, D. G. Compton in sweet and sour mood calibrating taped memory, pestish artificial intelligence, dire missionaries from space, the absolute remorseless media landscape of a reporter's unsleeping eye tracking a dying woman to her last gasp for the delectation of undying millions—D. G. Compton, indeed, persuading some hapless UK publisher to allow him to title a time travel novel *Hot Wireless Sets, Aspirin Tablets, the*

Sandpaper Sides of Used Matchboxes, and Something that Might Have Been Castor Oil.

I did a quick comparison of the populations of the USA, UK and Australia, and found a rough ratio of 77:18:5. When I counted from Abbott through Jones among my sf paperbacks, I found 74.3 percent were Americans, 21.6 percent British, and the rest were . . . well, everyone else. David Pringle's British tally of the 100 best sf novels in English since Orwell lists 75 from the USA, 24 from the UK, one Australian (mine, as it happens). So the proportions hold up: somewhere between a fifth and a quarter of the best sf has been by British writers, a little greater than their numbers and low commercial visibility might suggest. An American, however, would perhaps provide a different weighting.

There they stretch in the archives, from Sir George Tomkyns Chesney and his prophetic *The Battle of Dorking*, Erwin A. *Flatland* Abbott, Richard Jefferies, Robert Barr, George Griffith, Wells and Kipling and J. D. Beresford whose 1911 *The Hampdenshire Wonder* beat Stapledon's *Odd John* to the high-IQ superman punch and is unjustly forgotten (well, but also pretty unreadable, especially if you're not a cricket-playing Englishman), and S. Fowler Wright and Stapledon himself communing with the god of cosmological gaps, and Gerald Heard who thought flying saucers must be piloted by bees (Dennis Wheatley, his friend, took up the notion in one of his thick awful novels). Then the leap to the true thing, what we know when we point to it: `Hobbyist' by E. F. Russell, that early shaggy-god story written in a grating pseudo-Yank voice that is, again but even more so, almost unreadable today, at least by me. The lone astronaut is stuck on some out-of-the-way planet, out of fuel and out of luck:

> Steve pulled an ugly face and said, `Darn!'
> The face didn't have to be pulled far. Nature had given said pan a good start. That is to say, it wasn't handsome . . . Well, he wasn't going to feel at home anymore; not unless this brooding jungle held intelligent life dopey enough to swap ten-gauge nickel-thorium wire for a pair of old boots. (in James Gunn, *The Road to Science Fiction, Vol. 5*, 216)

And so on, more than half a century ago in *Astounding Science Fiction.* The voices mutated somewhat as stories were bought by UK markets once more, as they had been in the time of Wells: astronomer Fred Hoyle, a sort of right-wing scientific triumphalist successor to Wells, those two hackmeisters John Russell Fearn (a.k.a Vargo Statten, a.k.a. Volstead Gridban) and R. L. Fanthorpe, John Christopher and William Temple. John `Ted' Carnell's somewhat thumb-fingered editorial hand nurtured other writers at *New Worlds* and *Science Fantasy* and *New Writings in SF:* Colin Kapp, with his Unorthodox Engineers and psychotic, misogynist supermen, John Rankin (Douglas R. Mason), Lan Wright, A. Bertram Chandler, E. C. Tubb (even more significant, and these days shamefully forgotten), that sturdy workhorse Kenneth Bulmer, Arthur Sellings, Dan Morgan, no doubt other reliables.

Thirty years later, British writers sounded instead like this, as one aged spook speaks to another in a world where God has returned and is established in northern England, running endless convoys of trucks along His immense Causeway to some mysterious end:

> `. . . I grow orchids, and that is sufficient—in the old days I asked for nothing more; and you—why, you sit at a cafe table in Southend, or some *estaminet* of Antwerp, with perhaps more freedom than before to exercise your wit, your (if I may say so) rather impractical and gauzy cynicism . . .'
>
> He nodded slowly. `It is an argument. It is *the* argument . . . I have considered it. I chafe.' He gazed sadly out to sea, moved his hands. His face slackened, aged; for a brief moment, a hunger I can't describe illuminated his eyes, and I saw the whole superb pose, insouciance, iconoclasm and all, collapse into vacancy. (493)

Thus, M. John Harrison's `Settling the World'—published by one of the few Americans able to match him trope for trope at that time, a generation ago, Thomas M. Disch, in his notable anthology of skewed mythology, *The New Improved Sun* (1976). Nowadays, of course, everyone can write that well—everyone except the benighted writing machines churning out hexalogies and war-in-space series and routine fantasies, all the detritus of market success. Ambiguity and layering in every word. We are a long way from Eric Frank Russell's explosive farces (and how I loved them as a kid, how I bust a gut laughing), a long way from the self-satisfied civilities under convenient stress of John Wyndham.

Academic and writer James Gunn's sequence of anthologies, *The Road to Science Fiction*, attempted a definitive sampling of what he dubs `the characteristic fiction of our times' (1998, 9). Sometimes I find myself making the same lunatic critical bid, but then I get a grip on myself.

Certainly sf is one among many characteristic narrative inventions or turns of this last century. I don't think—and I doubt that James Gunn truly believes—that in the 25th century, art connoisseurs will place sf at the head of the list, or the heart of the bush, of our artistic attainments. Here's how Gunn launched his enterprise, back in *Volume 1: From Gilgamesh to Wells*, in 1977:

> Science fiction is the branch of literature that deals with the effects of change on people in the real world as it can be projected into the past, the future, or to distant places. It often concerns itself with scientific or technological change, and it usually involves matters whose importance is greater than the individual or the community; often civilization or the race itself is in danger. (1)

No greater danger exists to `the race' (that curiously olde worlde expression for the human species) than the risk we each face, and have never, so far, managed to evade: the looming threat of personal death. As Gunn closed his fifth volume with Stableford's tale of an ambiguous triumph over mortality, `And He not Busy Being Born,' he noted:

> The mainstream preoccupation with how people ought to behave in the face of inevitable death meets sf's concern with problem solving, to produce a new vision of immortality. (1998, 607)

The routine complaint about sf performed `the British way' is that it revels in gloom and entropy (Moorcock's mocking icon for the New Wave), in sardonic *fin-de-siecle* embrace of the grim reaper, in evasion of the optimistic fruits of high science and technology. I have never found this persuasive. The best sf from the United Kingdom has been as various as any in the world, but often it does escape the fatuity and one-dimensional Can-Do Galactic Conquest narrative vortices first stirred up by the pulp editors now all long laid to rest.

V

Fortunately there are ways to splice these traditions.

Gregory Benford has characterized Colin Greenland's rip-roaring space opera *Take Back Plenty* (1990), with its invocation of a kind of left-radical hard sf, as announcing `the lukewarm end of entropy-trans-fixed sf' (2003, 13). In *The Entropy Exhibition,* Greenland's spirited 1983 study of British New Wave sf, he had briskly depicted its dismal precursors. A typical tale of the early 1960s knew that `Women in space, like women at sea, are trouble. . . . When their space-liner is wrecked, Miss Krand's hysterical demands for attention infuriate and imperil the other survivors until one of the men comes up with a solution. They lobotomize her' (27). Disturbing, such glimpses into yesterday's tomorrows. In *Take Back Plenty,* Greenland tore up the last traces of that old rule book in a nonstop romp which rejuvenated a kind of story-telling that hit its nadir in *Star Wars,* with its Air Ace in Space mock heroics.

His tongue was not exactly in his cheek because the medium he colonized was over the top to start with, but he did not scruple to borrow back from Douglas Adams such wonderful absurdities as the Infinite Probability Drive (it takes you anywhere, but your engines are likely to turn into dead leaves or barking seals; you know the sort of thing). Tabitha Jute is a chunky, sexy, tough, competent but short-tempered driver of, well, space trucks. No sane man would take it into his head to lobotomize her, though inevitably she falls foul of several who try. With the aid of her trusty space truck *Alice Liddell,* a kind of mechanical *idiot savant,* she negotiates the wonderlands and looking-glass worlds of a solar system embargoed by the dread Capellans, whose giant smooth foreheads hide secrets that Woman Was Not Meant to Know.

There is a surprising measure of nuance, sense and sensibility in this good-natured Space Extravaganza (as its subtitle candidly describes it). Yet it really is sf as childhood regained: marooned in the steaming jungles of Venus, chased by little critters along the dredged canals of Mars, visiting the speaking dead on the orbital habitat Plenty, captured and (I am sorry to report) raped by pirates flying something like a gigantic spiny cactus leaf, breaking the solar system free of the ghastly clutches of the Capellans, their dog-muzzled Eladeldi space cops, their Frasque foe who stare like mad trees. . . . To tell you the truth, I kept drifting off and laying it aside. Even a *tour de force* of poker-faced parody that, yes, carries forward the classy space opera tradition of Delany's *Nova* (1968) and M. John Harrison's *The Centauri Device* (1975), not to mention the Australian radio serial *Captain Miracle* in the late-1950s, even a rip-snorting generic resuscitation of cosmic proportions can get dull for a grown-up reader. But it undeniably fits Greenland's account of postmodern sf: `It illuminates our enslavement to the idea of the future and to our own technology. It subdivides reality and adds provisional worlds, each flickering unsteadily, whose reflected light does not always draw our attention back to the source we know to be there' (1983, 190). Taken in bites, this sort of exuberant narrative is lush, demented, and greatly entertaining.

Greenland was not the first nor the last of the British writers to revisit space opera. Iain M. Banks made his reputation with several freaky post-modern novels of high-wire psychopathology. Without the middle initial, he erupted into British letters in the mid-eighties with such brio that Fay Weldon dubbed him `the great white hope of British Literature'. She had in mind *The Wasp Factory*, with its gristly psychopathic brilliance, and a handful of other technically adventurous mainstream titles. A closet sf fan, he was enabled by their success to publish a bounteous space opera, *Consider Phlebas* (1987), an exuberant amalgam of every big-screen science fiction invention since (and including) Larry Niven's Ringworld, a gold bangle the size of the Earth's orbit. With its T. S. Eliot title and its gaudy tale of interstellar conflict, it introduced a fully stocked universe as ample as anything in sf's alternative future histories. Banks has returned repeatedly to this delightfully detailed universe of a post-scarcity Culture. In *The Player of Games* (1988), for example, world-weary Jernau Gurgeh is apparently an amateur Culture expert in strategy and tactics, chockablock with specialized genofixed glands, nurtured (and perhaps owned) by whimsical and snide machines. Gurgeh is snookered into a hustle on a planetary scale; duped agent of his rich anarchist culture, he climbs the ranks of a barbarous game-structured society, learning something of empathy and involvement. His tale enveloped the story of a single intellectual combatant in the endless conflict between Banks's machine-loving hedonistic Culture (good) and its foes (pretty nasty): brutality, credulous faith, political hierarchy, war.

Perhaps Banks's finest sf novel to date, *Use of Weapons* (1990), is a drastically complex biography of a soldier taken from a world not unlike Czarist Russia and sent into the field again and again for centuries, supported with only the most ironic ambiguity by subtle Culture intelligences human and artificial. Frozen to death, he can be healed (if they reach him in time); decapitated, revived. A poisoned worm of memory remains hidden from sight, however, baffling the labyrinthine plans of even the Culture's most beguiling minds. Banks somehow works a narrative miracle, a triumph of generic engineering, fusing thriller and moral parable, reeking detail and clinical distance, fanciful invention and heartfelt pain. Almost. Perhaps he is too consummate. The novel winds on itself like a double spiral. The main story carries us forward; its parallel runs backward, in leaps of traumatic memory recovered. In the end, all certitudes are broken. Anything may be used as a weapon, however personal, ugly, ruinous to the wielder. The novel is a coiled maze; many ways lead in, as many out, all of them refuting determinacy even as they insist upon it. And for all that, the book is *fun*. Colossal artifacts with facetious names like the *Very Little Gravitas Indeed* roar across the galaxy, while enhanced humans and snide machines frolic within their protective fields. The happiest moment, exactly catching Banks's way of taking sf's geegaws and doing rude things with them, is this:

> `To the Culture,' he said, raising his glass to the alien. It matched his gesture. `To its total lack of respect for all things majestic.' (259)

At the heart of sf as an enterprise (if it has one, if there is one, to the extent that it surmounts such national boundaries), I think I see exactly what James Gunn hinted at: the hungry wish *not to die,* not to be cast into nothingness *just when the story is getting interesting.* Thus, sf's interest in time-dilating starships, in cryonic suspension into the future, in characters who upload their minds into secure computer substrates, who hybridize themselves by a dozen paths into persistence. Why should anyone *really* want to go to Mars, let alone the planets of distant stars? Maybe it would be a cool thing to do, in its way. But maybe it is a metaphor, after all, like the Banksian Culture. `Can I get there by candle-light? Yes, and back again!'

vi

I have been engrossed in reading science fiction for the last half century, in writing it professionally for some forty years and, for about as long, tussling critically with its texts, with varying degrees of theoretical sophistication and technical insight. This book is a consolidation (and frequently a reappraisal, in a frank variety of voices) of those readings, drawing upon reviews and essays published in many places, from fanzines such as *Science Fiction Commentary* and *Australian Science Fiction Review, Second Series* to my decade in the 1980s as sf reviewer for the metropolitan *Age* newspaper, and especially to longer pieces presented lately in that wonderful small magazine edited by David Hartwell and his ever-changing krewe of volunteers, *The New York Review of Science Fiction.* In two previous books, *Reading by Starlight* (1997) and *Transrealist Fiction* (1999), I followed the path of the academy, examining the way `modern' (but not modernist) science fiction transformed into the thousand flowers of postmodern sf, and one method, transrealism, for enriching its own distinctive possibilities. I shall try to avoid any considerable overlap in this book, putting to one side especially writers and texts read closely in those earlier volumes—Aldiss, Dick, Egan, Rucker, Jameson, Suvin, Todorov, a dozen more—although I shall begin my journey with a return to the jolting encounter with one tutelary theorist of those earlier studies, Samuel R. Delany.

1: THE SPLENDOR AND MISERY OF SCIENCE FICTION

`Where do you get your ideas?' [a writer] wanted to know.

I said, `By thinking and thinking and thinking till I'm ready to kill myself.'

He said, with enormous relief, `You too?'

`Of course,' I said, `did you ever think it was easy to get a good new idea?'

Isaac Asimov, *I. Asimov* (208)

i

How did all this come to pass, this rise and rise of Gunn's `characteristic fiction of our times' even as authorized cultural taste-makers regarded it with contempt? What did it look like to spectators and participants observing the ambiguous four-dimensional graph that maps science fiction and fantasy, those twinned paraliteratures?

Writing and reading are solitary acts, yet they are social to the core, embedded in plural histories, situated in the flesh and bone of individual humans born in tribes yet severed from one another by consciousness, partitioned inwardly, at war with self and others, hungry for companionship, jealous of the private space and time spent communing within the phantasmatic spacetimes of imagination, eager to share what reading and

28

writing have created and found there. In that awareness, this book is not intended as a distanced, formal treatise. When we are lucky, we speak of the books we adore and revile, one to another over a meal and drink (or as if so), when we find others who share our tastes closely enough for that conversation to be better than idle.

Leslie Fiedler, that great twentieth century literary scholar, exemplary reader of love and death in American letters, spoke more than once with burning clarity about what it is that works, and what doesn't, in critically reading these paraliteratures. More than twenty years ago, his commentary eerily shot down in advance the tedious excesses (I write as an insider, a fellow of an English department) of certain academic appropriations and disavowals:

> [I]t is [. . .] my conviction as a literary populist, impatient with the alienation of current critical writing from the large audience and all the fiction they especially relish, that I find the attempt to transfer to sf approaches which fail to do justice even to Mark Twain, Dickens, or, for that matter, Shakespeare, especially devious, duplicitous, unwittingly hypocritical, or worse, unconsciously self-parodic.
>
> Typically written by a younger generation of university `scholars,' who grew up loving hard-core science fiction, but concealed that fact until it no longer seemed an impediment to academic promotion, such articles try to justify a passion rooted in the naive responses of childhood and early adolescence in a language appropriate only to the most sterile hermetic discourse about equally hermetic books. (1983, 8)

Without such candor, what forgiveness? So:

Once upon a time, long ago when I was a strapping youth and you, my smalls, were not yet born, three-quarters of all the world's sf appeared head to toe in the form of dwarf Siamese paperback twins, with titles like *Slave Brains of the Female Centaurianesses.* Against all accepted laws of genetics, each such book was born fused at the spine with another of different parentage. It was terribly embarrassing to be seen with these Ace Doubles while traveling to school on public transport, although you could do simple tricks with them like masking one cover and giving the old lady sitting opposite the queasy sense that you were reading upside down. If she had a printer in the family, or was one herself, this trick would not impress her.

In those far-off days, the young in Melbourne, Australia, where I lived, were very poor and had to steal their books once they'd exhausted the local municipal library's slender sf stocks. There was one alternative; from a seedy alleyway, though a doorway into a warehouse, they could jerk and haul on an ancient rope, propelling a wheezing hydraulic lift, eventually condemned as terminally unsafe, up its dusty shaft, and thus enter the sublunary trove of the Melbourne Science Fiction Club. Cast your minds back, therefore, if only in doubting imagination, to those fabled virgin days of 1963, and imagine encountering on hidden shelves a Double by Samuel R. Delany with a disagreeably vulgar title: *Captives of the Flame*. This was dismal but characteristic for Ace Books, but even so one recoiled. The previous year, Ace had published *The Jewels of Aptor*, endorsed at once in the pages of *Analog* by its reviewer P. Schuyler Miller as `outrageously fantastic, romantic and gorgeously implausible . . . full of fantastic bits and glimpses of bizarre beauty.' Certainly that sounded to me like science fiction's fabled sense of wonder, but Miller's claim proved, upon inspection of the clumsy text (and, as it turned out later, clumsily hacked and truncated by publisher Don Wollheim), to be fantastically outrageous and implausible. Then again, Delany had published it when he was just 19 years old.

Captives of the Flame was announced as the first of three. An industrious writer, at least. In due course the trilogy, *The Fall of the Towers*, was completed, then *The Ballad of Beta-2* came out in 1965, and the following year the last of the Delany Ace Doubles hit the shelves: *Empire Star*. A title romantically gorgeous! Gorgeously implausible it proved, full of charming little literary jokes, droll references to Rimbaud and the rest (`Oscar and Alfred', `Jean C. and Raymond R.', `Wiley and Colette' (1966, 68), epigraphs by Auden and Proust, a candid homage to sf's legendary poet Theodore Sturgeon (67). A character called Muels Aronlyde was obviously `Samuel R. Delany' with one letter changed (why? a point not resolved in his following book, *Babel-17*, actually written earlier, where Muels Aranlyde—author of *Empire Star*—is mentioned; but we did not then know that Delany suffered from dyslexia). The book was delightful.

The critic John Foyster did not agree with my enthusiastic estimate of *Empire Star*, and soon supported his disapproval with a letter from Delany apologizing that the book had been written in eleven days, with a final draft adding another three or four. `I don't write as quickly as this normally, and don't want to do so again,' was Delany's summary. In 1966,

Babel-17 achieved an Ace volume all to itself, amazingly clean and attractive, in its way, and shared a Nebula with Daniel Keyes' *Flowers for Algernon*. I read it on the Sydney-to-Melbourne train some days after kicking the nicotine habit, a slow trip of a thousand kilometers, and I didn't crave a smoke the whole time.

I liked Delany's work pretty well by this time, and went back and read the trilogy. It was awful but portions of the final volume were more ambitious than most sf I'd read before. Delany was drunk on words and word structures, and many people felt his purple and extravagance were pretentiously out of control, but what I found finally was the pleasure of the text. Later, he worked for years on the enormous *Dhalgren* (1975), going mad in the process, then the transgressive space opera *Triton* (1976), and a considerable body of theoretical material. The first gathering of these reflections was collected as *The Jewel-Hinged Jaw* (1978) where Delany's infatuation with the critical discourse of structuralism shaped his practical insights.

`I was in a remedial reading class in elementary school,' Delany explained (1978, 5). `Reading for me has always been hard work. I want a lot out of it because I don't do it easily.' His correspondence and manuscripts are said to be easier to interpret than alphabet soup, but not much. Dyslexia is a drawback for a writer. It can sometimes be mistaken for retardation, though Delany had the benefit of an excellent school and well-off parents (some compensation for the drawbacks of being a black gay man in a white bigoted culture, judging from his memoir *The Motion of Light in Water)*. Delany has been called by editor and author Fred Pohl `perhaps the only true genius in our field,' and his fiction is notable for combining a quite excruciating intellectuality with a visual manner verging on the garish. Consider this *Star Wars*-style passage from *Babel-17*: `Drop a gem in thick oil. The brilliance yellows slowly, ambers, goes red at last, dies. That was the leap into hyperstatic space . . . Fling a jewel into a glut of jewels. This is the leap out of hyperspace . . . ' (1966, 58). Literary writing? No. But it is pictorially vivid in the prismatic manner of expensive motion picture special effects.

The basis for this variety of metaphor is Delany's distinctive brand of heightened visual imagination, described and employed in some detail in *Jaw*. The words of a story create mental images, he argued, cognitively and emotionally charged pictures in the head, and each additional word modifies those images.

`A story begins: *The*

`What is the image thrown on your mind?' (A rather cinematic metaphor itself in that question.) `Whatever it is, it is going to be changed many, many times before the tale is over. My own, unmodified, rather whimsical *The* is a grayish ellipsoid about four feet high that balances on the floor perhaps a yard away. My *a*, for example . . . is either much farther away, or much smaller and nearer' (1978, 25-6).

To me, this was absolutely astonishing news. Like a large subset of the human race, I have never had a literal mental image in my entire life. It took me two and half years studying English Literature at university to realize that the reason they kept using the word `image' about poetry was because most people got pictures in their heads when they read words. Extraordinary! It was like learning that a neighbor possessed authentic psi powers. *Images!* I cobble my own narratives together by *thinking it all through*, not by annotating the free mental movie. So reading Delany's account of his own procedure (which most writers and readers, apparently, recognize at once, to some degree, from the inside) fascinated me. Look at its instantiation in the opening untabbed paragraphs of *Empire Star*. This might too easily be dismissed as pulp recitative; I read it, with delight, as a kind of gaudy, erotic poetry thoroughly in tune with its generic specificity:

> He had:
> a waist-length braid of blond hair;
> a body that was brown and slim and looked like a cat's, they said, when he curled up, half asleep in the flicker of the Field Keeper's fire at New Cycle;
> an ocarina;
> a pair of black boots and a pair of black gloves with which he could climb walls and across ceilings;
> gray eyes too large for his small, feral face;
> brass claws on his left hand with which he had killed, to date, three wild kepards that had crept through a break in the power fence during his watch at New Cycle (and in a fight once with Billy James—a friendly scuffle where a blow had suddenly come too fast and too hard and turned it into for real—he had killed the other boy; but that had been two years ago when he had been sixteen . . . (1966, 5)

and so on, for another four paragraphs, until we reach this instant, surprising narrative crux:

Before he began to lose, however, he gained: two things, which, along with the ocarina, he kept until the end. One was a devil kitten named Di'k. The other was me. I'm Jewel.

I have a multiplex consciousness, which means I see things from different points of view. It's a function of the overtone series in the harmonic pattern of my internal structuring. So I'll tell a good deal of the story from the point of view called, in literary circles, the omniscient observer. (6)

It is a postmodern move in pulp disguise, somewhat startling in 1966. The whole concatenated passage is a demonstration, too, of Delany's emerging theory of the text and its realization in syntactic linkages that modify, constrict, amplify the images they build, flowing word upon word.

Delany was wholly conscious of theory, in a self-taught, exploratory fashion that took him, earlier than most academics, deeper into structural methods and then poststructural interrogations. In his first critical book, you might bark your knee from time to time on idiocentric opacities like `Together, the convention of ideohistories and the convention of idiocentric omissions (or opacities) generate the basic s-f dialectic' (1978b, 250). When the young Delany runs his long sensitive fingers over Ursula Le Guin's ordered prose, though, it can make your back ridge and jump (to borrow a different variety of Delany locution).

There are many pretty little insights along the way, some of them now famous epigrams. Consider his guess that the spaceport on Trantor, in the *Foundation* sequence, was actually Asimov's transformed image of Grand Central railway station, in his home town of New York, rather than, as we tend to read it nowadays, of an international airport. Or his suggestion that pliant cowering heroines on the movie screen are derided by male adolescents because `it looks all too much like an allegory of what he has come to the movies to escape: an encroaching social role in which, he has been told, the responsibility is *all* his' (201).

ii

Chip Delany, then, is a mirror for sf observers. Before he was 40 years old, he twice convulsed science fiction into something larger and more exciting. In his own person he embodies that jolt to the imagination which sf offers as its first charge:

He's black.

He's gay, and a divorced father, a literature professor who has shared his life of late with a street person.

His stories are forceful, strong as myth.

His storytelling is, by turns, baroque, light-splashed, elliptical, hideously mannered, excruciatingly intellectual.

The man is so smart and so full of curiosity that sometimes he has dropped out of sight, up there ahead. He cares so much, he is so genuinely *nice,* that this is not an affront. (Though it can seem that way, as you battle with his latest multilevel trip report.)

Delany cares about his themes and he cares about his words. He cares, as well, about other people's words. His first volume of criticism contained astute studies of his coevals Thomas M. Disch, Roger Zelazny and Joanna Russ, and climaxed in a long and enthralling ax-murder of Ursula Le Guin's *The Dispossessed.* His second critical volume was a staggeringly detailed Barthesian examination of a Disch short story, moving from deft anatomization of telling details to stunning structuralist barnstorming. His most recent quasi-critical text, as I write, is a volume cunningly titled *1984*—Orwell's was *Nineteen Eighty-Four*, although it is not often shown spelled out, as *Moby-Dick* is usually given as *Moby Dick*—that gathers a revealing selection of his private correspondence between late 1983 and early 1985, at the crossroads of sex and writing.

Published when he was 24, his novel *Babel-17* was an admired and reviled landmark, a seed around which crystallized the intelligent revival of pulp adventure. *Nova, The Einstein Intersection*, the stories of *Driftglass*, carried that impulse forward with joyous flamboyance and a keen eye to detail. Something even more interesting happened when, after a silence of years, a bleaker, tougher Delany gave us *Dhalgren, Triton,* the tormented experiments in social scrutiny and challenge that continued with his Derridean/Foucauldian/Lacanian sword & sorcery fictions, and his masterpiece to date, *Stars in my Pocket Like Grains of Sand* (1984). To the bafflement of many of his readers, including me at the time, in these later works it became clear that he was making sf over for the second time. Unfashionably, I find it irresistibly impelling to draw a parallel between Delany's creative restlessness and the convulsive questings of Bob Dylan. The third volume of Delany's early trilogy, *The Fall of Towers*, was dedicated in part to Dylan—although that nod to an old acquaintance from the Village vanished in subsequent editions. Listening to Dylan today is an ambiguous pleasure, as with reading the new and newer Delany, as with the work of anyone who has cranked open rusted apertures.

It was depressing in 1978—brow-smitingly, hand-wringingly depressing—to read *Empire,* a large comic book format narrative written by Delany and drawn by Howard Chaykin (advertised as 'illustrator of *Star Wars*,' hardly a recommendation). *Empire* is simply absurd. A technical analysis of why it is so awful would be out of place at this late date, but a couple of points might be mentioned. Delany used Catastrophe Theory, at the time a mathematical innovation for analyzing jumps in rates of change, as a metaphor for social revolution, in somewhat the way Lawrence Durrell used Relativity as a metaphor in *The Alexandria Quartet*— that is, for its flashy buzz value—without caring what it really means. And by doing so in graphic form, he reduced an attenuated cerebral gag or pun to an overliteral embodiment or concretization. 'We had learned to freeze information itself, to halt its free flow through a society. All our information about information—we call it meta-information—we re-crystallized in the separate shape of a demon, and we called her Meta-Max' (1978, unpaginated). This is painful, offensive technobabble or worse, the kind of silliness which once explained that rockets fly because their exhausts push against the air. More specifically, it is exactly that magic use of the emblems of science that early comic superheroes went in for, mumbling the secret formula which, like a mantra or a spell, changed them into their invulnerable and smartly-caped superforms. As in a *Doctor Who* episode or computer game quest, Delany's heroes battled through the galaxy searching for the fragments of the Meta-Max. Rejoined, these would allow the pure at heart to throw off the horrid tyranny of the Kunduke, whose Empire had an information stranglehold on humanity. Delany echoed that comic book tradition in full awareness, but at a higher level of obfuscation. Oddly, given 1980s' cyberpunk's acknowledged debts to Delany's early space opera prose and imagery, this earlier text botched its chance at visualizing the empire of information.

Was I disillusioned by the severally renewed manifestations of Delany? Certainly not. I forced myself to read the first hundred convoluted pages of *Dhalgren* before sliding happily through the next eight hundred. Even *Triton's* tormented prose, and the semiotic contortions of the *faux*-prehistory *Neveryon* sequence, paid off for the exploration Delany led us on. Instead of taking saunas and beating myself black and blue, from 1976 to 1987 I read Samuel Ray Delany's new works and tried to come to terms with them. Despite my pleasure in his earlier redemption of that despised sub-genre space opera, this was no easy or a joyful task. Like me, and therefore a point in his favor, Delany was crazy about unusual words and hard notions. At the end of the decade I was well placed to pursue a doctorate in poststructural approaches to the textuality of letters and sciences alike, but at the outset I found this new discourse very difficult to accept. *Tales of Neveryon* (pronounced Ne-VER-y-on) proved to be the sort of sword & sorcery novel crammed with words about words, like *syntagmatic*, making it, perhaps, a words & sorcery novel. Published in September, 1979, it contains epigraphs from Jacques Derrida's *Of Grammatology, The Archaeology of Knowledge* by Michel Foucault, and `Desire and the interpretation of Desire in *Hamlet*,' by the obtuse French psychiatrist Jacques Lacan, none of these texts at that time known widely beyond the confines of the humanities' academy and certainly unknown to the fantasy genre. It was hard to see exactly why anyone would do a book calling for a cover that bore a very large dragon and very muscly warriors and large Rubensesque ladies (with their breasts hidden, this being a non-sexist book) and a text ending with an appendix titled `Some Informal Remarks Toward the Modular Calculus, Part Three'. The astute reader of Delany did notice, however, that `Some Informal Remarks Toward the Modular Calculus, Part One' had appeared as the sub-title of his previous novel, *Triton*, while `Part Two' was that volume's Appendix B (but did not include A). `Part Four' comprised his second semiotic sword-swinger, *Neveryóna* (Ne-ver-y-O-na), and `Part Five' was the swollen Appendix A of the third volume, *Flight from Neveryon*.

One might suppose on this evidence that Samuel Delany was not a man with a sense of humor. On the other hand, there was evidence from Part Two of the `Informal Remarks Toward the Modular Calculus, Part Three,' that is to say, Sub-section Two of Part Three, which began:

K. Leslie Steiner was born in Cuba in 1945. Her mother was a black American from Alabama. (1979, 251)

This section was signed by the scholar S. L. Kermit in January, 1981 (264). So one surmised that K. L. Steiner's first name was probably Kermit, a conjecture is borne out in the appendix to *Neveryóna*. Kermit, of course, is not a black American but a green one.

All these genre-defying works are set in a notional pre-history when writing, counting, sex-role differentiation, trade and four-legged stools have just been invented. It is a world where money was invented four generations ago (75), where the inventor of the lock and key, one Belham, was known to one of the characters (61). Despite this, there are substantial cities, a topic Delany investigates forever in *Neveryóna*. There are real live dragons you can fly on if you are a bad girl, and more metaphors and exploratory games than you can shake a two-bladed sword at.

My copy of *Neverÿon* is spattered with marginal comments like (on 63) `this absolutely misses the point of pre-literate memory skills (but see page 64!)', and on 158 `this is all exactly like Heinlein's latest blather', and on the next page `... then again, maybe not...' *Neveryóna* carried this wild, tedious, endlessly provocative and irritating and interesting performance forward. Its cover art seemed pitched to appeal especially to buttocks-fetishists (like the covers of so many sf novels at that time, oddly enough). By the third volume the AIDS plague had descended in all its horror upon the gay world, killing many of Delany's friends, and his fictions closed in with a sort of coldly reasoned anguish on that experience, that dread, that betrayal of the ambiguously free body which his earlier work had celebrated. By the fourth, *The Bridge of Lost Desire* (1987), his paperback publisher Bantam seems to have given up on Delany; the book was published, in hardcover but in a small run, by Arbor House. In his persona as Steiner, he provided a Preface that appeared, perhaps inevitably, as an afterword, where the sequence is compared not to Howard's Conan or Leiber's Gray Mouser and Fafhrd series but `closer to *Der Mann ohne Eigenschaften* than *Die Frau ohne Schatten*.' (303). And the ironically self-regarding and therefore not self-regarding encomium Steiner cites from another sf writer is not without its justification:

Imagine going to a wonderful gallery exhibit with an intelligent, well-spoken, and deeply cultured friend, an expert in the period, richly informed on the customs and economics of the times, familiar with the lives of the artists and their models, as well as the subsequent critical reception of each of the paintings over every ensuring artistic period, a friend who you only wished, as the two of you walked from painting to painting, would shut up ... (303-4).

Of course that is not the end of the matter. But it was very close to the end of Delany's science and fantasy fictions, as he moved away into ever more ornate explorations of discourse and what the wider culture regarded as perversity, the disturbing realms of child abuse, the marginal worlds of street people, public masturbation in Times Square porn cinemas and endless sexual encounters in toilets, sadomasochism and coprophagy (in *The Mad Man* and elsewhere) and, most unnerving of all, the practice and academic teaching of poststructuralism.

iii

The alleged primacy of discourse in the construction and stabilization of culture, especially in its sexual aspects, was explored endlessly in Delany's late fiction. At about the same time, more women writers surged into science fiction at last, often using that same proposition as their narrative spring. Consider three exemplary novels of that period by women sf writers. Two are by Suzette Haden Elgin, a professor of linguistics, projecting a near-future dystopia in which dedicated and oppressed women snatch moments from service to their male dominators to construct an entire language of their own, capable of conveying with concision and beauty what is—we are told—the otherwise inexpressible experience of their oppressed gender.

Native Tongue (1984) established a rather implausible Reaganite America in which Nobel-winning research `proves' the genetic and intellectual inferiority of women, sanctioning a smothering paternalism far more crushing than high Victorian male sanctimony. In this future, extraterrestrials contact Earth, providing technology which effectively removes poverty and want. Their inhuman languages, alas, are available only to infants `interfaced' with aliens almost from birth. A `Lingoe' caste develops, gifted but despised; its women invent and disseminate their new `native tongue'. (In its lexicon, the word `disseminate' would doubtless find other expression.) *The Judas Rose* (1988) carried forward conspiracy via the pieties allowed silly, dithery women: the King James Bible is translated and hand-copied, its traditional male-centered theology rendered into something approaching goddess worship. This hardly seems to me, save perhaps tactically, a great advance; indeed, I find much of Elgin's story dismaying, and not for its feminism. If her premise is intriguing, and her multi-stranded method of telling it dexterous, the upshot appears to be a salvific quietism hardly distinguishable from some Nice Girl's Guide to Ideal Marriage in the happily-departed 1950s.

> Meanwhile, Laadan would spread; [. . .] it would continue to provide the women with the patience necessary to bring the men *out* of those endless loops of violence always begetting more violence. The day would come when they would have a war, and all of the men would look at each other and laugh and just go home. (1988, 355)

Oddly stereotyped in its own way, Canadian-Australian Nancy Corbett's *Heartland* (1989) offers a sweet-natured utopia of two separatist communities brought back together, very cautiously, after hundreds of years of sexual segregation. The WomanRight are five tribes of nuclear survivors near tropical east coast Brisbane where neither fallout nor climatic ruin intrude to ruin the arcadian bliss. Phoenix is an all-male high-tech society on the west coast. Corbett's people—so nice, if sometimes gloomy or mad—are plainly the living proof of their post-patriarchal utopia. Incongruously, much hinges on the idyllic joy of two gay couples who instantly find their opposite numbers, once found, wildly attractive; nature triumphs over culture, tah-rah. If culture reasserts itself by the close, our entrenched myths tell us it will not be for long.

What's wrong with that? Well, in *Dancing At The Edge of the World,* Ursula Le Guin wryly declared her goal as `always being to subvert as much as possible without hurting anybody's feelings' (1989, vii). Perhaps an embarrassing statement: as victims weep or fight for justice and bootboys and tycoons take what they please while the rest of us shuffle our feet, who can be happy with such cautious liberalism? Nancy Corbett tried to subvert without hurting anyone's feelings, and the chief outcome was blandness, even in an experiment in alternatives. By contrast, Le Guin's subversions in fact take the form of fierce and effective fictions. To read them is to know that cruelty and sexism are not glamorous but creepy and undesirable. `Narrative is a stratagem of mortality,' she wrote. `It is a means, a way of living' (39). But not just any narrative, least of all the narrative of fact: `Beneath that specious and arrogant assumption of certainty all the ancient, cloudy, moody powers and options of the subjunctive remain in force . . . Only the imagination can get us out of the bind of the eternal present, inventing or hypothesizing a way that reason can then follow into the infinity of options' (45). Le Guin, like Delany, speaks to that real world whose myths are all too often frozen into icy laby-rinths, and her verbal dancing is the liberative tarantella of a shaman-artist who asserts that the everyday `real' is just another, more rigid construct. It is not enough just to say so, however. We read Delany and Le Guin not because of their station at the top of the moral high ground (although Le Guin came perilously close to hanging the authority of her late novel *The Telling* on just that claim) but for their exceptional skills, their artistry, as storytellers.

2: NOVUM, VARIATION, REPETITION

... [The] formulaic stories [of American sf pulp-masters] are rendered in a language without distinction or grace. Yet despite their vulgarity (maybe, in some sense, precisely because of them), they manage to evoke a sense of wonder, rapture, magic, release of a kind notably *not* produced by much of the polite literature of the same period.

... Any bright high school sophomore can identify all the things that are *wrong* about Van Vogt, whose clumsiness is equaled only by his stupidity. But the challenge to criticism which pretends to do justice to science fiction is to say what is *right* about him: to identify his mythopoeic power, his ability to evoke primordial images, his gift for redeeming the marvelous in a world in which technology has preempted the province of magic and God is dead.

Leslie Fielder, `The Criticism of Science Fiction' (9-11)

i

Dr. Isaac Asimov, who died in 1992, was perhaps the most famous of the 1940s' sf Golden Age authors, nominated with cruel accuracy by Brian W. Aldiss as an sf `dinosaur'.[1] His greatest achievement was to propose a fictional future history operating by the supposition that its characters

---

[1] Chapter XV of Aldiss and Wingrove's *Trillion Year Spree* is entitled `How to be a Dinosaur: Seven Survivors'.

were statistics. Somehow this perverse achievement seems linked with Asimov's enormous continuing popular success 50 or 60 years after his first fictions, and that of his peers.

By the 1980s, in the post-*Star Wars* resurgence of sf, it was no longer feasible to talk modestly about the latest Herbert, Heinlein, Clarke or Asimov as if they were clocking on reliably in the pages of *Galaxy* or *Astounding/Analog*. Their images of the future had begun to invade the world at large. They spoke, it seemed, to the hearts of millions in a time when past had blurred abruptly into future, like that smearing, scary cone of light which was the *Star Wars* metaphor for zapping into hyperspace (and years later was tamed into a default screensaver for Windows).

And yet clocking on was *precisely* what those old war-horses were doing, by and large. Having agreed to extend his famous Foundation trilogy (launched in 1942, completed in 1953; the new books were *Foundation's Edge* [1982], *Foundation and Earth* [1986], *Prelude to Foundation* [1987] and the closing volume *Forward the Foundation* [1993]), Asimov swiftly did the same with his equally celebrated robot detective sequence. *The Robots of Dawn* (1983) carried forward the story of detective Elijah Baley and R. (for Robot) Daneel Olivaw begun in *The Caves of Steel* (1954) and *The Naked Sun* (1956), while *Robots and Empire* (1985) was borne with the extended longevity of Baley's Spacer lover Gladia to a point beyond his death. And while Frank Herbert had some success with *The White Plague* (1983), a `near-future' homily on the nastier consequences of recombinant genetic engineering, it was the world of Dune (which first collided with ours in 1963) which evolved unchecked until he died. After his death, lamentably but profitably, its backstory has been retrofitted on a gallumphing scale by his son Brian Herbert and *Star Wars* novelist Kevin Anderson.

Remarkably, one of Asimov's late novels was the mutant offspring of a film adaptation he committed in 1966 called *Fantastic Voyage*. Unhappy with the constraints inflicted on his scientific rigor by the script, which dealt with a team of specialists suffering miniaturization so that they might operate on a dying man from the inside, Asimov did what he could to render the tale into a Cook's tour of *Gray's Anatomy*. He plodded for a second time through the gooey itinerary in *Fantastic Voyage II: Destination Brain* (1987). Kidnapped to a fairly glasnostized but pre-fall-of-communism Soviet Union to help with the operation, his nerdish American hero triumphed via that oddly anti-heroic mode which always humanized Asimov's sf. Like all his late fiction, it screamed for drastic pruning. Of course Asimov was by then so celebrated (and bankable) one expected to see *Asimov's Annotated Laundry Lists*, but had to make do with *The Alternate Asimovs* (1986), a stout paperback containing the *rejected* manuscripts of three of Asimov's earliest novellas: `Grow Old With Me', later expanded into his first novel *Pebble in the Sky*; `The End of Eternity'; and the black original version of `Belief', his tale of scientific incredulity in the face of unpalatable data.

What is the meaning of this persistence, this single vision? Isn't science fiction the literature of change, of innovation, of shock and dislocation? How can it be that seminal ideas 30 or even 60 years old continued to propel books and their authors or surrogates to fame and wealth?

The facts at least of that resurgence two decades ago are undeniable, and astonishing (Jakubowski and Edwards, 1983). In 1966, an *Analog* reader's poll found Asimov's *Foundation* trilogy the best sf work of all time, and placed his robot books fourth. (H. G. Wells had to make do with second place). Nine years later, in a reader survey reported in *Locus*, Foundation had slipped to sixth place and remained there in 1987, knocked from the top by *Dune*, which also topped the poll in 1987 and 1998. (*Childhood's End* and *The Left Hand of Darkness* took it in turns for second and third places.) Even so, *Foundation's Edge* gained a half-million dollar advance in the USA, while *Heretics of Dune* won three times that amount. The first of the Dune books was sold to Hollywood for a million dollars, allowing Herbert to build a comfortable home for his dying wife in the more supportive climate of the Hawaiian island Maui.

Both Isaac Asimov and Frank Herbert were born in 1920, an auspicious natal year for sf writers. There the points of comparison diverge. Herbert only began writing sf seriously around the time Asimov withdrew to his self-imposed Wellsian task of bringing all the world's knowledge to the general reader. Asimov's style was direct, lucid, logical, while Herbert evolved a tortuous technique for conveying altered states of awareness and dark political intrigues that promote the mystical over the rational.[2] Asimov's plotting was clean, patient and somewhat dogged; Herbert throve on mystification, subtlety or its simulacrum, plots and counter-plots. Perhaps there is little of art in either. At his worst, Herbert

---

[2] Useful studies of these two writers include Gunn, 1982 (recently updated to take account of the late Asimov novels, but not substantially recast), and O'Reilly, 1981.

droned like an ecclesiastical bore. Both, it is true, created imaginary worlds on the greatest possible scale—galactic empires, intrigues deployed on time-scales to make the mind of a Spengler or Toynbee reel. But it is not only those similarities that explain their common success, or Tolkien's in fantasy.

One thing is evident: the Foundation sequence, the robot books and the earlier Dune sagas, and of course Tolkien's immense invented allohistory complete with new languages, constitute their own important *megatexts* or concatenated common alternative reality. (I discuss the idea of the sf megatext in *Reading by Starlight*, 1995.) The cumulative texts build consecutively toward enhanced understanding and enjoyment. Aldiss noted of Herbert's `density of internal reference' that the `later volumes in the sequence require not merely intelligent attention, but some knowledge of the previous volumes. Their webs of subtlety depend greatly on our catching the nuances. Without this knowledge, the story functions but lacks depth' (*Trillion Year Spree*, 398). In his later bestsellers, Asimov took extraordinary (and artistically damaging) pains to ease neophytes into his consolidated universe of human masses governed by the laws of psychohistory and intelligent machines governed by the celebrated Three Laws of Robotics. He succeeded chiefly in numbing the informed reader. Numbness was, sadly, Asimov's principal effect in his final fictions, as he strove, for his amusement and our own, to reconcile these drastically different settings into one triumphant unity.

A signal case was *The Robots of Dawn*, all 419 gum-booted pages of it. Every point is foreshadowed, rehearsed, stated, reiterated, flagged and finally beaten to death. Elijah Baley remains the middle-aged policeman from the earlier robot novels, a perfectly socialized resident of an over-crowded, claustrophobic Earth (those famous `caves of steel'). He is obliged, in a typical Asimovian essay at psychological depth, to risk his equanimity by venturing to the Spacer worlds where genetically improved folk laze about planning the future of the galaxy while robots do all the work. The racist Spacers mean to keep Earth bottled up; some of their number, though, see a place for the luckless denizens of the homeworld in seeding the universe. For political purposes, their spokesman is framed with a crime (a robot `murder') which only Baley and his humanoid robot associate Daneel can solve. As usual, the fate of the Earth is at stake. Readers of earlier Asimov volumes recognize in advance the nature and awful inevitability of this threat, for in the

Asimovian Galactic Empire universe the Earth was a barely habitable radioactive ruin. The `murder' case gives Baley an opportunity to further the romance which lent *The Naked Sun* its poignancy, and Asimov a long-delayed chance to write a warmly-observed love scene. The outcome is far-fetched, and getting to it is boring, yet its sales were substantial.

Arguably, that artistic failure was redeemed in its sequel, *Robots and Empire*. Asimov was clearly fond of his benevolent robots. They are sweet-natured creations, if a little dense when it comes to feelings and passion, controlled by a programmed ethic which obliges them to refrain from harming a human, to obey lawful human orders, and to protect themselves and their kind. Conflicts arise, naturally, and it is the ambition of an Asimov robot story to tease with paradox but satisfy with pure reason. It is easy to dismantle this brave attempt at mechanical morality, and indeed Asimov's own books did so progressively. *Robots and Empire* carried the argument to a tender, almost Dostoievskian moment of choice, when the humanoid robot Daneel Olivaw trembles at the edge of insanity in devising a `Zeroth Law', a transcendental edict that will finally cause robotic intelligence (in the person of the virtually immortal Daneel) to take over the governance of all human affairs while absenting itself from view. Thus, the Foundation universe emerges some 23,000 years later from a sclerosed non-robotic Galactic Empire. One might find this feat of logical juggling morally nauseating—humanity's future, apparently with Asimov's endorsement, being placed under the control of `ethical' machines—were one not anaesthetized by the bludgeoning blows of the Good Doctor's relentless stodge.

Intriguingly, Asimov's universes did not perish after his death. They have been carried on, largely but not always unsatisfactorily, by other hands, as we shall see.

ii

In the Clute/Nicholls *Encyclopedia of Science Fiction*, elaborate distinctions defined a runaway practice in sf: writers parasitizing other writers' ecological niches. Terms needed to anatomize this activity include Sharecropping (where the new works are done on a for-hire basis, forfeiting copyright), Shared Worlds (like *Star Trek* or *Wild Cards*, where an initiator invites other writers to play in an original and circumscribed fictional setting), Ties (in which new works spin off from old, sometimes in different media, as in movie `novelizations'), Open and Closed Universes (1993, 1091-3).

In a way, this has always been a disguised tendency in magazine or commodity sf, perhaps because there are only so many Large Themes and someone had to get there first. E. E. `Doc' Smith devised the hierarchical galactic history, Asimov bureaucratized it on a Roman model, Poul Anderson did the Kipling version, Pournelle ran a sort of conservative American pie variety, while Heinlein came back in his dotage and turned it into libertarian heaven. None of these texts was strictly a shared world or tie, but together they comprise a background of canonical assumptions, a kind of common grammar, that we all tend to operate by these days. (Michel Butor once recommended something similar to sf writers, to general derision; the smiles turned sour with the hegemonic triumph of *Star Trek* and *Star Wars*.) The same sort of genealogy might be discerned for time travel tales, or robot stories—at first very much restricted by Asimov's Three Laws, and then burst open by Clarke's HAL and real world AI research.

In this sense, the usual pejorative flavor of `sharecropping' is unwarranted. I'd argue that the slow emergence of sheaves of common assumptions and tactics—the megatext—is crucial to the success of sf as a mode or genre. And once we grant this truth, acknowledging that not every new book or movie need be utterly different from its predecessors (or even could be), it is possible to see the attraction of visiting the landscapes first sketched by the Masters, carrying their vision outward beyond the frame—even if that means, on occasion, deconstructing both the frame and the portrait. The impulse, in short, need not be low or mercenary. In some ways it stems from the very core of art (and indeed science) as a historical practice.

One shining exception to the schlock rule was Orson Scott Card's 1989 novella, `The Originist', perhaps the best Foundation story ever written. Card loved his work, and tells us he poured as much effort into it as he would usually expend on a whole book (1990, 270). Another, happily, was Roger MacBride Allen's *Caliban* (1993) and its sequels *Inferno* (1994) and *Utopia* (1996)—or, as the title pages make clear, Allen's *Isaac Asimov's Caliban* etc, which is how they are copyrighted by Byron Preiss Visual Publications, Inc. This is usually the stigmata of crass work-for-hire but plainly Allen soaked himself, as it were, in the Master's ebbing lifeblood.

There are grounds for saying that *Caliban* is the most searching Asimovian Robot story ever written, even in the face of its quite formidable but not particularly Asimovian kindred by Mark Tiedemann, *Asimov's Mirage* (2000), *Asimov's Chimera* (2001) and *Asimov's Aurora* (2002), also from the Byron Preiss franchise. The less said the better about Tiedemann's numerous direct predecessors in the dire *Robot City*, *Robots and Aliens* and *Robots in Time* sequences, from which he broke cleanly and decisively while retaining two leading characters authorized years ago by Asimov.

Allen, though, manages to capture Asimov's voice with some fidelity. Sheriff Alvar Kresh is a plausible Elijah Baley substitute, and if his robot sidekick Donald-111 sounds more like *Star Trek's* Lt. Commander Data than R. Daneel, this just shows us how thoroughly Asimov's calm voice permeated our stereotype of the rational, rule-bound robot. The storyline has a crime and plenty of suspects, though I knew who must have Done It within the first 20 pages. The book is impressive, however, for what the jacket copy calls its `searing examination of Asimov's Three Laws of Robotics, a challenge welcomed and sanctioned by Isaac Asimov'. Philosophers and cognitive scientists have mused for the past half century about whether the Three Laws were self-evident or completely unworkable. Research in AI suggests we make judgements on the basis of many thousands of small, often inconsistent rules (or maybe `neural darwinist' adaptive synaptic maps) that compete for air-time, their relative importance or `weighting' affected in turn by the semiotic frames or schematics we use to `read' the situations we happen to be in. This is so utterly unlike the Three Laws that they have long been hard to take seriously. Allen's achievement was to make the creaking old robots stand on their clumping great feet even as his up-to-date analysis cut them off at the knees.

The tragedy, from my point of view as a crusty pedant, is that he bungles a crucial datum that gives the game away. Avert your eyes, innocent reader, if you wish to discover the perp at your own speed. Caliban is a robot who, we learn very early, has highly unorthodox Laws, if any at all. `He' (but most robots have no sex, and hence only an ascribed gender) has been designed by the victim, robopsychologist Fredda Leving, as have other classy robots soon introduced: Donald `himself', and Ariel. All the names, it is explained, derive from Shakespeare. So it is deeply shocking to find that Ariel is referred to throughout as `she'. Like robots, the primeval spirit of Prospero's island has no sex, but he indubitably has a gender. (Strangely, another female Ariel features in the *Robot City* sub-franchise.) I wondered if this were ignorance on Allen's part, which seemed unlikely in such a canny fellow, but the predicted payoff for this verbal sleight comes on page 302. It was as infuriating as learning that Marilyn Monroe shot JFK because she was his disowned brother.

Asimov's own decision to rework as many as possible of his disparate sf novels and stories into a single monumental tapestry flew almost willfully in the face of current critical opinion, which praises plurality and abhors `closure' and `unity' (not that Asimov would have known or cared about the opinions of literary critics, whom he generally abominated). Robert Heinlein (in *The Number of the Beast-*, *The Cat Who Walks Through Walls*, and the last novel he published before his death, *To Sail Beyond the Sunset*), played the same game, combining all his work into a colossal solipsistic mosaic where characters from one book's `unique' universe sauntered freely through the next. This is intertextuality fetched to the airport paperback stands. Sf's peculiar narrative possibilities—its expanded dimensionality—had begun to breach the boundaries between criticism and text in ways neither were used to.

iii

A similar impulse drove Herbert's *Heretics of Dune* (1984) and *Chapter House Dune* (1985), the final volumes by the author himself in that particular saga, although it has been continued dismally by others (as has Asimov's Foundation sequence in a `prequel' trilogy by Gregory Benford, Greg Bear and David Brin). The immediate predecessor, the hectoring *God-Emperor of Dune* (1981), centered on the droning lofty `wisdom' of an immortal man-monster hybrid until finally he had the decency to do away with himself. Similarly, Heinlein's *Time Enough for Love* (1973) centered on the droning crackerbarrel `wisdom' of Lazarus Long, who dies only to be reborn. At its best, though, reading the complete Dune sequence can trigger the Zen-state one enters while playing multi-level computer games, or the condition attained three-quarters of the way through a fat middlebrow historical fiction such as *Shogun*—a poised, remote, interested acceptance, finger on the trigger and mind a-wing.

Presumably it startled many of Herbert's fans to learn that *Dune* and its sequels were not merely (and not meant to be) an exciting heroic romance. Below the power-fantasy surface, the sequence is a bitter exploration of the corrupting effects of just that mystique. Its Islamic roots give it peculiar prophetic cogency today. Dune, its prophets, messiahs and god-emperors, grew out of Herbert's fascination with `the messianic convulsions which periodically inflict themselves on human societies.' Unlike many sf novels, his series was meant to demonstrate that `superheroes were disastrous for humans' (O'Reilly, 1981, 153).

The early books dealt with Paul Atreides, futuristic avatar of Agamemnon's bloody house of Atreus. Child of a breeding program aimed at creating a prescient, totally conscious aristocracy, he is all that and more. Yet, Herbert insists, Paul's very authority cripples him and spoils his world. With each succeeding book, this thread of heightened perception and its discontents is wound tighter. Paul's son Leto II, transfigured into an ageless monstrosity, connives at his own death to set humanity free of his awful, stultifying omniscience. The last books propose complex results of that decision some thousands of years down the line, a world governed by the Bene Gesserit sisterhood and their enigmatic foes.

Female Jesuits in Herbert's ironic mythology (the punnish wordplay in their name is no accident, Herbert told me), the Bene Gesserit confront enemies from within and without their own system; courage is displayed, strange truths uttered, at last the world of Dune itself is shattered . . . and the saga opens out toward the next book, in which a new world is seeded with immortal sandtrout and Dune World is reborn. Like the dunes rolling irresistibly over all in their path, Herbert's extraordinary future history surged, it seemed, toward the 1990s and his next Hawaiian island; even his death has not ended the irresistible momentum toward yet another fat volume full of superhuman folk telling each other deeply cryptic truths and lies, vying for control of all space and history, dying horribly only to spring back to cloned or reincarnated life.

One might doubt the durability of a book like *Chapter House Dune*, concerned preposterously with conflict between the monastic Bene Gesserit and their crazed opponents the Honored Matres, a sort of Nazi coven of bureaucrats who use sexual bonding as their secret weapon. It was a little difficult to see why any reader should care. But the damned things sell and sell, and so do the inferior prequels. Build it, perhaps, and they will come?

Herbert's death in 1986, even more so than Heinlein's in 1988, can therefore be seen to mark the death of an entire universe. While that is true of each death, certainly of every artist's, his invented cosmos extended ahead of our own by thousands of years and light-years. In the public mind, the *Dune* series was the very definition of print-media science fiction. He was rivaled only by Asimov, Heinlein and perhaps Arthur C. Clarke—though, thanks presumably to the efforts of the Church of Scientology, the post-mortem presence of L. Ron Hubbard imposed at gruesome length once more on the sf marketplace an inept hand in the form of his (?) *Mission: Earth* `Dekalogy'.

None of this answers my original question. Why these ideas, why now? Perhaps because the claims of sf, presented in now-routinized or comfortingly familiar form, are at last seen to be just. There is no single future, says Herbert (even as he offers us one), unless we allow it to be imposed upon us. Imagination can create telling thought-experiments for us, and sometimes those will abut the real future. *The Robots of Dawn* is dedicated jointly to Marvin Minsky and Joseph F. Engelberger. Minsky was MIT's resident genius in the theory of artificial intelligence, a mathe-matical-computing discipline which did not exist when Asimov wrote his first robot tales. Engelberger founded Unimation, the first successful industrial robot company, in 1958, and sold it for over $100 million. He gives the credit to Asimov's fiction. While it is hardly true that fact has caught up with fiction, we can find many of today's shocking realities pre-digested in sf. Perhaps that is what makes Asimov's final writing alto-gether too close to pap, and Herbert's to mystagogy.

iv

`Our own grandchildren,' wistful Arthur Clarke wrote in the Afterword to *The Fountains of Paradise*, `may demonstrate that—some-times—Gigantic is Beautiful' (1979, 255) More apt might be `sublime'. The demonstration is not such a tough challenge. Try to estimate, for example, how many billions of tonnes of air go into making the average sublime sunset. Consider the size of the hydrogen fusion torch, better known as the Sun, which powers the spectacle. Of course, `Small is Beautiful' was a slogan aimed at engineers and bureaucrats. Nature is exempt from its strictures. The technological sublime aspires to attainments on scales rivaling those of brute nature. For the 22nd century protagonist of *Foun-tains of Paradise,* an Australian builder who starts by spanning the 58km Strait of Gibraltar before going on to grander schemes, gigantic is what he likes and stupefyingly enormous is what he gets.

By that date, Clarke speculated, much of the world's industrial plant and resources will be found in space. Since even the most efficient rockets are too filthy, noisy, wasteful and dangerous to serve as carriers in such an economy, Dr. Vannevar Morgan sees that the answer is a Sky Hook—a lift-shaft extending 40,000 km from earth to geostationary orbit and then beyond. A bridge, in fact, jutting straight out into space, with one end moving kilometers a second faster than the other, locked to the earth, sustained by tension. The central tension in much of the book is conflict between Morgan and the Sri Lankan monks whose sacred mountain must serve to anchor the elevator. The beauty and antiquity of their threatened temple is evoked with tender melancholy. Clarke is no voracious strip miner; if he dynamites in the name of progress, it is with regret. Brian W. Aldiss justly discerned `a dramatized sense of loss' as Clarke's predominant emotion; *Fountains of Paradise*, like most of Clarke's best work, is not without its dying falls, its fading embers.

Can a good novel be written about a piece of engineering, no matter how grandiose? Clarke claimed this as his best book, which raises a slightly different question. As a study in Vannevar Morgan's motives and complexities, it is no more valuable than most sf. Morgan is impelled, we understand, by a desire that he will live forever through his immense constructions; the flaccid irony is that they leave his name off. Still, by then the thing has been built. Our works are greater than our ignoble drives.

Perhaps the worth of such a book needs to be assessed in other than purely artistic terms. Like it or not, we approach the era of mega- and nanotechnology (see Broderick, 2001). Clarke's projection is useful, obliging us to go beyond the confused and urgent pressures of oil crisis, lead toxicity and microchips, to consider with some detachment and awe the ethics and aesthetics of a world made largely by human hands. The image of the colossal erection will gladden those conceptual theorists whose finest hour saw Christo Javacheff wrap up entire coastlines and islands with endless bales of plastic sheeting. In the end though, one is reminded of G. K. Chesterton's *The Man Who Was Thursday* (1908): `As he now went up the weary and perpetual steps, he was daunted and bewildered by their almost infinite series. But it was not the hot horror of a dream or of anything that might be an exaggeration or delusion. Their infinity was more like the empty infinity of arithmetic, something unthinkable, yet necessary to thought . . . He was ascending the house of reason, a thing more hideous than unreason itself.' Morgan's final, fatal ascension of the space elevator, the new Tower of Babel, is a climb into the unspeakable mysteries of the heart of reason. Arguably, this has been Clarke's journey as well.

We do need enigmas, of course, just as we crave explanations. The best sf is a balance between thought and dream, and its finest creations taunt and haunt us, needling the mind towards efforts to understand the mysterious even as they prick the pretensions of reason. That, surely, was the success of Clarke's most awarded novel, the 1973 *Rendezvous with Rama*. An artificial worldlet 50 kilometers long and 16 kilometers across, complete with an internal sea, hurricanes and organic robots, flashes through the solar system, utterly indifferent to human amazement. A party of explorers maps the vast artifact in a hurried sortie, and learns virtually nothing. Rama is an enigma, a projective screen for human wishes and fears, a hint of cosmic otherness. Only one fact seems clear: the Ramans do everything in threes. And there, with commendable tact, the book closed: as perfectly pent as Shelley's mocking Ozymandias: `round the decay /Of that colossal wreck boundless and bare, / The lone and level sands stretch far away.' But what if Shelley had given us Ozymandias II, III and IV and made a packet with movie sales? After all, why should we eager consumers be obliged to miss the king's early sexual frustrations, his retinue's in-fighting, court scandal, battle bloodbaths?

Such qualms were inevitable when Clarke contracted follow-ups to *Rama,* sharing out most of the writing to space scientist and scriptwriter Gentry Lee, who also co-authored *Cradle,* a movie deal which fell through. *Cradle* was meant to be the finny equivalent of *2001,* but as Clarke lamented `by bad luck, a whole string of underwater/extraterrestrial movies appeared around the time of the book's publication, and most of them sank without trace' (Clarke and Lee, 1989, 375-6). The *Rama II* gamble, in the event, seemed worth taking, but Gentry Lee's method was too neatly pitched to the new sf mass audience. His style veered away from Clarke's dignified plain chant into a nervy disco medley of airport blockbusters. When a second Raman megacraft enters our space, the crew sent to board it resemble the cast of, say, *The Towering Inferno:* former Olympic champion and life science officer Nicole des Jardins, a statuesque copper brown woman with `a complex French and African Lineage', the `lithe blonde' video journalist Francesca Sabatini, bitch and manipulator; Dr. David Brown, unscrupulous research thief; Shigeru Takagishi, whose hunger for knowledge drives him to hide a potentially fatal heart condition.

Nor was consistency preserved. In *Rama*, the planet Mercury was declared `the key to the solar system', rich in solar energy and heavy metals, ready to provide a cornucopia of wealth. The Mediterranean had been drained. Earth's population was down to a billion or so. Spacecraft had gene-engineered `superchimps' on board to do the dirty work. By *Rama II* these background facts were forgotten, presumably because they imply a background too flamboyant and alienating for a general reader-ship unaccustomed to the extrapolations of sf (and indeed to science and technology). Worse, a revival of Catholicism has permitted genuine mira-cles to be seen on global media, before the living saint in question is sent to a premature reward by a terrorist's neutron bomb. Is Saint Michael of Siena a manifestation, conveniently evaporated, of the mysterious Ramans? This odd intrusion of the supernatural, so uncongenial to Clarke's own robust materialism, was not explained in the succeeding and ever more dismal volumes *The Garden of Rama* and *Rama Revealed*, although perhaps it was in Lee's solo `Bright Messengers' quasi-sequels; I'll prob-ably never know.

Clarke's own sequels suffered similar fallings away. *2010* followed the arc of Kubrick's film rather than his own rather disappointing book version. There are two Clarkes. One penned beautiful, flawed, poetic masterpieces: *Childhood's End* and *The City and the Stars*. The other conceived orbital relays and boosted space flight, megatechnology and the Scientific Way. In *2010, 2061* and especially the travelogue *3001*, the two were uncomfortably spot-welded, and the seams show. If the Space Odyssey was (in part) a hymn to human ingenuity, it was also despairing, terribly—bracingly—bleak. Yes, humankind was after all the special creation of something like gods, but they were gods who did not really care all that much for us. We are merely a larval stage to something unutterable, the case presented earlier but more heart-breakingly in *Childhood's End*. More to the point, technology itself seemed lethally malevolent. The campy computer Hal was a murderer. What can you do when your own robots turn on you? Turn them off, yes, but this is not a satisfactory solu-tion to a technophile. In the books following *2001*, we learned that it was all our own fault. What brought Hal unstuck was human maliciousness. The poor honest creature was driven insane by its inability to deal with deceit and hypocrisy. Clarke may find this consoling.

There are, though, striking and even haunting images in *2010*. If the astronaut-turned-starchild of the film never really gels, and the Chinese expedition to Europa looks stuck on, and the ending is absolutely stony-hearted, still there were compensations in the vision of a plague of monoliths chewing up the giant world Jupiter and spitting out the pips.

V

Kingsley Amis famously found sf attractive partly because `it provides a field which, while not actually repugnant to sense and decency, allows us to frolic like badly brought-up children among the unstable atomic piles' (1963, 115). At the start of the 1960s, his much-disputed choice for best sf novel of all time was *The Space Merchants*, Frederik Pohl and C. M. Kornbluth's classic dystopia about a world run by mad-dog advertising. Pohl and Kornbluth made their meals off this sort of insane social comedy, shifting the White House to Madison Avenue some years before the real moving van arrived and took it to California and Texas. Pohl's later work, unlike that of Asimov and Heinlein, left the sf `Golden Age' well behind. His books place small, irritating thorns in the flesh to niggle after the Made-for-TV images have dwindled to grey.

Amis dubbed *The Space Merchants'* variety of frenetic, intelligent satire `comic-inferno'. Pohl tried many times to recover that first success. Rollicking, for all its bleak setting of insensate ad-mass madness and over-population, the novel can be contrasted many decades later with Pohl's own direct sequel, *The Merchants' War* (1985), and with his *magnum opus*, the crisp social commentary-extrapolation *The Years of the City* (1985). The city, inevitably and emblematically, is New York; its prospects, if it is not to rot or explode, might well follow his oddly unsurprising scenario in the next century. Pohl has no illusions about his fellow humans, so this grimy and realistic forecast of the building of a radical utopia—limited participatory democracy, abandonment of `expertise'—is the more compelling. Few of us would consider his domed megalopolis much fun to live in, but it is instructive to visit.

By contrast, Pohl's return alone to the hucksters' world, *The Merchants' War*, set 50 years on from the original, simply failed to work. His anti-hero Tennison Tarb is *so* dumb and gullible it is hard to see why he wasn't put down like an unwanted kitten at birth. And Tarb's triumphant liberation of the consumers is so starry-eyed that one wondered where Pohl's cynical savvy had got to. In fact, in the 1970s, Pohl had nearly abandoned the genre. His change of heart saw some slick writing, all of it produced at four pages a day, hail or shine while Pohl flew endlessly around the world, but he never quite made good his promise. *The Cool War* (1981), for example, was a cynical appraisal of international relations carried a tiny step forward in time, after the oil's gone, and managed to be smarmy, boring and melodramatic.

More interesting was *Starburst* (1982), an expansion of his well-known story `The Gold at the Starbow's End' (1972). Pohl remained sour about human beings and our prospects. His tale of forced evolution to an ambiguous and fairly repellent superior state is another variant of his dyspeptic vision. Even so, the book has its moments, as did his fine and quite deeply felt novel of a man physically re-built to suit Martian conditions, *Man Plus* (1976) showing that sf can achieve effects impossible in other media. The notion of alternative time-lines, for example, can be a powerful tool for investigating our weary prejudices. In his dreadfully-titled *The Coming of the Quantum Cats* (1987), Pohl set out to produce its very paradigm. If every choice creates a variant world and physics finds a way to leap from one virtual reality to another, we might confront our twin selves—strangely skewed by divergent histories.

Allohistory remains a thought-experiment fit to test every major doctrine of ethics and politics, but Pohl dithers between *realpolitik* and debased story-telling conventions. Alas, a book like this can have its greatest effect (genuinely mind-boggling) only on readers fairly innocent of sf's formulas—and they're the least likely to pick it up, which is a shame. How unnerving to find that President Reagan's name is Nancy, or that in yet another world Ronny is a relaxed white-haired criminal power-broker; that a beautiful concert violinist is quantum twin to a thumbless torturer; that eager, dopey Nicky DeSota, the protagonist with a Thousand Faces, can be stuffy Senator Dominic DeSota and gung-ho Major DeSota, D. P. Wish fulfilment? Yes, but philosophy in action, of a fairly simple kind, as well. Interestingly, Greg Egan denounced the book for its failure to confront the real challenges of quantum theory's Many Worlds hypothesis, which he himself met fascinatingly in *Quarantine* (1992).

Pohl continued his scathing assault on the American Dream with the award-winning *Gateway* (1977) and its sequels: a future of overpopulation mitigated by technical fixes, of ever more mind-wrenching perspectives in time and space seen through the eyes of a simple lad who risks Faustian damnation to become the Richest Man in the World. In *HeeChee Rendezvous* (1984)—an appalling title, if less dire than its companion volume *Beyond the Blue Event Horizon* (1980)—his guilt-ridden prospector meets the lover he abandoned all those years ago on the time-stilled event horizon of a black hole, solves the problem of international terrorism with some back-room diplomacy, discusses the secrets of the universe with his computer simulation of Albert Einstein (who twinkles his eyes to a frightening extent) and dies, only to be resurrected as an enhanced simulation. What is Pohl telling us in this extravaganza? Is he simply beguiling our out-of-work nights with a curious melange from the futurologist's pot, spiced up into some 21st century Rider Haggard yarn? The central institu-tion of his imaginary world, the Gateway Corporation, which governs the exploitation of artifacts left here and there by the vanished predecessors of humanity, is patently a guy for burning, a monstrous exaggeration of what we are doing with the world's dwindling resources. Yet Pohl is not just preaching. His tale is exuberant, each horror-story ending a springboard to a fresh flurry of optimism. If his hero dies, he goes to a sort of heaven. The universe is about to end? Someone Up there is reworking the blue-prints. In the subsequent End of Time trilogy, Pohl kept slogging on into the deep future, portraying the mortal Face of Satan/God, but for all the *gravitas* of his topic it seemed his own time had passed.

vi

Standing above this quarternity—Asimov, Clarke, Herbert and Pohl—Robert Heinlein was undoubtedly the most important (and infuri-ating). With his death in 1988, science fiction lost its most innovative writer since H. G. Wells. Heinlein's strategic and tactical brilliance was acknowl-edged even by Samuel R. Delany, his foe in ideology and style. Concurring with the Annapolis graduate that `Mighty little force is needed to control a man whose mind has been hoodwinked; contrariwise, no amount of force can control a free man', Delany offered tribute to `the man who, as much as any writer while I was growing up, taught me to argue with the accepted version' (*Starboard Wine*, 43). From a gay, black writer in a homophobic nation once riven by a war over slavery, this is an estimate to be considered carefully.

Heinlein famously perfected techniques for creating `lived-in futures', never *told* if he could *show*. He eschewed explanation; his characters simply went about their strange, fascinating business in the world of the 22nd century—an America run, as like as not, by religious fundamentalists, or lipgloss-adorned men, or anarcho-syndicalists—and the reader of the 1940s was meant to absorb all this through the pores. It is the essential technique of sf, difficult to acquire, demanding a kind of genius to carry off compellingly. In his fantastic futures, novelties in engineering, epistemology and politics hang from one another like the struts of a geodesic dome (one of the few breakthroughs he failed to forecast). His fiction had sufficient collective impact that his death drew a brief newspaper obituary, which dwelt on two points: that he was author of the 1960s cult novel *Stranger in a Strange Land*, and that in it he had predicted the water-bed. Old hippie communards fondly recalled the novel's buzz-terms `grok' and `share water', which spliced together outlandish religions and sexual permissiveness in an eerie anticipation of Orange People and Charles Manson both (although Manson, despite rumor, never read it).

The truth is odder still. The water bed was imagined by Heinlein not in 1961 but in 1942 (in *Beyond This Horizon*). In *Stranger in a Strange Land*, Heinlein hit quite a different unexpected target, not to be instantiated until revelations concerning the uses of Nancy Reagan's astrologer:

> Mrs. Douglas stood up. `Well, I can't waste time arguing intangibles; I've got to get Madame Vesant to cast a new horoscope. I didn't give the best years of my life putting you where you are to have you throw it away through lack of backbone. Wipe the egg off your chin.' She left.
> The chief executive of the planet stayed for two more cups of coffee. (74)

Perhaps what seized the campus enthusiasts for *Stranger in a Strange Land* was its sweetly inhuman hero, Valentine Michael Smith, a boy brought to manhood in the company of Martians. For Heinlein, an advocate of the linguistic hypothesis of Benjamin Lee Whorf, we are what we speak. Since Mike is a Martian by upbringing, he perceives a unique world. His iconoclastic reactions are no more `correct', perhaps, than ours—but they encouraged readers to argue with the accepted version. Above all, *Stranger* was taken by its young readers as a manifesto for free (but `mystical') sexual exploration.

Over the final decades of his career, the `Dean of sf' continued to give those initials a new meaning. Much of what Heinlein wrote subsequent to *Stranger in a Strange Land* was `speculative fornication'. A curious instance was *Friday* (1982), widely hailed as a return to commercial form in a writer seen as latterly corrupted by self-indulgence. Friday is a genetic construct in a near-future world secretly controlled by the energy utility which has made the beginnings of interstellar colonization feasible. She is a beautiful, smart, sexy woman of the future clearly meant to offend feminists and non-feminists alike. Just as the later Lazarus Long blockbusters elaborated Heinlein's earliest future history tales, *Friday*'s world was an extension of a notional pluralist fascism first conceived in a 1949 *Astounding* novella, `Gulf'. That story, with remarkable audacity when we recall how recent was the victory over Nazism, presented for the reader's approval and identification a select band of genetically optimum men and women who use assassination and terrorism to correct the world's problems, meanwhile gabbing at each other about the foolishness of democracy (a quirk of Heinlein's that persisted throughout his subsequent fiction).

He stopped and brooded. `I confess to that same affection for democracy, Joe. But it's like yearning for the Santa Claus you believed in as a child. For a hundred and fifty years or so democracy, or something like it, could flourish safely. The issues were such as to be settled without disaster by the votes of common men, befogged and ignorant as they were. But now, if the race is simply to stay alive, political decisions depend on real knowledge about such things as nuclear physics, planetary ecology, genetic theory, even system mechanics. They aren't up to it, Joe. With goodness and more will than they possess less than one in a thousand could stay awake over one page of nuclear physics; they can't learn what they must know.'

Gilead brushed it aside. `It's up to us to brief them. Their hearts are all right; tell them the score—they'll come down with the right answers.'

`No, Joe—We've tried it; it does not work. As you say, most of them are good, the way a dog can be noble and good. Yet . . . there is no way for us to give the man of imperfect brain the canny skill to distinguish a lie from a truth . . . The gulf between us and them is narrow, but it is very deep. We cannot close it.' ([1949] 1971, 63-4)

Friday continues this disagreeable tradition for many chapters, proving her doughtiness well beyond the aspirations of most Clint Eastwood heroes, before settling down to marriage and kids with other nice superfolk, including the man who raped her at the outset. What is especially noteworthy about the thematics of this novel is that the villains are *laissez-faire* multinational corporations, which settle their scores by obliterating rival aligned cities with nuclear weapons. Heinlein's rightwing cynicism veers so far that it collides with the radical left, which, interestingly, is where he began—as a political activist for Upton Sinclair's EPIC (End Poverty in California) movement (Wells, 1993, 1-7). During the Second World War, Asimov says, he was `an ultraliberal' (Asimov, 1979, 488). In a scorching analysis, Barton Paul Levenson has attempted to show that his final point was a version of fascism (Levenson, 1998).

No one would ever mistake a Robert Heinlein novel for an art-object, with his corn-pone authoritarian verities and cracker-barrel gags. The cruel but just European critic Franz Rottensteiner has pilloried Heinlein as `chewing gum for the vulgar' (1969b). The validity of this estimate is plainest, perhaps, in *Job: A Comedy of Justice* (1984) where Heinlein tried for the post of Voltaire of the vulgar. His hero's escapades in multiple universes do indeed prove amusing, diverting, very mildly shocking; the writing is typically self-indulgent and artistically shapeless—all the faults and virtues which sf readers came to associate with Heinlein's work after the end of the 1950s. Rottensteiner's critical position was uncompromisingly humanist. `The purpose of fiction is but one: to dissect a character, a situation, or a problem—to show what makes a character human, or a situation/problem humanly meaningful [. . . T]hat's what most sf authors, most of the time, fail to do. It surely isn't the purpose of fiction to boost the egos of the kiddies who want to read of invincible, omnipotent heroes, want to see "good" (or what they think constitutes good) triumph, and to see "evil" vanquished. What most sf presents is whipping pieces: and from them we learn nothing about the nature of good and . . . evil, or the nature of knowledge and . . . ignorance' (1969, 4). It is a position that continues to underpin most literate/ literary repudiation of sf as a whole, fusing with the much less generous motive deplored by Brian Aldiss: `ignoring [sf], as they do, because it doesn't conform to the conventions of the major nineteenth century novels they studied in the English schools of Oxbridge and Ivy League. Imagination is in short supply: a precious commodity that many fear' (*The Pale Shadow of Science*, 97).

The worlds of *Job* are 'lived-in presents', each different. Ever the gad-fly, Heinlein chose to mock his own mockers by offering as hero a likeable bigot, a man who knows in his revivalist Christian bones that women are meant to stay in their place, that blackamoors and Jews and Catholics are wicked if not outright inferior, that the world was created in 4004 BC—and is due to end in 1994. It was Heinlein's audacious bid not merely to teach this fellow some of the errors of his upbringing, but to create a fictional meta-universe where his basic beliefs prove to be correct. Incredibly enough, three-quarters of the way through the book the last Trump sounds and the elect are snatched up into a medieval Heaven, complete with St Peter as straw boss and God visible on His Throne. In the first fly-by of the elect, marshaled by angels, Alec sees Jesus taking the salute from a field throne. This image is, it must be admitted, wonderfully crass, as funny as a gag by Hunter S. Thompson:

> It was magnificent, carved out of a single diamond, with its myriad facets picking up Jesus' inner light and refracting it in a shower of fire and ice in all directions. And that is what I saw best, as the face of Jesus shines with such blazing light that, without sunglasses, you can't really see His features. (331)

Alec is a latter-day Job, tormented not by Satan (who, in hi-tech mode, befriends him and his spunky but obedient Margrethe), but by Yahveh in cahoots with Loki. The upshot seems tailored to please any fresh-faced college atheist, for Heinlein has the affair taken to a higher court, where sulky Yahveh is chided for his cruel incompetence.

Job has been compared with Heinlein's frolic *The Door Into Summer*, but actually it is a re-run of one of his very first stories, the chilling novella 'The Unpleasant Profession of Jonathan Hoag' (1942). Hoag's nasty line of work was art criticism, the whole world his canvas. Yahveh had botched his first sketch and lazily created this world on the palimpsest, leaving unspeakable Things lurking behind mirrors. *Job: a Comedy of Justice* really did nothing to extend Heinlein's early work, which lurks behind *its* surface as a rebuke. The book's ethics, artistry and characterization are of a piece with all Heinlein's late fiction: unsurprisingly sclerotic, too good-natured and *silly* to be truly offensive. Their tone can be conveyed definitively in this sample from the opening of *The Number of the Beast-*, where the narrator is allegedly about thirty years old (although, admittedly, from a slightly variant history from our own):

> I signaled a twirl by pressure; she floated into it and back into my arms right on the beat. I inspected her hands and the outer corners of her eyes. Yes, she really was young—minimum 18 . . . maximum 25 . . . Yet she danced like her grandmother's generation.
>
> `Well?' she repeated more firmly.
>
> This time I openly stared. `Is that cantilevering natural? Or is there an invisible bra, you being in fact the sole support of two dependents?'
>
> She glanced down, looked up and grinned. `They do stick out, don't they? . . . (1980, 9)

This oddly adolescent geriatric sex banter was to remain at the center of Heinlein's final works. The theme of *To Sail Beyond the Sunset* (1987), capstone of Heinlein's germinal `future history', employing every possible combination with the greatest proselytizing enthusiasm, was incest for fun and profit. Fathers and daughters, mothers and sons, brothers and sisters: this customary combinatory merely set the stage. Replete with strongly autobiographical elements, the book proved to be the 400-page confessions of Maureen Johnson, born 1882 and still going strong in the fifth millennium. Johnson is the mother of Heinlein's favorite rogue sage, Lazarus Long, the time-travelling immortal from *Methuselah's Children* (1957) and *Time Enough For Love* (1973), whose sexual entourage includes his own cloned sister-twins. Longevity, complete genetic mapping and a dash of time paradox makes a snip of having it away with your grandparents or your remote descendants. But, as Freud knew, mother is best. Heinlein mocks `Dr. Fraud', which is hardly fair, since his own crude biological determinism ensures that wives are dutiful (if feisty) and husbands masterful, or they are for evolution's scrapheap. His libertarianism of the Elect juggles pukkah zest for military virtues, discipline and patriotism with narcissistic sexual taboo-busting. In Heinlein's archetypal sf world, causality is abolished, human frailties are ignored; every emotional or ethical difficulty is, as Yvonne Rousseau has put it, `eerily smoothed away' (Rousseau, 1986, 36). So it is not the incest that is corrupting in Heinlein—for here he merely apes Voltaire, Shaw, Cabell and other iconoclasts—but the way his own dogmatism is uncoupled from the human heart.

vii

The persistence of the Heinleinian system of tropes, as well as its critique, is evident in the work of his admirers. At one time, the sf writer Joe Haldeman used a droll calling card bearing the slogan `Heinlein re-treads a specialty'.[3] Later, John Varley, Spider Robinson and John Barnes echoed something of the Heinlein narrative attack and voice, sometimes in ways their model might not have approved.

Half a lifetime ago, Haldeman recast the Vietnam conflict as memorable, award-winning science fiction in *The Forever War* (1975). His elite, technically-savvy troops battled an alien foe across light-years and centuries. Poignantly, each engagement cut them off from Earth by hundreds of years, as relativistic velocities flung them into their own ever-more incomprehensible future. At the end of the thousand year war, it all turned out to have been a mistake. And new humanity, now a standardized group-mind named Man, had more in common with the clone-like alien Taurans. Haldeman is sf's consummate story-teller, his tales always illuminated by a moral consciousness. Far from turning them dull or didactic, this is what makes his fiction memorable, decade after decade. It is no accident that a new British series of `SF Masterworks' chose *The Forever War* as its launch vehicle. Where can damaged veterans go in a universe like that? Haldeman returned in *Forever Free* (1999), more than two decades later in both reality and narrative time-line, to probe the consequences of the peace. William Mandella and his love Marygay Potter accept Man's offer of a world sardonically named Middle Finger (`up yours' or, even more frankly, MF). Here, unreconstructed relics of the war huddle from a universe repellent in its inhuman benevolence. MF proves to be the sort of welcome-home Vietnam veterans enjoyed—cold and hard. Technology, surprisingly, is not greatly advanced after a millennium. William and Marygay, and their adolescent son and daughter, now aquaculture fisherfolk, live in ice-bound rural Paxton (`peace town'), chafing under Man's benign supervision. If *Forever War* was a caustic reply to Robert A. Heinlein's *Starship Troopers*, *Forever Free* seemed ready to follow his *Methuselah's Children*: a stolen starship, a run for the edge of the

---

[3] Joe Haldeman and his wife Gay are perhaps the most beloved figures in science fiction, regular convention-goers in many countries. I am proud to have provided the title for one Haldeman novel, filched from Shakespeare.

galaxy, freedom boldly purchased. But Haldeman had larger fish to fry.

Can a wily, squabbling group of aging veterans defeat the omnipresent custody of their evolutionary superiors? Or is Man's non-telepathic group mind a blind end? If Mandella and his conspirators manage to flee relativistically into the remote future, what can they possibly seek that will not be worse than their current anguished alienation? Might they find God—and an answer to the horrors of the Forever War itself, and all of human history's suffering? The plot maneuvers of *Forever Free* are abrupt and startling. One conceptual breakthrough after another tears open our understanding of this universe, until finally Haldeman deploys a kind of Gnostic explanation for the world's pain. Gnosticism is a faith with few adherents these days, perhaps because it is not very satisfying—and its claims are just as dubious in fiction (except, perhaps, in Philip K. Dick's).

Oddly, a thematic sequel already existed—Haldeman's 1997 Hugo-winner, *Forever Peace*. Set in a different near-future, that novel proposed a cure for war and hatred in the tradition of humanistic sf, notably Theodore Sturgeon's: just the sort of empathic group mind that Mandella and his veteran friends find so creepy. It was if Haldeman restlessly tried out all the variants on salvation, determined to keep us entertained as he did so. Perhaps he is telling us that suffering is simply built-in to the cosmos, laced through it, unavoidable except at the cost of extinguishing the burning spark of individual awareness. The gratuitous cruelty that climaxes *Forever Free*, and its gratuitous redemption, lurches from comic-book excess to world-weary acceptance. The augmented fighting suits of this quasi-trilogy have morphed into a stifling enclosure of the spirit. But perhaps the deity Mandella finds at the end of his long road is just the manipulative author himself, Joe Haldeman gazing pitilessly at his creations behind the computer screen—yet another Heinleinian reprise: `It amused me,' the nameless god thing tells Mandella, `to construct your situation' (266). That is not far from Heinlein's playful pseudo-explanation for the concurrent reality of his inconsistent and mutually penetrating `ficton' worlds: `Eschatological Pantheistic Multiple-Ego Solipsm' (*Number of the Beast—*, 537).

viii

In general, though, Haldeman took from Heinlein only the most general tricks and usages of what Budrys calls `modern science fiction', the staples of *Astounding/Analog* editor John W. Campbell's stable from the 1940s on. In a well-received Hugo-shortlisted first novel, *Emergence* (1984), David Palmer appropriated the details, the feathers and eye glances and webbing on the water-churning feet, the odor and the grooming behavior, pretty well everything that makes a duck a duck. Palmer, in brief, colonized the Robert A. Heinlein Ecological Niche, abandoned a little earlier by Spider Robinson. He had the coloring, the voice (though some of the mating cries were muted—he was not quite as insistent on everyone calling everyone 'dear' and 'Boss'), the cropping habits: not so much a case of adaptive mimicry as of cloning.

In *The Moon is a Harsh Mistress* (1966, winner of the 1967 Hugo award), Heinlein's utopian anarcho-capitalists built their new world under a blood-drenched flag inscribed with their acronymic slogan: 'There Ain't No Such Thing As A Free Lunch'. The word for Palmer's intertextual gleanings is not 'tanstaafl', however. It is not exactly plagiarism, either, for no piece of explicit plotting, no complete character, no sequence of words is stolen from Heinlein—just everything that a simple-minded fan of his middle-period storytelling would recognize instantly as his imprint, his knack of doing things, his obsessions, his political tastes . . . This is a droll outcome, it must be confessed, to the intellectual and artistic career of a man who spent his life preaching that the competent individual makes his own path, goes his own way, respecting others in their god-given ornery singularity, and demanding his own prerogatives at the point of a nuclear weapon.

Palmer, jack of numerous trades including many of those attributed graphically and compellingly to his 11-year-old superchild heroine and her 13-year-old friend (car racing, flying, bird fancying, farming, karate and emergency medical expertise), seemed less to have *studied* Heinlein's stock in trade than *lived* it, breathed it, absorbed it as might a worshipper the incense of his deity.

In 1968, Alexei Panshin published a detailed analysis, much reviled—like the powerful, ideologically driven 1980 study by Marxist H. Bruce Franklin—by Heinlein's fans, of what made a Heinlein story or novel tick. He was not uncritical, but the component of his study that burned through was Panshin's clear wish to learn how to emulate Heinlein's mastery of a certain kind of very effective sf. Effective, that is, in seizing and holding adolescent readers, knocking them sideways with wonder and a sense of honor and decency and courage that they did not find in their 1950s' American world but which Heinlein told them would be the spine of the future, when tough-minded, practical dreamers would run the world right, if they had to kill every last Bug in the universe. Panshin learned his own lesson: the result was *Rite of Passage* (1968), a slightly left-wing variety of the standard formulation which immediately garnered the Nebula Award. It pays to study the masters.

Spider Robinson, as noted, did the same somewhat later, with similar success. He too extended the original range a little, introduced profanity to balance the sticky sentimentality, was more streetwise than hi-tech, but the essence was `Heinlein re-tread'. Palmer's first novel did it more convincingly than either. He failed to win the 1985 Hugo Award, though his Heinlein is better than Robert A. Heinlein's own attempt with the flaccid *Job*, also a contender; the competition from William Gibson's post-Bester *Neuromancer* was too great.

It is an oversimplification to credit Heinlein as onlie begetter. Palmer's story (increasingly *ad hoc* and full of holes as it is) goes like this: Candidia Smith (a perfect Heinlein name, reminiscent of Valentine Michael Smith and Johann Sebastian Smith) is orphaned, adopted by nice Dr. and Mrs. Foster (*sic!*) in, one might say, Smallville. Candidia is very very clever; her mother helps her read by age 2, calculus shortly after. Her father treats her like a child, which is a comfort to an infant who otherwise might be alienated by a sense of freakish difference. Mother dies, but soon a nice old Asiatic-American arrives in town to teach her karate and provide access to lots of books behind her father's back. At eight, she is a Fifth Degree Black Belt, and by 11 has self-induced hypnotic access to hysterical strength (deployed strikingly in a number of astonishingly violent scenes). This old gentleman proves (as is typical in such books) to have three doctorates as well as Eighth Degree mastery; Candy's country practice foster-father turns out to be something similar, as well as owning a nuclear bomb-proof installation 200 feet down under the mandatory white clapboard home, which saves Candy when the treacherous Soviets wipe out the Free World with radiation-induced viral megadeath.

Candidia is not just a classic Heinlein over-achiever, she is also that marvel of *Astounding*, the mutant superhuman. Mark Clifton's `Star, Bright' (1953) is the epitome of the tradition; that, or Wilmar H. Shiras's *Children of the Atom* (1953). Zenna Henderson's psychically gifted extraterrestrial but very human People are another variety. The point the sub-genre makes in its very structure is that *you*, lucky reader, might well be one of these fortunate souls in hiding—Homo post hominem, in the

Palmer avatar. In the frame of his narrative, true, this is unlikely, for one evidence of membership is lifelong immunity from illness. Many devoted sf readers, by contrast, became fans due to being rather smarter (and hence lonelier, often bitterly lonelier) than their peers, as well as sick, fat, scrawny, half-blind or disabled (and hence ready consumers for the consolations of fantasy and not quite so distracted from reading by the pleasures of rough-and-tumble sport or nascent sex). Still, though the standard sf reader is almost certainly *not* Homo superior, he and she are likelier candidates than their tormentors, and when they grow up and master science they will surely run the world! Until then, and in the absence of the existential pleasure of writing the worldly text upon the world itself, Heinlein surrogates of this kind provide the pleasures of the readerly text.

A considerable amount of research and imagination (of a kind) went into *Emergence*. Palmer conceives a plausible method by which the world can be depopulated of all but superfolk (don't *you* sometimes wish everyone would just *go away*?). He finds ways to make a cute little 11-year-old indispensable in Saving The World (don't you just know you too could drive a spaceship if they gave you the chance?). None of this expertise is entirely fudged: it draws on the NASA Shuttle Operator's Manual, consultation with physicians and specialists in Russian. Like Heinlein's own polymathic expertise, it pays off; the book is heavy with authenticity by comparison with the slick multi-volume series produced by (let us say) Jack Chalker and Piers Anthony.

But the sub-text is abominable, when it is not simply laughable. The world left to the superfolk is under threat by the last surviving *Homo sapiens sapiens*, bunkered in Russia. Inevitably, these are also Commie scum (the Evil Empire, in 1984, not having yet imploded), while the nice, handsome, healthy, brave, honorable, heartbreakingly American hominems are all Republicans. So the equation read back into our world: superman is to man as American is to Commie scum; but American is man, not superman; ergo, Commie scum is *sub*-human, and deserved to be nuked by Reagan as soon as possible. I am not claiming that Palmer introduced this syllogism deliberately, but it was shared in one form or another with much `militaristic' hi-tech science fiction; today the sub-humans are terrorists, usually Muslim.

Candy's friend `Adam' desires her underdeveloped body. So does virtually every other male she meets. This is a little odd, surely, but critics have found it before . . . in Heinlein. (Daniel Boone Davis, for instance, in *The Door into Summer*, consummates his love for Ricky, an associate's 11-year-old stepdaughter, by lingering in suspended animation until she is legally grown-up, but fortunately still besotted by him despite his absence during these formative years.) Men in their forties, their thirties, they are all eager for Candy. One of them, while putting this idea to her in a paradigm-cum-parody of Heinleinian reasoning—a gem of self-ridicule, carried off, I am sure, in full awareness of this fact—is very messily and satisfyingly murdered / executed. Radical feminists might possibly rejoice at this. Candy is appropriately remorseful (she is usually more sensitive to the value of the lives of those she dislikes than Heinlein's characters ever were), but by then the readers have enjoyed their surges of adrenalin. In any event, her older girlfriend Kim Melon (*sic!*) convinces her of the probity of her murder. Kim is `slim, willowy, long-legged. Waist-length natural Swedish-blond mane. Pretty face—correction, beautiful face—double-correction, movie-star face. Plus last name describes salient physical characteristics with unintended hilarious accuracy' (166). Such boyish `unintended' gags typical Heinlein.

Can we believe Candy is superhuman? She writes most of the book in Pitman shorthand—Palmer is a court reporter, the jacket notes inform us, when he is not being a racing driver—and as a mark of her superlative intelligence leaves out all the unnecessary words: verbs, pronouns, articles definite and indefinite, and so on. This makes her sound (a convenient side benefit) rather like Manny Davis (Davis again), the narrator of *The Moon is a Harsh Mistress*, but clots some of the text so foully that it is tempting to skim. Palmer's error is that natural language speakers do not employ redundancy from stupidity, but as an important syntactical and semantic aid. It might save Candy time to write it that way; decoding it merely slows *us* up to no good end.

ix

At quite a drastic remove from both Palmer's and Haldeman's methods, an alternative avatar of Heinlein's impulse and methods arrived, most startlingly, in the guise of the late E. P. Thompson, New Left historian of *The Making of the English Working Class* (1963) and that corrective to Althusserian dogmatizing, *The Poverty of Theory* (1978). His satire *The Sykaos Papers* (1988) placed a Marxist version of Valentine Michael Smith in England's green and increasingly unpleasant land and watched the world spin madly around this Candidean angelic figure: spin and topple, finally, into the SDI nuclear holocaust which Thompson spent so much of his energies before his death trying to forestall. If Thompson lacked the deftness of an sf writer as fully schooled as Palmer in Heinlein's methods, he made a fair fist of it by virtue of knowing so much about so many other things, or at least by focussing engagingly on those he knew extremely well—humans military and academic, high and low, the dubious powerful and the poignantly sane.

Fetched here for a pre-colonization reconnaissance from the iced-up computerized world Oitar (Ratio, Reason, as the adjective from Sykaos—our Earth—is, with regrettable elephantine joviality, `Sykotic'), Oi Paz crashlands. When he appears name-reversed as Sapio the Spaceman in a TV exploitation show, he is taken smartly into custody by security and dispatched to a Research Establishment for what amounts to psychological vivisection. The novel is a collage of his notes (in a charmingly sustained and revealing patois), fragments of interviews, and the diaries and notebooks of the conscripted feminist anthropologist, Dr. Helena Sage, FRAI.

Like Heinlein's Smith, Oi Paz is an innocent abroad, showing up our best and worst features. Unlike Smith, he is no superbeing. A kind of copper-skinned adult Apollo, he speaks in the piping tones of a pre-pubescent, which he is. Luckless Oi Paz undergoes the joys of sexual awakening in our fallen world. Dr. Sage observes with postmodern sagacity, is observed, becomes involved with her project. Thompson sustains these shifts in narrative voice, funny names and all, shifting from satire to sentiment and back through parody. Only in his redemptive close does the dynamic falter, jettisoning half the text's achievement, a plausible non-sexist picture of people who are more than their biological essence.

By contrast, Palmer's very minor work is typical of two factors in generic sf: its dependency, even to the point of near-plagiarism, on previous exemplary works and interests, and its tendency to repetition, almost to entropy. In part, of course, these traits are automatically entailed by the notion of generic categorization, but it is instructive to turn now to an examination of the constrictions and liberations available to more genre-challenging writers who, while potentially reordering the canon by their presence, nevertheless continued to work within the web of the sf megatext. In the chapter following, we shall look at certain writers operating additionally within the world-inscribing megatext of that threatened nuclear apocalypse, now either in abeyance or redoubled by terrorist urgency—which is a classic locus of sf, the harbinger, in the `real' world, of the end of all texts.

3: THE OWLS ARE NOT WHAT THEY SEEM

i

As a beardless youth, I once gatecrashed a social gathering held by a distinguished professor. Nostalgic among cronies, he reminisced over his own undergraduate days. He had been much exercised, it emerged, by the Ontological Problem.

So far as I could make out, this had to do with the question whether anything actually existed or merely seemed to, and if it did what it was really like, and in any case why it should.

Eventually I was introduced to the professor. Lying in my teeth, I told him I was a postgraduate philosopher.

`Really?' he cried, pouring cabernet sauvignon. `And what's your specialty?'

`An unfashionable area these days, I'm afraid.' I lowered my voice. `The Ontological Problem.'

`Bless my soul. Tell me, what's the current state of play?'

`Actually,' I said, `we've just about got it licked.'

He nodded thoughtfully, and called for more wine.

Of all literary and paraliterary forms of imaginative writing, it is science fiction that plays the most formidable games with such primordial questions. A marvelously clever British writer, Ian Watson has licked the Ontological Problem at least a dozen times in novels and short stories. At the start of his career, I read the general tenor of his attack as Sufism, the mystical branch of Islam that long attracted Doris Lessing's admiration, resulting in her *Canopus in Argos* sequence of sf allegories. Watson's version was arabesqued from the outset with flaming darts of Chomskyan linguistics, high-energy physics, advanced molecular biology, the cosmology of black holes and Big Bang, all tied together in a nervy style replete with recondite puns.

This must have seemed to most literary readers strange material to build novels from. Perhaps only science fiction has the cognitive room to let such hares run, unencumbered as it is by the over-riding and sometimes dictatorial demands of character, psychological density set in a frame of recognizable and exquisitely limited quotidian reality. Watson's characters are rarely better than thin, but they are *exemplary*. Their thoughts and actions embody a dynamic totemism. They move in a realm close to the logical transformations of a mathematical theorem, but one which permits infinities to lodge in its equations.

Infinity draws endlessly at Watson's characters. Their anxieties yearn toward the metaphysical. In his impressive debut novel, *The Embedding* (1973), Watson bravely if somewhat unsuccessfully juggled assorted human, parahuman and alien characters in a fictional demonstration of generative grammar and its capacity to shape its speakers' life-world. If nothing else, it was a triumphant exercise in radical linguistic relativism. Noam Chomsky, as is now well-known, dwelt on the astonishing fact that by using only a couple of hundred words even the simplest competent speaker can generate an indefinite number of different meaningful sentences. This can be done most primitively by embedding dependent clauses, even though the meaning of such sentences is monstrously diffi-cult to decode (which might be thought to subvert the claims for `native speakers'): `The rat the cat the dog the man kicked teased chased ran' is, for Chomsky, a legitimate sentence built up by embedding. Watson uses that idea as a powerful metaphor for the literally unspeakable mystery that consciousness represents in a vast but finally limited non-conscious cosmos of atoms and galaxies.

Both in the structure of most of his novels, and in the concepts he evoked from cognitive science, Watson retained the key notion of embed-ding. *The Martian Inca* (1977) has a spore returned to Earth from Mars, a splendidly conceived alien lifeform whose DNA encapsulates an entire ecology. The alien biological information serves to catalyze a theocratic revolution in Latin America (rather as Islam was later to do in Iran and Afghanistan and might yet in Iraq), reviving at a higher level Inca society, that ultimate hierarchical order.

Perhaps such descriptions make Watson's strategies sound arid. It is part of his gift, however, to evoke sensuous settings, often exotic. One of his finest early novels, *Miracle Visitors* (1978), moves swiftly from the Malcolm Bradbury/David Lodge territory of a British red brick university 'Consciousness Research Group' to the idiotic subculture of UFO contactees (thoroughly researched and accurate, and in advance of the later boom in UFO 'abduction' hysteria), to the Cairo headquarters of a Sufi Master. Reality blurs, fragments, opens out like Jamil Nasir's *Distance Haze* (2000; see chapter 14) into transreality (Broderick, 2000). Events and their explication prove endlessly recursive, a typical Watson tactic. Under hypnosis, a young man 'recalls' his kidnapping by sexy UFO crew members. Their names derive from Blake's *Zoas,* and the 'recovered memories' have a clear Freudian significance. But so too, at the next level down, does the investigator's interest in the pretty youth's case, to his wife's chagrin. So too, indeed, do the motives of the otherwise hard-nosed UFO buff who gives credence to the youth's grotesquely absurd story.

For the Sufi guru, none of this narrative decoration is essential: the events have a numinous quality transcending any reductive account. UFO happenings, like other miracles, are an intrusion into prosaic reality of the larger metaphysical realm in which we are embedded. Indeed, for John Deacon, acolyte to the new religion, 'saucers and their kin did not intrude *into* the world. The world was actually within them.' Human consciousness is drawn into evolution from without: UFOs are 'intrusions of higher-order knowledge into a lower-order system, namely the human mind, to draw it upward. The alien was the miracle from now on' (Watson, 1978, 188). It is a perspective that engaged the imagination of American sf master Philip K. Dick at around the same time, culminating in such novels as *The Divine Invasion* (1981), *Valis* (1981) and *The Transmigration of Timothy Archer* (1982), each of them derived in turn from Dick's own epiphanic 'experiences' of an alien intelligence touching him with strange data and physical insight.

ii

Everyone was talking about God in sf at the start of the 1980s. In the oddest of his late novels, *Valis,* Philip K. Dick turned from paranoid crypto-gnostic sf to a kind of explicitly theological fiction. In the guise of

Horselover Fat (a sort of Greek translation of his name fore and aft), Dick had a nasty shock some years earlier when he was vouchsafed a vision of Absolute Evil. The Three Stigmata of the devil. Entropy rode the range, sucking everything down into gluey oblivion. Life wasn't easy for Horselover in those days; happily, a redemptive revelation showed Mr. Fat that he could be snatched out of the fire. It turned out to be a sort of . . . spirit or . . . Force . . . watching over us, imbuing us, hinting that after all, in the face of all that grim evidence, everything is really all right. (Can it be an accident that Darth Vader so greatly resembles the demon-soaked pilgrim of Dick's earlier and much applauded hallucinatory 1964 novel, *The Three Stigmata of Palmer Eldritch?*)

Horselover Fat meditates on the nature of the world, and human misery, for most of the novel's 213 pages. In between the meager narrative events, in which a species of Messiah or AntiChrist or something is born to a pair of unusually clean popstars, Horselover mulls over, bit by bit, his diary jottings. They look like this:

Entry 30: The phenomenal world does not exist: it is a hypostasis of the information processed by the Mind.

That might strike us as a fairly old fashioned idea, as does this, from Entry 48:

The Godhead is impaired; some primordial crisis occurred in it which we do not understand.

The twelve pages of this insight-packed revelation are not left scattered incoherently through the body of *Valis*, but neatly reprinted in an Appendix at the end, presumably for easy reference and spiritual guidance. *Valis* is a very bad novel *qua* novel, but fascinating as a casebook in the disintegration of a mystic science fiction writer. One kept wanting the author of *Ubik* and *Dr. Bloodmoney* to take command of the typewriter, but that was obviously impossible, and an unfair request. Dick had moved into stranger habitats. *Valis* is perhaps best regarded as a by-product of the Seventies' California Mindfuck Trip, to be enjoyed as such.

iii

On the other hand there was Philip José Farmer's endless Rotary Club cruise up and down the River of Cosmic Meaning, begun promisingly in *To Your Scattered Bodies Go* (1971). After *The Fabulous Riverboat* (1971), the next sequel *The Magic Labyrinth* (1980) was advertised as the concluding volume of the Riverworld series proper, but turgid endless Philip José Farmer publicly threatened more, and went on to deliver it, mighty additional volumes, *The Dark Design* (1977), *Riverworld War* (1982), *The Gods of Riverworld* (1983), little stories and snippets and for all I know encyclopedias of addenda and marginalia..

Something had gone badly wrong. After the first volume of the series appeared in book form, a close, careful and reasonably admiring analytic scrutiny was published, assessing the improvements Farmer had wrought in language and character since its earlier magazine publication. The author was John Foyster, the Australian killer critic. Impossible to imagine Foyster paying the same kind of attention (or any at all) to the later volumes in the series. Farmer visibly thumped this stuff out like a cook in an army camp hurling bangers and mash onto tin plates as fast as he can, while the hungry troops march muddily past, endlessly. (I do not wish to imply that Farmer abandoned his previous artistic standards for mercenary motives.)

Plainly, the flaws in writing and thinking did not disturb the great majority of Farmer's enthusiastic devotees. Sf readers, by and large, are word-blind. Consider a fan critic's verdict on Joan Vinge's best-selling Hugo winning Barbara-Cartland-in-space *The Snow Queen* (1980): `If I had read it without knowing the author,' confessed the critic, `I would have said it was by Ursula Le Guin.' In any reasonable court, that would be grounds for damages and a horse-whipping. The docks would be filled, though, since sf readers generally cannot tell the difference between Vinge and Le Guin, or if they can they don't care, or between Farmer on those rare occasions when he got it shockingly, brilliantly right, and the rest of time when he flopped down those unending piles of burnt sausages.

Yet the Riverworld series was not without considerable ambition. Like Haldeman's work, like Watson's, it was about enigmas: the meaning of life and consciousness. Everyone gets resurrected on a world where the basics of life are provided free. Sin enters at once. Greed, lust, aggression, anxiety (you didn't know anxiety was a sin?), suicide. Yet suicide is no longer a sin, for self-destruction merely triggers further rebirth into healthy young adulthood. Ultimately, the Riverworld series suggests, one ought to live for passionate intensity. The higher the passion, the fiercer the flame, the greater will be one's respect for those other conscious beings who share one's physical and psychic universe. Ethics emerge from ripeness, not staleness, not constriction, not cowardice and self-restraint. And the final goal and reward of true ethical passion is transcendence. The developed soul/mind/body passes out of this world into the mysterious and unknowable Bosom of God.

In short, the Riverworld series contains assertions (or speculations) about the nature of humanity, about our purpose in a blind universe, and it contains as well a full-blown multi-level metaphor for those speculations. Yes, there is also an `explanation' at the end which ties all the mysteries up in a dingy bow, forcing the loose ends under in the hope that they won't pop back out until the book is closed, but that explanation is not really important. It, too, is a metaphor, dragged in at the terminus with such speed that I assume even Farmer considered it marginal. Basically, its claim is this: the universe produces complexity of all kinds, but something extraphysical is needed to ignite reality into meaning. Farmer postulates a *wathan*, or soul; personally, I find this as unnecessary and distasteful as von Daniken's argument from about the same epoch that we need to invoke extraterrestrials to explain the great human achievements of the past. Curiously, even as Farmer's series rolled on toward bathos, this question of the origins of consciousness in a world of matter was being explored beautifully and in depth in Douglas Hofstadter's wonderful *Gödel, Escher, Bach: An Eternal Golden Braid* (1979).

The real problem, I suppose, and one common to much ambitious sf, is that the Riverworld books proposed a literary project far beyond Farmer's powers. Despite some embarrassingly heavy-handed attempts to define his characters through speech register, they clump about the stage like zombies. The background data is loaded in clumsily. Inserting such quantities of information gracefully is, admittedly, a hard trick to pull off upon so broad a stage; Tolstoy strikes the modern reader as ham-fisted in this regard.

iv

Not for a moment do Ian Watson's sf novels and stories smack of tawdry von Danikenism. Like the magical Tom Stoppard, and to a far greater extent than Philip Dick was able to manage, Watson from the outset blended the undergrowth of the human imagination with a fastidious attention to complex intellectual nutrients. In one astonishing apercu in

Miracle Visitors, he unites Barthesian semiotics, then fashionable in the academy though hardly in popular fiction, with quantum theory:

> If events in the `real' world were all thoughts—processes by which the universe thought out its own reality—and if one learnt to think of these events as thoughts; if one grew aware of the universal thought processes rather than the `events' which were their language—why then, the landscape would be symbolic: a `virtual' landscape directly manifesting symbols—rather like dream imagery, yet operating not privately within one's own personal consciousness, but instead publicly and collectively. (1978, 200)

Is this the stuff of a novel? Surely it is, although ideative fiction like this typically causes shudders of loathing in the breasts of those wedded to Anglo-Saxon Attitudes of commonsense and geniality. On the other hands, enthusiasts for postmodern profundity might well be outraged by Watson's merry impertinence. A coruscating free-wheeler who gives scant shrift to classical notions of character and social minutiae in fiction, Watson preferred formal structures of great inventiveness and wit. In *Chekhov's Journey* (1983), for example, he intercepted the Russian playwright's famous trek to the convict island Sakhalin, deflecting poor Chekov into a mare's nest of squabbling alternative selves. Deftly borrowing characters from the plays, Watson amuses himself and us with such absurdities as spacecraft Commander Anton Astrov (pinching the doctor from `Uncle Vanya'), hijacking the Russian theorist of spaceflight, K. E. Tsiolkovsky, diverting the 1908 Siberian `meteor' impact to the previous decade, and doing all this in a format remarkably redolent in style and mounting to one of Anton Chekhov's own plays. Equally profligate are his several collections of short fiction. In *Sunstroke* (1982), he taunted Austen fans (`To the Pump Room with Jane'), envisaged the ultimate movie (`The Thousand Cuts') and stranded us in a splendid Sufi parable, `The Rooms of Paradise'.

This method does not always work. A quality of wonderment is central to most memorable sf, which calls for some deeper engagement than mockery or game playing, precisely the large dimensionality of Watson's first novels. Sf's comic element goes dreadfully elephantine in *Converts* (1984), an avowedly slapstick farce about evolution, divinity and genetically improved apes. I liked the apes. In more traditional garb, Watson's trilogy *The Book of the River*, *The Book of the Stars* and *The Book of Being* (1984-85) took his sprightly feminist heroine Yaleen from one rather silly shock and world and Worm and Godmind to another. This series was, by the look of it, a highly intelligent gameplayer's shot at reaching a mass audience with regular thrills; it was followed by a two volume retelling of the Finnish Kalevala. None seems to have been very successful, perhaps explaining Watson's apparent shift away from sf as his preferred medium. Sometimes the owls *are* what they seem, and they seem just now not to be terribly promising for so fecund a fabulist as Ian Watson.

4: THE NUCLEAR FAMILY

i

Looking at a mathematical graph one day, I was surprised to find my throat tighten, a pressing emptiness in my chest, blurred vision, grief: I was crying. At a piece of algebra.

The last time anything like this had reached me so shockingly was during Ken Russell's calculatedly poignant BBC hymn to composer Edward Elgar's heroic melancholy. In a slightly jerky newsreel clip, a brisk officer herded one wounded man after another into a straggling queue, each man's hand to the shoulder of the fellow ahead. The stumbling line forged across the screen: fifteen of them, thirty, more. And suddenly you saw why they were clutching one another like this. Heads wrapped in dressing. Blinded, every man-jack of them, poor damned blind sods from the corrosive gas fields of Europe, after the war to end all wars. And swelling on the sound track, `Land of Hope and Glory', Elgar's glorious bombast.

The graph which made me cry was in Douglas Hofstadter's *Metamagical Themas* (1985). You take a piece of paper and rule it into 121 squares, 11 by 11. Then you fill each square, all but the central one, with a tight array of 50 dots. Place a single lonely dot in the middle square. Now you have one dot surrounded by 6000 others.

The solo dot represents all the firepower used in World War Two, including both atom bombs. The rest of the dots were the nuclear weapons ringing the world near the end of the twentieth century, waiting for deterrence to break down.

Numbers do not mean much to the emotions. They don't speak to the heart. That graph reached inside me, as the blinded men from the smashed fields had, and made me weep.

Science fiction has often thought about the unthinkable, usually with unthinkable stupidity and relish. James Morrow's *This is the Way the World Ends* (1987) is like a punch in the mouth by the Angel of Death in the garb of a stand-up comic. It was quickly compared to Jonathan Schell out of Kurt Vonnegut, which was spot-on.

George Paxton is a tomb cutter with an `adorable daughter' and a wife `who always looked as if she had just come from doing something dangerous and lewd' (15). His neighbor sells *scopas* suits, for Self-Contained Post-Attack Survival. The suits do not work, in the event. Here is part of Chapter 5, `In Which the Limitations of Civil Defense Are Explicated in a Manner Some Readers May Find Distressing':

> Townspeople marched down to the river . . . arms outstretched to lessen the weight of their burned hands. Many lacked hair and eyelashes . . . A white lava of melted eye tissue dripped from their heads; they appeared to be crying their own eyes.
>
> A seeing-eye dog, its scopas suit and fur seared away, licked the face of its dead master. `Somebody put the fur back on that dog!' George shouted. (58, 60)

It is not sentimentality to be moved by these images of carnage and horror. Nor is it ghoulish to laugh with Morrow at the black, bleak post-holocaust progress of George Paxton, his good-hearted Candide. In the twenty-first century ours might no longer be the worst of times, after the collapse of one wing of this appalling calculus of global death; nor is it the best of times, for international terrorism and the forces underpinning its threat ensure that George's world might yet ignite around us. Morrow's splendid novel, already in some measure superannuated by political shifts, lives on; it cannot help but stiffen our resolve to resist the lunatics who are preparing to kill us all.

ii

If Martin Amis had his way, he would take us by the scruff of the neck and frog-march us across the lawns and shove our stupid, feckless faces right up against the Keepers, his metaphor for weapons of mass destruction, and hold us there until we throw up, or throw them out.

> For the Keepers are a thousand feet tall, and covered in gelignite and razor-blades, toting flame-throwers and machineguns, cleavers and skewers, and fizzing with rabies, anthrax, plague. Curiously enough, they are not looking at the children at all. With bleeding hellhound eyes, mouthing foul threats and shaking their fists, they are looking at each other. (29)

Isn't it strange? Megatons and seasons of nuclear blight and half a million years of mutating poisons fail to touch us. Skid off. Razor-blades and cleavers do it, though. Slam the children up against the foul things, slash their soft flesh, force them to breathe in the fumes of anthrax. Does that help? Has Martin done the trick for you? Are you frightened enough to wet yourself? I suppose that is asking a bit much. Global ruin is finally too abstract, even when it is wrapped about in gelignite and skewers, too abstract to loosen the bowels. Maybe we shall just have to boil and char, after all, and watch the skin peel away from the children's soft flesh.

Alike in this, if nothing more, the writings of Amis *pere* and *fils* are each clever, cruel, bilious and funny. Sir Kingsley was the tall one with seamed and rosy cheeks, as befitted the author of several books urging the merits of booze. Martin is pale, small as a weasel. Kingsley staggered slightly, well to the right, lugging his Booker Prize (for *The Old Devils* in 1986); Martin crouched to the left, lacking one (although shortlisted for his quasi-sf *Time's Arrow* in 1991). Everyone but the Booker judges agreed that Martin's *Money* was, in its year, far funnier, crueler and certainly no less clever than *The Old Devils*. Nobody presumes to assay or apportion the Amis bile. You could easily get the impression that they had in common a gene for misanthropy, but actually it seems to me to speak of the bitterness of thwarted, disappointed love for humankind.

> At the multiracial children's teaparty the guests have, perhaps, behaved slightly better since the Keepers were introduced . . . but standards of behavior are pretty well as troglodytic as they ever were . . . Although they are aware of the Keepers, they don't want to look at them, they don't want to catch their eye. (29)

The Rachel Papers came out when the lad was, what? 23? It is shockingly clever and reads as if Martin had been swotting away like the very devil at his Dad's *oeuvre*. Most of my friends felt quite sick when they'd finished it, if they did. (I relished it.) Their stomachs were hardly settled by later courses. *Money* and *London Fields* and especially *Time's Arrow* (with its time-reversed Nazi doctor) tidied up the meal with a good purge. You can't complain. Satire is like that. If it doesn't make you throw up you get your money back.

But it is facile to nominate misanthropy as a motive. You do not need to hate your fellows to pound their tripes with your metaphorical, metafictional boots. There is love and fear, after all. *Einstein's Monsters* is sparked by love and fear, as Frankenstein's was. Can we love the Bomb, as Kubrick sardonically suggested? Freud thought we love death, and fear love. Can we, for that matter, *fear* the Bomb? Perhaps not. Perhaps we do not want to look at it, even now; we do not want to catch its eye.

Amis is ferocious and it is hardly his fault if his attempts to allegorize Armageddon failed to ignite. *Einstein's Monsters* is five short stories and a polemical, furious essay on `Thinkability'. Do the stories catch this unprecedented horror? Not for me, not for a moment. In this case, this one case, I wonder whether it is possible to speak obliquely without giving away that hot terror which must be thrust again and again before the self-blinkered gaze.

Even his opening polemical essay falls away into the lure of rhetoric. Brilliant images turn wrong, once the mind brings them to focus. `The man with the cocked gun in his mouth may boast that he never thinks about the cocked gun,' Amis tells us. `But he tastes it, all the time' (13). But he *does not* taste it, you see. That is the whole problem. The human brain works by editing out the habitual. The man with the cocked gun tastes it no more than the man with the amalgam filling. Remember that vile chill at the edge of your tongue? Gone in a day. You cannot even *will* it back.

Amis was cross with his allies in this most holy of late twentieth century wars. Yes, E. P. Thompson had tried to show why the Strategic Defense Initiative (`Star Wars') was a criminally stupid idea. `But he will devastate nobody—indeed, he may even subvert the converted—because he has no respect for tone.' Perhaps so. Three pages on, Amis flays one Capt. T. Kalogroulis, irresponsible writer of *Civil Defence in Nuclear Attack: A Family Protection Guide.* `Not everyone (by definition) is as thoroughly, as exemplarily subhuman,' Amis concludes, `as Captain Necropolis' (22).

How many waverers will swallow this flourished barb? It's okay by me, I think the capt. should be put against a wall and shot, but I am not too clear on Amis's consistency of tone.

I have called the stories allegories, which Amis denies. They `were written with the usual purpose in mind: that is to say with no purpose at all—except, I suppose, to give pleasure . . . ' (Author's note). `Bujak and the Strong Force *or* God's Dice' shows a man turning from revenge even in the moment of its cruelest temptation. I was not convinced, but stranger things have happened. As a political fable it misses the distinction between personal impulses and State imperatives, the fundamental glitch in this whole enterprise. Soldiers do not kill out of anger at the enemy. Politicians do not exterminate all life on earth because of rage, although the Mutual Assured Destruction regime did seem nicely set up to make that the motive of last and inevitable resort.

The other pieces are progressively weaker. `Insight at Flame Lake' parallels the diaries of a dutch uncle and his schizophrenic nephew in a way reminiscent of Fowles' *Collector*. `The Time Disease' purports to be a homage to J. G. Ballard and shows with poignant clarity how little Amis grasps of the tropes of science fiction, as does the impeccably boring and obvious `The Immortals' which closes the book; its `secret' is disclosed as early as line 7. The longest story is a genuine fable, `The Little Puppy That Could', which reminds me much more of Thomas Disch than of Kafka and Nabokov, whom Amis claims. It is effective enough, although—unlike Disch—in a dumb way. Alas, most of the Booker-fanciers who dived upon this slight (127 page) collection will probably never encounter the sweet pleasures of Disch's whimsical prose, perhaps because his father was not named Kingsley.

That is too unkind, however. Martin Amis has written several exceptional novels, and extremely fluent and gratifying cultural critique, and doubtless shall again. And for all its errors and lapses (a pound of uranium is not so awesome a thing as he suggests, for he confuses Einstein's formula for total conversion of mass to energy with the very much more modest yield of a fission chain-reaction; strategic overkill ratios were irrational but not stupid, since it was assumed that most missiles would fail to reach their targets), *Einstein's Monsters* helped remind us that

If only they knew it—no, if only they *believed* it—the children could simply ask the Keepers to leave . . . The party has not been going on for very long and must last until the end of time. Already the children are weepy and feverish. They all feel sick and want to go home. (30)

iii

So when *The Joy of Sex*, *The Joy of Yiddish* and all their uplifting kin caught the book market a while back, I sourly mused on the chances of a bestseller entitled *The Joy of Killing People*.

Wander into an arcade computer-game parlor, watch the zap-fest of concussive roars and blinding lasers, see unemployed kids being programmed with idiotic glee for World War III in simulations called *Missile Attack*. Whoops, lost New York, another dollar down the tube. This evil sanitation of what ought to be literally unthinkable was furthered, I think, by novels such as *Footfall* by Larry Niven and Jerry Pournelle. That was an enormously successful sf blockbuster aimed at those huge audiences outside the narrow sf genre, a hymn to grit, xenophobia, manifest destiny and the Joy of Nuclear War.

American paperback science fiction has always tended to a gung-ho conservatism. It is largely adventure fiction, after all, and combat is the traditional stuff of thrilling heroics. Even so sensible a humanist as Isaac Asimov (notable for his abrasive onslaughts against `Star Wars' research) once wrote: `The dropping of the atomic bomb in 1945 made science fiction respectable . . . Believe me, there can be nothing duller than tomorrow's headlines in sf.' To the sf fan, Shute's *On The Beach* seems, he commented, `very milk-and-watery. So there's a nuclear war to start the story with—and what else is new?'

Like their earlier bestseller *Lucifer's Hammer* (about the global cataclysm of a cometary impact), *Footfall* was palpably a metaphor for US/Soviet nuclear war. Their interstellar invaders, the baby elephant Fithp, are a herd species, a fact gratifying to the novel's commissars before Russia too gets pounded. Fithp science, though, is hand-me-down, so their defeat is merely a matter of dogged human determination: *Hogan's Heroes* in space. Dr. Wade Curtis, a character modeled closely on co-author Pournelle (who wrote spy novels under that name) recommends: `Nuke `em till they glow, then shoot `em in the dark' (694). The US President's military subordinates mutiny to forestall not cowardly appeasement but conditional alien surrender, and an Orion space battleship driven into the sky on a column of detonating nuclear bombs hammers the aliens into absolute submission. *Footfall* captured the Reagan 1980s even more vividly than the movie *Rambo II*.

iv

It is an odd feature of the fantastic genre that its more reckless writers con themselves into delusional belief systems just as screwball as the worlds they dream up. L. Ron Hubbard, founder of Scientology, was the most infamous. One of the most successful horror writers, Whitley Strieber, announced in the late 1980s, to his richly rewarded astonishment, that he has repeatedly been abducted by little bald varmints in UFOs—and subjected, like many other claimants since, to sexual tampering aimed at breeding human-alien hybrids. Not to mention the dreaded anal or more properly rectal implant, a mysterious and humiliating procedure presumably with a different aim.

This ludicrous claim was unleashed in Strieber's testimonial *Communion* (1987), for which he was paid a million dollars. One follow-up, *Confirmation* (1998), also had a sacramental title, although *Confession* has not appeared. Just another tawdry example of pop gullibility and extreme unction? Strieber has not deserted the horror genre—*The Wolfen* (1978) and *The Hunger* (1981) made his name, and the vampire sequel *Lilith's Dream: A Tale of the Vampire Life* was released in 2002—but he added several intense novels of apocalyptic warning. Co-authored with the scholarly James Kunetka, *Warday* (1984) and *Nature's End* (1986) were almost dirty realist in style, and dealt passionately with real nightmarish hazards: nuclear conflict, and overpopulation. Strieber's adventures with aliens, whether they are compensatory fantasy or well-timed cynical exploitation (think of the Raelian Clonaid's fake reports of human cloning some years after Dolly the lamb), are not characteristic of *Nature's End*. Using techniques developed by sf writers in the past half-century, but without many of the insiderly nudges and quirks that alienate non-sf readers, Strieber and Kunetka constructed a thoroughly detailed and plausible portrait of a future which seemed at the time almost unavoidable, and still might be.

In 2025, the world gasps in noxious smog, Brazil is ablaze, the poor eat poison while the rich do not age if they keep up the payments. Into this global pillage steps Gupta Singh, a death-obsessed charismatic whose

Depopulation program proposes the voluntary euthanasia of a third of the world's human number. Singh has honorable ancestors in fantastic satire, notably Gore Vidal's *Messiah* (1954) and *Kalki* (1978). Against him stand four privileged white Americans, practitioners of a genuinely intriguing new art: the `conviction'. Combining voice-stress analysis, global data bases and artificial intelligence computer processing, a conviction is a total AI simulation of its chosen victim: Presidential candidate, corporate criminal, would-be messiah. Unlike the human original, a conviction program has no inhibitions. It will answer, with crucifying candor, any question put to it.

Would such power be licensed in a foreseeable future? Probably not. But then we do have senate inquiries and investigative journalism which sometimes (unlike much of the `embedded' journalism of the 2003 Iraq war) offend the wealthy and powerful. Indeed, the narrative of *Nature's End* is as much the terrifying nemesis wrought by the powerful upon these public gadflies as it is a tale of global cataclysm. If the book is tritely optimistic in its close, too eager to see a solution to technology's mayhem in a genetic boost to the intelligence of selected children, that is its bow to Hollywood and sf's dream of a Good Fairy in a white laboratory smock. It remains a striking document, welding imaginative extrapolation with effective storytelling skills, committed and involving. If it is the benign result of coaching by Grey aliens, we should all watch the skies with interest. We must hope, at the very least, that alien intellects vast and cool and unsympathetic do not drop by to nuke us until we glow, and then shoot us in the dark. Or, more realistically, that we refrain from doing it to ourselves, however exciting it seems on the big screen.

5: MARTIAN GOTHIC:
FAMILIARITY AND AFFECTION

[Estrangement effects] discovered by recent critics in the conventions of science fiction may result in a dulling of the audience's sense of reality, in shell-shocked acceptance rather than critical intransigence. . . . Whether fantasy makes us more critical or merely more solipsistic and self-indulgent depends finally on whether it is accountable to something that is not fantasy.

Gerald Graff, *Literature Against Itself* (1979, 99-100)

i

Is putting a hovel together out of compressed soil and scrap iron the same human activity as building a skyscraper or a Gothic cathedral? Are they both `architecture'? Do identical standards of excellence apply? (Or is the hovel, a structure intimately on a human scale, automatically superior?)

Ray Bradbury, most famous and candied of all twentieth century sf writers, was elevated to semi-literary status out of the pulps during the glossy mid-century triumph of Mad Ave. At first glance he was the gee-whiz kid from Green Town, Illinois (his favorite nostalgic if imaginary setting), dancing his innocent rapture in the mid-American moonbeams of Halloween, even on Mars, roasting chestnuts over the burning leaves. Then one saw that the leaves were torn from gutted books, blazing at 451 degrees Fahrenheit. Above all else, even when he seemed the very model of dated small-town celebration, Bradbury's enduring topic was conformity's hatred of imagination.

While urban blight is not Gothic, the decayed remnants of machine hopes certainly are. Those rusting starships in the expensive special effects movies and television series, those crammed steel cylinders in orbit or beneath the ocean, winking in the dark with a million lights, creepy with muscular aliens hidden against plastic surfaces they resemble: these are the Gothic ruins of the millennium we have blundered into.

Bradbury knew exactly where this paradox dwelt, and in his late novels he went there: not to Mars, nor razor-wired Belfast, but rhapsodic Ireland and Hollywood in the fifties. Hollywood especially, where dreams, vulgar and gorgeous alike, were distilled into light and song and sent out to colonize the world. Who is the wizard sitting up there, running Oz? What murders might be done in the flickering darkness? What ruin of soul and body? Who better, finally, to tell the tale than Bradbury's own alter ego? In his 1930s' Midwest rites of passage, a landscape of dark carnivals and feverish pubertal hungers (*Dandelion Wine* [1957], *Something Wicked This Way Comes* [1963]), he always played the starring role—but split: innocent, driven, the white-haired bookish kid, the black-haired scamp. In two moody thrillers (*Death Is A Lonely Business* [1986]and *A Graveyard For Lunatics* [1990]) the identification was clearer than ever. Indeed, in the latter, the dark twin was drawn explicitly upon his own childhood friend Ray Harryhausen, a celebrated creator of animated movie monsters:

> Roy laughed, and held out a big fat copy of *You Can't Go Home Again.*
> `He was wrong,' said Roy, quietly.
> `Yes,' I said. `Here we *are,* by God!' (21)

For Bradbury, home is the *only* place you can go again.

Consider the screenwriter narrator: `a real honest-to-God idiot savant. A real fool, not a fake one. Someone who talks too much but then you look at the words and they're right . . . The good things come out of your hands into words' (273). As they do from Roy Holdstrom's, into miniaturized landscapes, alternative realities constructed for a movie set:

> vistas so alien and beautiful it broke your heart and mended your
> terror and then shook you again as shadows in great lemming mobs

rushed over the microscopic dunes . . . fleeing a doom already promised but not yet arrived. (28)

The story in *A Graveyard For Lunatics*, perhaps inevitably, is almost irrelevant to one's reading, a collage of all Gothic stories, as it must be: the dubious priest, the beautiful woman with a ghastly secret, tombs and vaults and catacombs, a face as scarred as a gargoyle, deaths and worse in graveyards. While it makes very little plot sense, neither did Poe, Bradbury's great forerunner. Yet its images, its cool tendrils, its not-quite-cloying sweetness, persist when traditional horror tropes fade away.

ii

These late Bradbury works are not sf, certainly, and hardly fantasy. They might, perhaps, be regarded as *slipstream*. Consider, for calibration, two examples of distinctly non-fantastic fiction at the farther edge of slipstream—hardly novels at all, by canonical standards. Michael Herr's *Walter Winchell* (1990) is, confessedly, a screenplay masquerading as a novel masquerading as a screenplay grounded in detail upon the biographical facts of its subject. Philip Roth's novel *Deception* (1990) is, in effect, a radio drama drawing poignantly upon the death by cancer of his English mistress. By no means science fictional . . . and yet . . .

Walter Winchell was an influential American gossip columnist and broadcaster between the thirties and fifties, a supporter of Senator McCarthy in his crusade against leftists, a friend of celebrities. Most of the other important figures in Herr's novels are also drawn from life: Damon Runyan, press agent Irving Hoffman, Hemingway. In a *faux*-diffident preface, Herr noted: `Personally, my most ambitious claims for it are as an entertainment in the tradition of the Hollywood biopic, with the undertones of history spreading beneath the jokes in various bitter shades of dark' (v). Certainly the novel reads like a popular `biopic'; even better, like a free adaptation of the film-script format. As I mentioned in the opening chapter, sadly deprived people like me, more numerous than is generally recognized, lack almost completely the capacity to form pictorial mental images. Word-strings evoke music, ideas, feelings, but not those photos for the inner eye which implicitly support the metaphor `image'. It is a shock, therefore, that I remember watching Herr's novel on television—a slick, fast-moving, made-for-TV special, something like Dennis Potter's *The Singing Detective*. In reality that did not happen, but despite my deficiencies it is lodged that way in my memory. So Herr's formal experiment was triumphantly successful at least to that extent. It shares the flushed surrealism of Kurt Vonnegut's novel *Mother Night* (1962): ` . . . we see Walter Winchell, Jr., walking down Third Avenue, late afternoon. He's dressed in the uniform of an officer of the Waffen S.S., a horrible, arrogant sneer on his face' (Herr, 146).

The scriptwriter, Herr says with a certain bitter regret, `cannot make *mise en scène*' (vi), a power usurped by the director. But we as readers can and do, through whatever imaginative modalities are available to us, directing and casting idiosyncratic movies from the scriptwriter's hints, dialogue, jump cuts. We always have done so, reading any fiction. Herr's book was thus less an appropriation to print fiction of some alien formal device than it was a forceful proof that these days we all speak motion picture fluently. Bradbury proves it.

Winchell is an arresting vehicle for Herr's textual borrowing precisely because he was not exemplary of those visual media whose rise simultaneously provided the most glamorous of his roster of celebrities but stole his own medium when television temporarily supplanted talk-radio in the 1950s. A failed stage dancer, a compulsively grabby gossipmonger and opinion-maker for newspaper and radio, habitué of nightclubs (most of the novel is set in New York's legendary Stork Club), friend of gangsters, womanizer, an anti-Nazi Jew in complacent Wasp New York, Winchell was a vulgar, go-getting verbal explosion. Can such a man possess sufficient stature to make a tragedy of his rise and fall? Only in the degree to which he was a projection of America in its greatest and its worst period. Because Herr understood this emblematic quality in his character, he pared away any depth of authentic feeling (for the death of Winchell's child, for example), feeding into the text instead fragments of biopic sentimentality with a deftness that makes us wince at Winchell and the whole history of the media exemplified, and which at the end flung him off like the exhausted genie of an expired technology.

iii

If Herr confessed his limitations in the control of *mise-en-scène*, Philip Roth eschewed it entirely in *Deception*, a suitably self-referential title for a novel that deploys truth for its own purposes while subverting it in the interests of ours. Roth presents undated entries in a writer's notebook, recording dialogues between `Philip', his English lover, previous inamoratas, a wronged former friend, the writer's wife. Aside from a very few stage directions (`Undressing him'), all we are given is this stark polyphony. Although sophisticated readers have been well trained in avoiding autobiographical fallacies, this approach throws us into a circuit of ontological doubt as unnerving as Philip K. Dick's. This `Philip', like Roth as he wrote the book, is in his 50s, has written Roth's novels, suffered Roth's rather too frequently documented victimization at the hands of his narrow or malign enemies, those indignant rabbis, those clutching women, who assail with philistine literalness his fictional portraiture. We cannot fail to ask (as we don't, not quite, of impotent Nathan Zuckerman in *The Human Stain* [2000]), in the midst of all this strenuous demand for decent distance, if these women, this lover awaiting her CAT scan, this wounded friend, are after all drawn straight from Roth's real life?

But we know the answer to these vulgar suspicions. The writer *invents!* This woman with her well-bred ankles over `Philip's' hairy shoulders is a conflation of many women and none. This cuckolded friend who berates him has had no cause to, the wife is unmolested, the reported complaint is therefore an invention as well. Why must the writer's wife ache with jealousy at these women who exist only in lines on the page? But which wife do we speak of? Is she not also an invention? We are sophisticated readers; we are not naive. Is not the whole thing merely a true story in the guise of a deception, played out at our readerly expense?

It is a novel, a fiction, as is Herr's appropriation of Winchell's biography, or, let us say, E. L. Doctorow's use of historical figures in postmodern narratives such as *Ragtime* (1975) and *Billy Bathgate* (1989). Despite one especially low point—an annoyingly crass rejoinder to Roth's feminist critics that serves only to bolster their indictment (113-17)—*Deception* is no less than the *tour de force* of technique we take as our due. And despite all the distancing Brechtian apparatus, it is effectively, emotionally moving, after the fashion of traditional mimetic fiction.

iv

It might be, then, that the best work at the edge of slipstream will have, inevitably, like these novels, a Ballardian character, moving from outer to inner space, or from fantastic mimeticism to magic realism and transrealism. That, you will recall, is Rudy Rucker's term for a mode of near-sf that uses the devices of extreme imagination to portray the inner world, and/or thickens the fantastic with the grit, nubbles, swollen erections and inward turmoil of real life. It is another way of performing science fiction (or at any rate another way of reading it), the step out of `immediate reality' and into `the higher reality in which life is embedded' (Rucker, 1999, 301), a topic I have explored extensively in *Transrealist Fiction* (2000). Even when its debts to sf are visible only to the insiderly observer, much writing today inscribes sf's own lexical and voluptuous spaces.

Each of these exemplary yet transgressive novels shows how perfectly ordinary it is nowadays for fiction to wander very far indeed from traditional canons of realism. This flexibility in narrative strategy and concerns has provided the ecological niche for sf's expansion into a new and more open landscape of its own, even as slipstream fiction (consciously or not, most not) has colonized some of the fabulist domain first opened up and tilled by science fiction writers. Each also shows that there are limits to how far mainstream fiction may move in the direction of slipstream before it shears off into some other modality: ornamented confession, allegory, film script.

One way of going entirely wrong is located, alas, in the disputed ground between sf and allegory. In Kenneth Cook's *Play Little Victims* (1978), the little victims are a doomed race of mice, temporarily reprieved by divine oversight in a Rentokil operation meant to sanitize the earth of all life. Taking over humankind's truncated sovereignty, the mice breed and rediscover the need for purpose and breed and reinvent technology and breed and recapitulate the horrors of industrial society and breed. The pitch of Cook's laudable intention was caught precisely by the blurb: the book `would be amusing if it weren't so horrifying,' and vice versa. More: it `could well be as accurate a forecast of the future as was George Orwell's *Animal Farm*.' It is none of those things. Orwell, a convenient yardstick, possessed a piercing analytical eye. The subject of his savage wit was

always held in close focus, and merited its flaying. Cook unerringly casti-
gated symptoms, apparently taking them for causes, and treated the
plight of our decaying social order with the acumen of a Sunday newspaper columnist. The one sin Cook avoided was coyness. No Swift, he
sustained a degree of astringency in his allegory. But his targets are wrong,
he scampers away from all the potentially rewarding difficulties he has set
himself, and his indifferent style is inadequate. Consider the sheer
badness of the third paragraph: `God contemplated His handiwork for a
split fraction of Infinity, then said, "Oh God!" or words to that effect' (1).

Cook's central failure is twofold: in his treatment of humans, and his
treatment of mice. Clearly, he thinks human beings are collectively insane.
His mousy protagonist Adamus and the rest of the mice mimic the ways of
Man, under the primary dictum `God is Love.' Imperiled by their own
drastic population explosion, they comically conclude that the ills of
human civilization (war, road toll, you name it) were measures of deliberate triage, a self-culling of our numbers. Voracious readers of human
books, the mice are curiously selective: they never stumble on Freud, say,
or any elementary treatise on sociology. Their supposedly chilling,
rational interpretation of human history is a straw mouse. If we kill
because we are intractably insane, why aren't the jackboots stamping day
and night in every street? Covertly justifying this myopia, Cook's mice are
blank, malleable, bereft of instinct or emotion. One can forgive them for
being other than human, but they are also innocent of any micely traits.
They are stooges, puppets for a series of propositions with no trace of intellectual validity. When T. H. White sent Wart, the Once and Future King,
into the worlds of badgers and ants, his ethological parables got all their
considerable grit and charm from a ruthless adherence to observation.
White knew how ants and badgers live. If you think this a stuffy, pedantic
objection that misses the enchantment of it all, ponder the value of a fable
where anything can mean any other thing at all.

V

Despite the links between such boundary texts (with their Martianized
familiarity) and sf, I often wonder if science fiction and fantasy are after all
fundamentally *different in kind* to the sort of writing exemplified by, say,
Henry James and James Joyce and Joyce Cary. It could be that Isaac

Asimov's sf is quite legitimately nearer in effect and intention to his instructive books on science and technology than to Proust or John Irving. What, though, are we then to make of consummate literary writers who choose to employ the language of sf or fantasy, no ifs and buts? Among the greatest is Ursula Le Guin; consider her collection of short work *The Compass Rose* (1982), which cannot be placed in a box. One of her oddest stories makes this very point, I suspect, combining elements of madness, surrealism and quantum mechanics. In the world of `Schrödinger's Cat', metaphor merges with reality. The narrator meets a couple who are coming apart, *breaking up*. The wife is `finally reduced to nothing but a mass of nerves: rather like fine chicken wire, in fact, but hopelessly tangled' (42). The Cat of the title is, famously, the subject of a cruel thought experiment in quantum theory. Locked inside a booby-trapped box, it has one chance in two of surviving. Until the box is opened, though, quantum theory seems to insist, it is neither alive nor dead. Le Guin cheats quantum theory, and those who insist on categorizing (is this my pun or hers?): the cat has vanished from the box. The price, though, is the loss of lawfulness from the world.

If this sleight seems merely tricksy, many other tales by Le Guin are beautiful, deep, austere, politically wise and sad, and often very funny. These days Le Guin is published as often in *The New Yorker* as in sf anthologies. For her, at least, the barriers of genre are down. This might be true, too, for M. John Harrison, whose controlled and lovely prose built enigmatic images of a decadent city, *In Viriconium* (1982) and related texts: *The Pastel City* (1971), *A Storm of Wings* (1980), *Viriconium Nights* (1985). Viriconium is a terminal landscape, used in previous fantasies by Harrison to represent a paralyzed future where technology long ago corroded into virulent quicksands: `umber iron bogs, albescent quicksands of aluminum and magnesium oxides, and sumps of cuprous blue or permanganate mauve fed by slow gelid streams and fringed by silver reeds' (1971, 60). For *In Viriconium*'s version, the city has a *fin de siècle* feel to it, as the fashionable portraitist Ashlyme seeks to salvage his consumptive friend Audsley King from the shadow of misery and numbness which creeps like an existential disease across Viriconium. The city is plagued as well by a pair of farcical gods, the boisterous, drunken Barley brothers, whose final wounding will waken the city from its `long, grey, debilitating dream' (121). The atmosphere is everywhere dreamlike, slow, fated, punctuated by wonderful creations: the Grand Cairo, the city's corrupt constable; the

Fat Mam who reads cards which shape book and Viriconium both; Ashlyme himself. It is a splendid, mysterious novel, and while it is clearly sf it is just as clearly not limited by genre. Harrison's delicious inventions span fantasy and sf. In *Viriconium Nights*, poetic princes hunt mutable lamias, ancient polluted bogs run with corrupt metals, fireworks pop each night above the arena as criminals are burned and quartered, burly paid sin-eaters swallow the wicked deeds of the dead. Merged landscapes of past and future served with equal effect in *The Centauri Device* (1975), a bravura pastiche of pyrotechnic fifties' sf. Harrison added his own wicked jests: interstellar anarchists with spaceships named for Swinburne and Wilde (*Atalanta in Calydon*, *Green Carnation*) whose exhausts burn, in Walter Pater's recipe for artistic success, with gem-like flame (71).

More accessible, once you get past the apparently twee opening, and equally beautiful, is John Crowley's fantasy *Little, Big* (1982). Here was a book pushed for the big time, like John Irving's quirky, incest-driven *The Hotel New Hampshire*, and while it had a fair success in the USA somehow it never caught the wind elsewhere. This is understandable, but depressing, for it is a memorable, affecting invention. Two aspects will block the path for many readers. Crowley chose to use emblematic names for his characters and places, and I for one really did not wish to know about people called George Mouse and Daily Alice Drinkwater, and places called Edgewood. When I learned that these people were notable because of their affinity for the Little People, I put the book down with a thump. Still, Thomas M. Disch had recommended it with all his might, and Disch was toe-to-toe with Le Guin for the title of the world's finest sf writer. So I picked it up again and slowly Crowley's magic penetrated my cynicism. *Little, Big* is not cute, not sentimental, though it is full of warmth and caring and feeling. It is a parable, I suppose, about the true purpose of building for human beings (it has the world's most wonderful house, which seasons break, inevitably, justly), and its pastorale is balanced by some stingingly credible and funny scenes in feudal New York, at the turn of that fabled millennium which in reality turned without fuss, until the two great towers were broken. If those moments are now superseded by the inevitable turning of the calendar, that in its own turn is perhaps a suitable shading of the great traditional tones in Crowley's memorable text.

vi

And yet—

Traditional literatures tell us: this is how things are, always have been, always will be. The crisis literature of the last century modified that message only a little: this is how things *should* be, and they're getting out of control, help! Sf, by contrast, takes change in its stride—not always relishing its surprises (few readers *enjoy* holocausts) but accepting their inevitability. Most mass-market fantasy tales retreat instead to a neverland of magic, happy feudalism and dragons. Significantly, as noted earlier, fantasy currently outsells sf by a hefty margin. By contrast, Bruce Sterling is a prophet of hyper-realist sf, fiction devoted to headlong change. Sterling was in the 1980s a (perhaps *the*) vociferous propagandist for cyberpunk, futurist writing that combined hard-edged, hi-tech gloss with a cynical posthumanist sensibility. His novel *Schismatrix* (1986) proposed a world hectically different from our own, but anchored in it, the human species split into warring `clades' while plunging toward a collective break with history to which even our strange descendants prove unequal. That invented universe was first evoked in a series of stories as gemlike as Harrison's rocket exhausts, equally filigreed with complex detail work, set in the era of conflict between Shapers and Mechanists (Sterling, 1990). In line with genetic research currently underway, the former literally remake themselves via DNA engineering, enhancing intelligence or intuition, beauty or longevity. The latter treat flesh as a disposable way station to cybernetic utopia, transcending biological limits with machined replacements. Neither path was likely to appeal to twentieth-century readers, but Sterling's Posthumanist future is altogether convincing, in the twenty-first, as a parable of unchecked change.

Like Sterling, twenty years ago, William Gibson came from nowhere to prove that all was not lost in a mode first spoiled for art by its pulp origins and a prudish disdain for those associations, by then already corroded by commercial success. Famously, his cyberpunk novels *Neuromancer, Count Zero* and *Mona Lisa Overdrive* (1984, 1986, 1988) won awards and astonished notice. In this sequence of novels set in a near-future of cyberspace, the computer-mediated notional universe of virtually realized data swarmed with global multinationals, addicts, Yakuza, rogue artificial minds passing as Haitian *loa* and on the run from the Turing police.

Gibson's stylistic roots in the spare, evocative prose of hard-boiled 1940s' thrillers conveyed his fast-lane, sleazy dystopia in swift jabs of laconic wit. Wisely, Gibson changed gears and lanes at that point, just in time to prevent the flattening of his original charge into habit. With Sterling, in *The Difference Engine* (1990) he reinvented the mid-19th Century (`steampunk'), so that Charles Babbage has built his gear-driven Difference Engine—a mechanical computer—instead of merely planning it, while Lady Ada Lovelace invents Gödel's Theorem and artificial intelligence. In a dark satanic-mills version of the *Neuromancer* trilogy, this machine divinity plots to create its opposite number in England, and its plot tangles up characters from Benjamin Disraeli's 1845 novel *Sybil* and such real historical personages as Sam Houston, Laurence Oliphant, Lord Byron (Prime Minister and leader of the Industrial Radical party), and Karl Marx (crafty Leninist leader of the Red Manhattan Commune). If the book never quite attained the depth and verbal agility of a John Fowles or a Peter Ackroyd, it made up the measure in sheer inventive stamina and abundance.

An equally remarkable concussion of a book that bent the generic razor-wire perimeters, but without embracing the posthuman, was Jack Womack's *Ambient* (1988). If feminist and posthuman sf remind us that startling new content hollers out for shocking new forms to express it—*is* the new forms at play, in the final analysis—the gas-plasma illuminations of cyberpunk science fiction slammed doctrine into imagery. Inheritor of Alfred Bester's decaying Spanglish American future and modernist wordplay, Gibson's sleazy crack-wired street wisdom, and (reaching back to roots which took two decades to bud, and then as lurid weeds) Anthony Burgess's Clockwork horrorshow argot, Womack turned the Greenhouse-ruined future into a chainsaw adrenaline circus. The story was minimal—Old Man Dryden owns the world's stock of dirty secrets, and most of its wealth, following the Ebb; his son Mr. Dryden would like him offed; bodyguard Shameless O'Malley and his true love, Mr. D's doxie, Avalon, try to zap the Old Man and find themselves on the lam through a Manhattan more inhumanly gruesome than anything remotely possible, even in the war-ravaged Middle East. The decoration, though, is lush. Damaged by corporate drugs, the Ambients are a sub-class of freaks and their fans, who pay crooked doctors to remove limbs or breasts and implant nails in their scalps. They speak, by a kind of cultural compensation, a delicious Elizabethan argot:

`A look as death redoubled finifies you,' said Margot, turning to eye
Avalon. `Wherein did mewly press you on?'
`Pardon?'
`Flying you after airy promises and painted allure?'
`What?'
Margot laughed. `New bonnets for old boneache.'
`You'll pick it up after a time,' I told Avalon. (165)

So do we, along with the business patois of Mister Dryden, the Rasta
razz of their Jamaican driver, the loping voice of Seamus the
Candide-innocent narrator. If finally, in the bitter humanist rebuke of its
ironic Grand Guignol, the book itself is unreasonably innocent, that's a
small enough price for the pleasure of its unchecked text.

vii

Well, then, maybe science fiction is the crazed biker of literature,
sloppy-grinned, barreling back down the wrong side of the road into the
shrieking traffic. Zest and paranoia, plus some maudlin nostalgia for the
lost breast at the birth of time. Certainly one principal science fiction
vector seems to be pointed firmly toward the past, and I do not just mean
its often reptilian conservatism and no-nonsense story-telling. Science
fiction dotes on monuments, vast and trunkless, the corpse of God in an
infinite desert, or its shadow on the future.

In a famous preface to his play *Cromwell*, Victor Hugo suggested that
civilization echoes its history in the evolving forms of art. Primitive lyric
sang the praises of an ideal time beyond time, ancient epic strutted
Homeric heroes, modern drama portrays the realities of life. Science
fiction reverses this neat scheme, often enough, gunning backwards from
realism through larger-than-life adventure into a mythical lyricism not
easily distinguished from religious exultation. Hugo's idea could not
stand up to scrutiny, but perhaps its science fiction inversion does, if we
add that this curious retrogression is often worked through within the
span of a given novel—the ordinary yielding to the grand, and then to the
awesome. Arthur C. Clarke is notable for it, beginning his stories in scrupulous research and computerized calculations (how long to get from here
to there, hmm, what delta-vee will we need, mumble mumble), and

finishing in swelling vistas of grandeur: the cosmic Child hovering over the world in *2001*, the artificial Mind Vanamonde waiting to do battle with something rather like Satan at the end of time in *The City and the Stars*.

Greg Bear's work plunges along exactly this trajectory, and has stretched the genre's boundaries from the outset. If the excellent early novel *Beyond Heaven's River* (1980) was cool, complex, artful, his ambitious novel *Eon* (1986) started in gritty detail with a devastating nuclear war, switching from that nearly genocidal stupidity to a cleverly devised redemptive tour through the Way, a mega-light-year habitat in superspace created by the transcendental technology of our wiser descendants. In *Eternity* (1989) Bear pursued this ambiguous utopia through to the end, which is to say, Monsieur Hugo, through to the beginning as well—of the universe, in each case. The Way turned out to be a sort of hairball caught in the future's throat, and must be dismantled: think of it as Chartres Cathedral on the scale of the Milky Way and one begins to appreciate the tragedy. A narrative of such magnitude cannot readily be encompassed within the viewpoint of a single, well-developed character, that hallmark of the Rothian `literary' novel, and Bear's future characters tend to be multiple, tomorrow's citizens sending `partials'—independent agents that simulate them for a limited task—into collective virtual space. While Bear is no Tolstoy, he very nearly surmounted the impulse to turn his multi-stranded tale into a pair of airport blockbusters. It was clearly an exhausting task; often the books turned from one prodigy to the next with a gasp of relief. Who can blame them? Bear was re-creating the universe entire, combining new physics and old generic formulae, and elevating it to a final state where individual consciousness sublimed into a kind of unfolding natural divinity. Inevitably, the testament was a touch anticlimactic, as Bear seemed to confess in his closing words:

> First, Mirsky told his companion, we start at the beginning.
> And then? Lanier asked.
> We search for points of interest, until we come to the end.
> And then? (1989, 399)

6: REPORT ON PROBABILITY NULL-*A*

`Carter's sure he can hide me. He has software that can break up my model and bury it deep in the city's algorithms—as a few billion trivial redundancies and inefficiencies.' [. . .]

Peer continued to show Kate his body sitting in a chair, thinking it over, while in truth he rose to his feet and walked across the room, escaping her formidable gaze. [. . .]

In twelve short real-time years as a Copy, he'd tried to explore every possibility, map out every consequence of what he'd become. He'd transformed his surroundings, his body, his personality, his perceptions—but he'd always owned the experience himself. The tricks he'd played on his memory had added, never erased—and whatever changes he'd been through, there was always only one person, in the end, taking responsibility, picking up the pieces. One witness, unifying it all.

The truth was, the thought of finally surrendering that unity made him dizzy with fear. It was the last vestige of his delusion of humanity. The last big lie.

Greg Egan, *Permutation City* (1994, 66-8)

i

Seeing the self as fractured, partitioned, an evolved ensemble of specialized modules, is becoming part of the standard narrative background of the sf mode, long after this device was introduced crudely but with mythic power in A. E. van Vogt's *Null-A* novels of the 1940s. Just as Lacanian psychoanalysis and *apres*-Marxist decolonialism provide templates for both poststructural literary theory and postmodern fiction, these assumptions from the rival disciplines of cognitive and neuroscience have entered the sf megatext.

Making these new myths of the future, sf writers build not simply from the great narrative invariants and patterns of literary tradition, not even by inverting or subverting them, but by cross-circuiting as many schemata as possible. So when Michael Swanwick devised worlds in which his characters could plug in optional personality implants, as in *Vacuum Flowers* (1988) and *Stations of the Tide* (1991), we may read his dashing fictions through multiple lenses: as a complex meditation on Lacanian ruptured subjectivity, as a mocking play on the strictly incommensurable modules of cognitive science, as imaginative ventures into the constructed ontologies of virtual reality. In Bear's *Eon* and *Eternity*, `partials' can simulate conscious actors for a limited task. Bear's ornate *policier* of the 21st century, *Queen of Angels* (1990), used nanotechnology to enter the fragmented neural architecture of a political dissident, paralleling that voyage with the quest in an artificial intelligence for true selfhood—something it attains only by doubling itself into self-reflexivity.

The future will be *different*: surely this is sf's primary postulate. Will it be better, or worse? That is the wrong question. In fifty or sixty years' time, today's children will be the elderly, and their standards will not be the same as ours *whatever* happens. Bear's *Blood Music* (1985) introduced a form of nanotechnology, viruses or perhaps machines built on a molecular scale, and melted the world into transcendence. Less drastically, *Queen of Angels* remained challenging, audacious, nothing if not ambitious, attempting to portray an American world of 2047 real in every fiber of the text, as utterly different from our own time as ours is from the Elizabethan. The neuro-therapied rich live in combs, vast hi-tech termitaries. Between these arcologies, in the Shade, dwell the untherapied. Society is rich; nano machines can literally build gourmet food from garbage, construct full-scale robot devices (arbiters), even transform human bodies. An artificially intelligent probe investigates the planets of Alpha Centauri B, beaming back data and opinions for dispersion through LitBid interactive media programs ample enough to give a Ted Turner wet dreams. Crimes are solved with ease by highbrow pds—public defenders. And the mind/brain itself is giving up its secrets. In this endlessly inventive utopia Emanuel Goldsmith, the world's most famous black poet, runs amok, murders eight of his friends, vanishes. Transformed pd Mary Choy must track her suspect, but more importantly she needs to understand his crime. The immensely wealthy parent of one of the victims, capturing Goldsmith, seeks to use prohibited psychological techniques that permit an observer to enter another human's Country of Mind. In Bear's Jungian mythos, this is the substrate of mental agents, talents, sub-personalities that comprise each self. In an eerie parallel, the AI four light years away struggles to become the first non-human 'self'.

Bear's narrative never remains stationary, shifting voice and point of view, adapting techniques from Dos Passos first borrowed for sf half a generation earlier by John Brunner in *Stand on Zanzibar* (1969). The reader does not slip gracefully through this story; it can be a slog, but with an enormously satisfying payoff. Bear is genuinely prodigious, and his future assembles itself from a multitude of brilliant details, builds with a disturbing conviction. Simultaneously, one is aware that this *is* a construct, a kind of artistic thought experiment that echoes the fundamental model of mind that Bear employs. That model was itself entirely up to date, at least for the end of the Eighties, paralleling with remarkable fidelity the cognitive psychology of, say, Howard Gardner or Roger Schank. Things come in at least threes; there are no brutal oppositions of right versus wrong. Self and Other are met halfway by the self's Jungian double. Human and machine AI are mediated by the transform. Crime is not opposed simply by punishment, but by therapy (and understanding). So the book is not merely the demonstration of an academic theorem; it has a heart: Marvin Minsky meets Dostoievsky.

ii

It would be all too easy to list the titles of books that embody these inter-pretations of mind, brain and their social ecology. In physicist Gregory Benford's *Great Sky River* (1988), *Tides of Light* (1989) and *Furious Gulf* (1994), for example, humans in the far future plug into their spines chip-personalities, or Aspects (often nested one within another, like this sentence), of their ancient relatives, and go through life nagged by the dead. *Great Sky River* is a Hemingway title for a somewhat Faulkneresque novel that follows the exhausting travails of a far future band of micro-chip-implanted humans in flight from a machine foe. This mechanical species, whose convulsive evolution is impelled as much by Lamarck as by Darwin, infests an unusual world in orbit about a black hole binary star. The tale of Cap'n Killeen and his son Toby is wrought with a certain brutal grace, even anthropological nuance. It is possible to esteem these families on the run, seeing in them a genuine shadow cast on our future by the artificial intelligences that AI specialists hope to construct. This is not to make lofty literary claims for the book, which is finally a clever construct in an adventure genre. Yet this exotic postulate dramatizes Benford's very contemporary understanding about the partitioned or segmented nature of selfhood.

Writing about `style', Benford has made an observation any cognitive scientist might share with any Lacanian or discourse theorist: `For our words are chosen, all right, but not by "us"—that consensual, passing parliament of the mind we call consciousness. The subconscious lines up our words for us, so that even as I begin this sentence not all of me knows how it is going to end—hence, style samples the dark netherworlds, with Freudian slips on banana peels' (Benford, in Slusser and Rabkin, 1992, 49). He had toyed with such ideas closer to the beginning of his career. In 1978, he had published *The Stars in Shroud*, a substantially revised version of his first novel, *Deeper Than the Darkness* (1970). Written when Benford was in his late 20s, this maiden effort later struck him as `dreadful'. He went through it carefully, trying once more to pin down the `fragile images' which were in large part `a memory of teenage excitements, of vast sweeping imagination' (1978, concluding Note). His main complaint, however, was with the blithe, cocksure heroes of space opera. `I kept asking, where did they come from? Who were their parents, to have such impossible children?' Although by trade Benford is a high-energy physicist, his fiction has tended subsequently to emphasize this interest in the psychological reality of his characters, not neglecting a social dimension. The shadow of Heinlein is visible often in this regard: there is more than one hyped-up fundamentalist religion in Benford's work. Orientalism is more important, though—Chinese, Japanese and Hindu elements, often with complex social ritual functions, recur in his writing.

In a collaborative novel now forgotten, *Find the Changeling* (1980), Benford and Gordon Eklund also entered the realm of variable identity. A step backwards for Benford, and no great addition to Eklund's uneven catalogue, there was no sense of truly imagined life in the book; part of the problem was unearned claims. Two killers are sent from an oppressive totalitarian regime on Earth to assassinate the last of the Changelings, a genetically engineered variety of humanity that can alter its physical form. One is a simple soul repeatedly bruised by his contacts with reality, the other a trained psychotic traumatized early by witnessing the minions of authority literally incinerate a scientist in his living room while his son watches. The Changeling's mind perceives form and order as wicked, sees flux and instability as painful but necessary: it is a sort of sanctimonious bomb-throwing masochist, and thinks inwardly in prime late-1960s Silverberg, a kind of prose crafted to be taut, thrilling, and deeper than the darkness. The final revelation is genuinely shocking (though hardly new; Eastern philosophies have incorporated it for millennia), but the cop-drama plot trivializes it even as the text claims to be presenting profundities. Given that Benford has gone on record in favor of unmarked trails he seemed the last person in sf warranted to offer what he has so pungently dubbed `plastic epiphanies.'

iii

Two exemplary Nineties' sf novels accepted as a working hypothesis this trope of the multiple and concatenated mind: Walter Jon Williams's *Aristoi* (1992), and Alexander Jablokov's *Nimbus* (1993). Another was the wonderfully inventive *Permutation City* (1994) by Greg Egan, cited in the epigraph to this chapter.

Aristoi is a highly romantic tale set in a meritocratic fascism of the remote future. The aristoi are a sort of Confucian elite, selected for their super-abundant talents and, more importantly, by their capacity to contain multitudes. An Aristos is the product of study, examinations, surgery and inner disciplines. Above all, he or she is the cognitive and affective focus of specialized Limited Personalities or *daimones*, deliberately partitioned fractions of the brain dedicated to specialized tasks, making themselves known to the primary consciousness as distinctive voices not unlike the dissociative personalities so beloved by viewers of Oprah Winfrey. And beyond this inner company, each Aristos or Ariste may commune with a vast informational cyberspace, the Hyperlogos, and in simulated projection enter its Oneirochronon (or `dreamtime') artificial realities. The narrative follows the increasingly cosmic intrigues of laconic Gabriel Aristos, bisexual genius and master of the many Mudras and Formal Postures of this baroque world. Williams has devised an effective and engaging textual strategy in deploying his fabulous melodrama: occasional parallel sidebars to the on-going consciousness of his character, in which *daimones* and nanosystems report, advise, and sometimes dispute (24):

Gabriel undid the buttons of Marcus's dressing gown and revealed the smooth, porcelain-skinned body that had caused him to nickname Marcus `The Black-Eyed Ghost'. The rain of sensation from Cyrus fell away, replaced by the pressure of Spring Plum. Spring Plum was a Limited Personality, the most complete and self-possessed of his LPs yet revealed to Gabriel, and though she was as complete a

SPRING PLUM: `*The expression of a well-made man appears not only in his face, / It is in his limbs and joints also, it is curiously in the joints of his hips and wrists . . .*'

GABRIEL: «kisses»

SPRING PLUM: `*To see him pass conveys as much as the best poem, perhaps more.*'

RENO: Pulse 92, pressure 139 over 90.

BEAR: The boy is too nervous.

CYRUS: «the silver curl of Corinthian caps . . . »

Inevitably, even a superman like Gabriel runs into trouble and loses control of his Limited Personalities. He is saved, also perhaps inevitably, by a *daimone* even he has been unaware of, a sort of Norton Utilities, just the kind of thing you're glad you bought when the hard disk of your primary self goes bad.

What is especially interesting about novels like this is their deliciously deplorable blend of high and low, gorgeously vulgar plot and setting yoked with advanced concepts from the cognitive science lab. Jablokov's *Nimbus* is less gaudy but no less melodramatic. In the nearish future, the Devo Wars have wasted much of Europe, and the Sons of Glen Canyon eco-terrorists in the USA are turning the place into a typical *Mad Max* wide-screen trashed future. A group of orphans has been the subject of a military experiment, in which tacky stuff is done to the inside of their heads, and they are conditioned to obedience with dubious memories by a child-abusing psychologist. Years after the war, one of the Nimbus team finds that his dispersed companions are being murdered—apparently by the cruel psychologist. The only problem with this explanation is that the psychologist has been dead for years. People who live in partitioned brains, of course, can never be quite sure who else is sharing the bathroom with them. Jablokov's detective story is neat enough, and his mutually cathected victims poignant (rather as in Iain M. Banks's *Against A Dark Background* [1993]), but the pleasure of the text is in its details of a world where high executive officers and top researchers have much of their brain encrypted by the company, so they cannot even call their thoughts their own.

Why is this trope of fractured selfhood so prevalent in today's sf? Do we seek anxiously for an extended sense of self, an enhancement of subjectivity in a world that seems all too willing—like the antihumanism of poststructuralism—to crush the self into an effect of discourse? But then what could be more disturbing, more destructive of any heartfelt security of tenure within the self, than the idea of plug-in personalities and optional identities?

7: THE STARS MY DESPERATION

I remember in reviewing one of Jim Blish's books, `For God's sake, Jim, will you go out and chase ladies, gamble, rob a bank, do something. Get experience, because although your science is great your characters are completely unreal.'

Alfred Bester, Schweitzer Interview (13)

i

Alfie Bester's strategy was always to lead the reader a merry dance, not to say a *danse macabre*, to leap from concealment with shouts and firecrackers, to lurk and entice and disguise and . . . unmask! Explosion! Concussion! When he was in form, his pace, attack, payoff were exemplary, dazzling. Out of form, he was . . . not flabby, as you might expect, but strained, herniated, desperate, clattering maniacally with his varicose veins on a stage stuffed with burst toys, while the last of the audience gritted their teeth in humiliation and pity.

Damon Knight noticed all this half a century ago, when Bester was writing at the top of his form:

> Dazzlement and enchantment are Bester's methods. His stories never stand still for a moment; they're forever tilting into motion, veering, doubling back, firing off rockets to distract you. . . . Bester's science is all

wrong, his characters are not characters but funny hats; but you never notice: he fires off a smoke-bomb, climbs a ladder, leaps from a trapeze, plays three bars of `God Save the King,' swallows a sword and dives into three inches of water. Good heavens, what more do you want? (Knight, 1967 [1956], 234)

When I was fourteen or fifteen, I loved Bester like a father. (I loved Arthur C. Clarke like a Father, the sort with a white reversed collar and a vision of the City of God built out of science, transcending science. Strange chariots!) Yes, imagine how it would be if your old man had a brain like that, sizzling with lunacy, knowing, cynical but flushed with a baroque unashamed romanticism that was not all that common under the grey banner of the close of the 1950s. Later I had the guilt of conspiring with the other siblings, spiteful and oedipal, in trying to kick the old man off to Sunshine Acres, making it plain that he should have taken himself there while he still possessed some decent control over his sphincter.

The Demolished Man (1953) and *The Stars My Destination* (1956) were unforgettable neon poetry blazing against the suburban night. But it is hard to remember anything at all from *The Computer Connection* (1976), also known as *Extro,* also known as *The Indian Giver.* That last variant offers a clue: wasn't there a wild-man Native American in it? And . . . a bunch of immortals who had defeated death by yielding to it at the nastiest possible moment. And . . . some super-intelligent slugs, first of a new breed of Homo Superior. And . . . a global computer? And . . . a narrator whose name was given both as Daniel Curzon and as Edward Curzon, which perhaps indicated exactly how riveted Bester himself was by the whole exercise. In a 1979 interview with Charles Platt, he called it `a disaster . . . that confounded book': `There was something vitally wrong with that book, and I knew it when I finished it, and I couldn't patch it then, and to this day . . . I can't understand it, so I can't profit by it' (in Platt, 1983, 243).

Some two decades earlier, Bester's masterwork left one in no doubt of the protagonist's name. The Penguin edition back jacket blurb caught it with vulgar precision:

What is Gully Foyle? . . . Saviour, liar, lecher, ghoul, walking cancer . . . a man possessed . . . a blazing hero of a science fiction novel that transcends its category.

This last claim, however, is precisely wrong, for the book is a quintessence that exactly epitomizes, emblematizes its genre category. Samuel Delany, who rightly esteems it, noted that `The Stars My Destination (or Tiger! Tiger! in its original title) is considered by many readers and writers, both in and outside the field, to be the greatest single sf novel. . . . It chronicles a social education, but within a society which, from our point of view, has gone mad' (Delany, 1978, 35). More than that, it is the apogee of Bester's consistent struggles with a single theme: the heightened image of a compulsively driven individual bursting through the prison bars of nature and nurture both, marked by demonic and transcendent stigmata, a Bergsonian emergent evolutionary salient embodied in one passionate, driven creature who hurtles through a world stripped to hard, brilliant, teleological metaphors.

Here is Bester's crucial notion, now long abandoned by practicing biologists and philosophers: that Nature is in some sense a Designer with a Plan and a Purpose, shaking the bottle of *elan vital* until it seethes and spurts. Bester's books are overgrown with grotesque coincidence, lucky accidents of history that have the obvious narrative merit of advancing the story with maximum attack but through their failure to offend us conveying as well, and more importantly, a subterranean awareness that in *these* universes Nature is a participant, a partisan, rooting for the seed-bearers.

In an incompetent way *The Computer Connection*, Bester's belated return to the sf novel, persisted with this theme, but blurred its expression hopelessly by skeining the dialectic, shortsheeting the narrative, splitting the typical Besterian dyad into a multitude of funny hats performing comic capers, some of them not so comic. *The Demolished Man*, Bester's bravura mystery story set in a world policed by telepaths, evoked that dyad stunningly in Ben Reich/Lincoln Powell (criminal/detective), Ben Reich/Craye D'Courtney (upstart/tycoon, and son/father), Ben Reich/The Man With No Face (conscious/unconscious selves). All of those were subsumed, quite deliberately on Bester's part, into an archetypal mandala of contest which can be represented (at some cost) as Eros/Thanatos, Life/Death.

In *The Stars My Destination*, the dyad is above all Gully Foyle/Olivia Presteign, each at once the other's sibling Other and Self. This is true at least in terms of narrative impulse, but the dialectic between them points to something grandiose and in individual terms almost unspecifiable:

perhaps the emergent salient of Life itself, set against the frigid, uncaring vacuum of spacetime. On the social level, the ground halfway between the psychological rampaging of individual compulsion and the final magisterial epiphany of Foyle-as-god, the dyad is manifest as common humanity versus power elite. Foyle effects a one-man revolution in human consciousness and power by dispersing PyrE, a kind of primordial Schopenhauerish element, to the brutalized masses of the world. PyrE is the primal stuff of the universe, latent force in its purest form, responsive only to Will and Idea. On the one hand, Foyle's act seems precisely an unwitting metaphor for mid-fifties liberal aspiration. On the other, it is an intriguing figure (no doubt overdetermined) for the devastating potential of both art and science in the conduct and context of human affairs.

ii

A quarter century later, Bester had recused from the social dimension. *Golem*[100] (1980) revived the dyad abandoned in *The Computer Connection,* as male/female, although this is not self-evident, since the male component is further bifurcated, without thereby generating a triad. Its imagined society, shared with *The Computer Connection,* is a pot-pourri of gaudy images with no underlying texture, no embeddedness in gritty reality. While this is true also of *The Stars My Destination,* in that book the apparent cartoons are clearly emblematic, at once shimmering with wit and satirical laughter and darkening into depths of authentic pain, cruelty, aspiration. The Guff of the later books—most loathsome sector of the Northeast Corridor—is `a lunacy of violence inhabited by a swarming population with no visible means of support and no fixed residence' (1980, 32). It is `a raree show', curiously premonitory of William Gibson's Swarm (a conurbation running down the eastern edge of his cyberspaced future America). Portions of Third World cities already fit his description, but Bester's adoption of the locale possesses no rationale beyond his patent wish to strut his exhausted obsessives one more time on the peep-show stage—a desire confirmed in his final novel, *The Deceivers,* a terminal case of frenetic technique in the service of nothing beyond its own tired exercise. (A dire posthumous collaboration with Roger Zelazny, *Psycho Shop* [1998] is better passed over in silence.)

The story line in *Golem*[100] is surprisingly frail. Eight bourgeois `bee' ladies with twee `secret names' while away their bored lives in the protected redoubts of the brutal Guff, playing at raising the devil. Their rituals bear fruit only when a husband, Droney Lafferty, `the celebrated necrophile' and piebald haploid, introduces a radioactive catalyst into their incense. Awakened and given focus, `the brutal cruelty that lies buried deep within us all' (10)—as Bester simple-mindedly characterizes Freud's *Id*, evidently having learned nothing after the same simplifications in *The Demolished Man* were lambasted by critics—emerges, expressing its nature in atrocities. These crimes defy normal explanation, to the chagrin of Police subadar Adida Alkhand-Sarangdar-ind'dni (whose palindromic names hint at some ontological mirroring or antinomy). Events from Bester's 1974 short story `The Four-Hour Fugue' were modified and incorporated as an alternate narrative strand. Scent chemist Dr. Blaise Shima (previously Skiaki) is slacking at work. Warlock Salem Burne (sic!) and psychodynamician Gretchen Nunn determine that Shima's supernal olfactory acuity, coupled with his neurotic self-pity, make him obsessively vulnerable to human pheromone trails: specifically, the trail of would-be suicides. In the reversed or inverted mask-persona of `Mr. Wish', Shima tracks these unfortunates and becomes the occasion, though not the agent, of their demise.

For no clear reason, the Golem monster-from-the-Id makes its presence known in such a way as to implicate Nunn and Shima in its roster of crimes. To clear themselves they must find the monster and defuse it. Their attempts to do so merely destroy its original embodiment, the eightfold `hive', and provoke Gretchen Nunn (meanwhile revealed as `the new Primal Man') into re-establishing the hive with herself as Queen. As part of the murderous nuptial flight preceding this consummation, Nunn couples with numerous `drones', including a dog, and climaxes by tearing Shima's penis from his body with the muscles of her clenched vulva. Awakening, she learns with horror (perhaps) that the honest policeman Ind'dni has been replaced by his negative self, a perverted being from the same Collective Under-realm which gave birth to the Golem. Luckily, he is now an extraordinary lover, a Primal Man fit for a Queen. He is, in fact, Golem[101].

Bolstering this inane and attenuated plot were, firstly, the usual Besterian helter-skelter pyrotechnics, inventive setpieces, and concrete poetry formal variants, segueing to and from, secondly, about a hundred pages of quite fine integrated graphics by sf artist Jack Gaughan, doing by and large what could not be done by text alone. Alas, the fireworks were no better than bizarre variants on Bester's genuinely original and brilliant games of the fifties. Replacing Lady Olivia Presteign, albino heiress blind to all but the infrared, is Gretchen Nunn, Watusi genius who sees through the eyes of others (a singularly unworkable notion) and in the cosmic ray spectrum through the `cloud chamber' of her own flesh (a singularly useless ability). Visual disabilities or variants crop up repeatedly in Bester. Shima himself is color blind, Salem Burne semiotically `sees' the meaning of physical gesture. No doubt this emphasis is motivated by Bester's own eye troubles: `my eyes failed, like poor Congreve's' (`My Affair With Science Fiction', 450). This is no accident in any case, for the second great theme in Bester is perception: sight and insight, sleight of sight (the Man With No Face) and enhanced perception (telepathy; the obsessional rhythms of the Pi Man; a Baudrillardian replacement of vision by sheer motion, in teleportation; the Promethium-induced visions of *Golem*[100]). Unhappily, the variants forced in his late novels like stones from the urethra are agonizingly *constructs,* with no imaginative life.

Above all, in these late texts Bester's own artistic perception and tact seemed crusted with cataracts. In a schoolboyish note of lavatory puerility, a character named Phlegmy utters this Pukebox song (admittedly quite prescient of the rap lyrics popular two decades later):

> Vomitation. Vomitation.
> Retchitation. Retchitation.
> Spew. Spew.
> Upchuck, daddy,
> With a solid pour. (374)

Presumably this was intended as a scathing if-this-goes-on satire provoked in the early 1970s by, say, Alice Cooper. But the sexist and night-marish play-format scene on the next page is there for its relish:

> *(A Hang-Glider sails low overhead, slowly descending. A man hangs by the neck from the glider, the strangling noose knotted into the traditional 13 turns of the rope.)*

PI

Ooo look, Miz Gretch person. I seen a lot of suicides but never like this one before.

*A gaggle of crones follows the falling glider avidly absorbing the emissions
from the spasming penis of the suicide.) (375)*

At one level this is familiar territory to readers of William Burroughs.
On another, it is an extreme extension of the Extrapolation Theory of sf
proclaimed by Bester in his electrifying short story collection, *Starlight*
(1976):

Here's my definition:

Extrapolation. The continuation of a trend, either increasing,
decreasing or steady-state, to its culmination in the future. The only
constraint is the limit set by the logic of the universe.

`And good luck,' he added, `to the late, great Alfred Bester, American
author' (377-78). He needed more than good luck to persuade us that the
Hang-Glider scene (a pun with all the spritzig of the Salem Burne jest) fell
within the logic of the social universe inhabited by human beings. In
another introduction in the same gathering, Bester declared against
pornography:

A Puritan streak in my nature has always stifled the slightest temptation to do that sort of work. I'm strongly opposed to censorship in any
form, and yet I confess to being disgusted by the passages that diagram it
for you. (321)

From the outset, Bester builds clues to his sociobiological culmination.
The eight middle-class nitwits are referred to as `charming bee ladies' who
meet in `the hive'. This parallel is not pressed immediately: `They were not
all cut from the identical pattern like insect-type bees. They were intensely
individual human-type ladies'. Nevertheless, the leader is Regina
(pronounced Re-JYN-a), `the Queen Bee'. They `buzzed with gossip ... did
bee-dances ... gorged on sweets ... butted heads to establish an informal
dominance-order' (7-9). At the outset we learn that one of the husbands
(not Regina's; she is a virgin) is nicknamed Droney. The moment Gretchen
Nunn inveigles her way into the hive, she is dubbed `Black Beauty' (for her
Negro good looks), or BB, or, to spell it out, Bee-Bee. After a time the reader
becomes dazed, over-eager to seize this motif. When the Glacial Army sing

a revival hymn entitled `Where You Beez Come God's Big Freeze', one's attention is stung, perhaps in error.

This is textual ontology with a vengeance, utterly overdetermined. The irruption of the inverse Ind'dni from the contra-universe is specified like an Attic fate in the shape of his palindromic name: not merely Ind'dni, the short form of his patronymic, but in his first name, mentioned once and neglected thereafter.

Midway between these manifestations of the World as Word and Idea are the characters' names: Blaise Shima, the Japanese raised as a French Catholic (`Shima' is the Japanese for `island', an opportunity for the horrendous pun `Hero Shima'). Gretchen Nunn reeks of metaphor and metonymy. Some of the other names are purely for fun, if that is your idea of fun: the thespian Sarah Heartburn, the lesbian Yenta Catienta (a Yiddish pun), the twins Oodgedye and Udgedye, which Bester tells us is Chekhovian Russian for `Guess Who' and `Guess Which'.

The impulsive conceit, of the bee-ladies and their hives, seems consequent on the original story, `The Four-Hour Fugue', and its preliminary exploration of the pheromone-compulsion motif. Bester took the lazy way out in developing this concept to novel length. Yes, pheromones are typical of insects, not humans. This is a good reason for supposing that humans do not use pheromones to organize their sexual drives, rather than for supposing that *if* humans *did* use pheromones they would become like insects.

In his late work, Bester turned to an always-present but previously-contained taste for Grand Guignol (the nickname, after all, of the narrator of *The Computer Connection)* and it became the more schoolboy unpleasant in its execution. Shima's castration is unexceptionable, true, the stuff of archaic myth, harvest festivals, turned to sf usage more than once by Philip José Farmer and postmodern use by, say, Martin Amis, Iain Banks or Will Self. But the ugliness of the Golem atrocities is unrewardingly disgusting:

> The man was circling a pillar stub of the decayed opera-house portico; crawling, falling, rising, stumbling, crying piteously, shrieking, calling on Christ and cursing his gods. There was a gash in his belly that oozed blood and extruded intestine. One end of his gut had been fastened to the pillar, and as he circled and circled it was torn out of him, inch by inch, to garland the column with a bloody, grey hawser. (28)

My reaction on reading this botched book, despairingly confirmed by the novel that followed it, *The Deceivers* (1981), was simple dismay. Leave aside the discussions of masks and persona theory in Jung, the way Bester got Freud ludicrously wrong in his gutter psychoanalysis, how finally the supposed theme of transcendence got its comeuppance in the Epilogue (set 105 years on, but on internal evidence clearly meant to stand at the beginning), how the book's proofreader could not spell `architectonic' correctly or decide on a consistent abbreviation of the element Prome-thium (Pm, or P-M, although on p. 88 it is explicitly spelled out), how Golem to the hundredth power is a rather larger quality than 100 times Golem, which Bester meant, how impoverished the Apollinaire *calligrammes* had become in their fall from *The Demolished Man* to Sarah Heartburn's tawdry expostulations. All this detail dimmed to irrelevancy before the heartbreaking wish to cry out (now superfluously): Give the game away, now that you have lost your skill at it, the late, great Alfred Bester, American author. Break your staff and bury it. For Bester, and perhaps for widescreen baroque sf, it was too late for reprise, for recovery, for the persistence of memory. Like the bloated late fictions of Isaac Asimov's, these depressing texts were, awful though it is to recognize the fact, nothing better than a final spastic fouling of the nest.

8: R.I.P.

i

Disturbing fictions that exceed the bounds of realism need not, of course, transgress the expectations of popular genres. The most accessible and immediately powerful mode, though perhaps the least interesting, is contemporary horror. Consider `Metastasis' by Dan Simmons (1989), an adroit transition from surreal metaphor to unsettling and quite concrete, if banal, mimesis. Louis Steig, victim of a car crash that has left a sliver of bone deep in his brain, attends his dying mother. Through sorrow and headache, he glances at her hospital bed in a wall mirror. Inevitably,

> Something was sitting in the chair he had just vacated . . . .
>
> The small figure leaning over his mother had a large, shaven head perched on a thin neck and even thinner body. Its skin was white—not flesh-white but paper-white, fish-belly white—and the arms were skin and tendon wrapped tightly around long bone . . . .
>
> The thing had slowly, almost lovingly, pulled down the thin blanket and topsheet which covered Louis's mother's chest until the opening of that obscene proboscis was scant inches away from the faded blue-flower print of her hospital gown. Something appeared in the flesh-rimmed opening, something grey-green, segmented, and moist. . . . The great, white head bent lower, cartilage and muscle contracted, and a five-inch slug was slowly extruded, wiggling slightly as it hung above Louis's mother . . . .
>
> [T]he moist slug fell softly onto his mother's chest, coiled, writhed, and

burrowed quickly away from the light. Into his mother . . . Louis could see the slightest ripple of flesh as the slug disappeared under the pale flesh of his mother's chest. (Simmons, 1989, 135-7)

The language is adequate, although for immediacy and shock value the vile imagery is already superseded by state-of-the-art television special effects. But a curious ambiguity lurks in this Oedipal fertilization-by-death, a simile more distressing than the surface blend of Nosferatu and the small grey alien `doctors' of UFO abduction myth: `Louis could do nothing but stare at the image of pale flesh, sharp bone and bruise-colored shadows. He thought fleetingly of concentration camp inmates . . . .' (136). The authentically monstrous iconography of Auschwitz, of the slandered victims of state terror, is ruthlessly appropriated. I do not mean that Simmons intended his image to work in this way; certainly, though, his own poetic-horrific imagination captured some deformed reverberation from a century steeped in totalitarian malignity.

Why, though, need a fiction writer take such long additional steps into the uncanny, the horrific, the sublime, the fantastic? Ought it not be sufficient to avoid the traps of kitsch romantic or thriller formulae, to dispute received, comfortable patterns of narrative impulse? The weird end of the fantasy spectrum, devoted to bloody horror, boomed for a time, fell away, is on the rise again. Perhaps it was a spin-off from all those video nasties where frustrated maniacs dismember lissome girls and parent-figures with chainsaws. One early and typical analysis was offered in Glen St John Barclay's *Anatomy of Horror* (1978). Barclay is a droll intellectual—an historian and specialist in international relations rather than a literary critic—clearly fond of occult tales. His slim volume had nothing in common with academic narratology's schematizing and scholarly approaches to critical anatomy, nor indeed to Northrop Frye's famous ground-breaking efforts in *Anatomy of Criticism* ([1957], 1973). Barclay's ambit is established slyly at the end of his first chapter, `The Lure of the Occult', following a string of encouraging citations from the traditional canon (George Eliot, Henry James, Conrad, Dickens, Tolstoy): `The fact is that many and perhaps most of the major novelists concerned with presenting authentic visions of the human experience, have felt required to include occult intrusions as elements of that experience' (20). In short, an enthusiasm for the occult (or its motifs, at least) is sanctioned by prior art. This argument from celebrity is admittedly thin. After all, there have been writers who have devoted most or even all of their literary output exclusively to the occult. Most of them have been very bad and very unimportant, and it is reasonable to assume that their chief motivations have been lack of ability to work in any other area of fiction, or the simple desire to make money in the easiest possible way, by cultivating their readers' fears or prurience. (20)

Thus, not only were these mainstays of horror bad writers, often incapable of penning a fresh or even a lucid sentence, but their efforts were pitched at the beast in us. How, then, might a sophisticate justify a taste for this prurient trash? Perhaps (and this is my comment, and Jung's, not Barclay's):[4] in much the same way Freud dealt with his own obsessional interests. The fan of what we have just been assured is a degraded and unacceptable form of imaginative arousal is instantly reprieved, redeemed, recuperated into the station of biographical sociologist, explorer of mass desire, lured by some small hope of illumination from unlikely sources.

[T]here are still others who by their treatment of occult themes have somehow managed to create or revivify legends, or have themselves become legends in their own lifetimes. They include some of the most popular and certainly most assiduously emulated and plagiarized authors of the past hundred years. They are remarkable phenomena in their own right, and as such they are certainly worth close investigation. They might even have a message for us. (20-1)

Granted, every critic shifts in some measure into uninvolved abstraction by virtue of her critical stance, his detached angle of appraisal. Traditionally this adoption of distance has been authorized in the interests of getting a better, more `objective', view of texts. Rarely, until the rise of reception aesthetics and reader-response theory and cultural materialist accounts, was the primary goal to obtain a superior hold on the `remarkable phenomena' of their authors and their readers. While Barclay's subtitle was `The Masters of Occult Fiction', his principal promise was to

[4] For example, in Carl Jung, *Memories, Dreams, Reflections*, ed. A. Jaffe, Collins and Routledge & Kegan Paul, 1963, p. 149: `Freud never asked himself why he was compelled to talk continually of sex', etc.

anatomize the writing. Perhaps he shifted ground to shield himself (and his readers) from the embarrassment of his topic.

When the emphasis does turn to formal considerations, particularly on the plentiful occasions to flay bad writing and the quirky tricks of the horror game, Barclay is an amusing guide. The noxious Dennis Wheatley is dispatched delightfully:

> Wheatley can seriously claim to be the greatest living master of the cliché. One can find on almost every page whole passages that might have been assembled by a computer, programmed to regurgitate nothing but certified banalities, as for example in this alleged love-scene from *Star of Ill-Omen*: `Flushed and trembling, she had consented. Once inside, their passion mounted to fever heat . . . During hours that sped all too swiftly, they gave free rein to the lovely madness that had seized upon them both, and, quite oblivious of past or future, reveled in the highest delights that youth can give.' (117)

Wheatley's language—far more reduced than that found in his contemporaries, let alone in today's supple horror textuality from, say, Ramsay Campbell—functions bluntly in the service of fantasies predominantly of sexual viciousness:

> By contrast [to Rider Haggard], Dennis Wheatley's approach is wholly unerotic and titillating above all else. There is literally no symbolism in his occult stories, no images of unadmitted or concealed desires. . . . One gets instead the unabashed presentation of woman as a sexual object, to be exhibited, enjoyed, raped, tortured and on occasion murdered. Indeed, the paraphernalia of the occult itself is introduced not for any symbolic purpose, but simply to provide opportunities for the exposure and abuse of the heroine. (114-5)

What Barclay found most notable in Wheatley was his espousal of Manicheism. For if the world is seen as the devil's creation, or at least his demesne, if the devil is as powerful as God, a distinct tension arises with the other reactionary values worked out in his writings: if nothing else, it might alert the naive reader to some of the perverse concomitants of hierarchical conservatism. So the one-time popularity of his books might, after all, `have a message for us'—perhaps that it is not the sexual permissivity of consumer society which is doing us in, but its non-permissive supplement, the Joy of Cruel Infliction.

One might easily extend this kind of analysis to the ever-increasing list of mass-market horror books and films that matched the non-realist tastes of the 1980s and 1990s as Heinlein's and Asimov's science fiction caught the mood of the 1970s: I mean the works of Stephen King, Peter Straub, Ramsey Campbell, Clive Barker, Ann Rice, Dan Simmons. Even for a book published a third of a century ago, before the truly popular upsurge in horror and vampirism, Barclay's was remarkably narrow in its range. He comments of *The Exorcist* that it `would have to be the most obscene and revolting book ever written' (108), which suggests a certain innocence about Undergrowths of Literature prior to the liberal victories over censorship in the late 1960s and 1970s, let alone such breakout works as Philip José Farmer's horror trilogy *An Exorcism*[5] which includes castration by steel dentures, a phallic symbiont bearing the shrunken, hungry head of Gilles de Rais which devours the entrails of hapless fornicators (a pre-AIDS creation perhaps even more disturbing than Simmons's vampiric cancer), a woman who fragments into independent organs—

> Presently, the many-legged cunt, still followed by the many-legged uterus, walked toward him. . . . The odor from it was clean and faintly musky, and under other circumstances he would have enjoyed it very much. . . . Vivienne's head appeared from under the bed and stalked slowly towards him. Her tongue was sticking out from her lax lips, and her bright eyes stared at him. (*Blown*, 1969, 31-2)

—and an entire psychiatric or oneiric checklist of other repulsive images. (That last trope—the literally decentered, disseminated self—was subsequently employed to darkly comic effect in John Carpenter's re-make of *The Thing* [1982], causing one stoned character to blurt: `You've gotta be fuckin' *kidding!*')

---

[5] *Ritual One: The Image of the Beast*, [1968] Quartet, 1975; *Ritual Two: Blown*, [1969] Quartet, 1975, and the non-pornographic *Traitor to the Living*, Ballantine, 1973.

ii

The same zany zest is at work in a number of novels and stories at the margins of sf, fantasy and horror by today's greatest fabulist, Gene Wolfe. Wolfe is humane, adult, a person who can actually write about human beings because he cares about them, and can do so in this richly transformed way because he has a sufficiently powerful imagination. Plainly, Wolfe understands suffering and hope; the four spiritually damaged characters in his *Free Live Free* (1985), dossed down with their mysterious benefactor Ben Free in a house condemned for urban renewal, seek physical treasure and find kindness, *caritas*, in a tale part fantasy, part Boy's Air Stories for grown-ups, part parable. Each voice speaks clear and recognizable, and if the denouement is baffling, why, so is life's. No fan of franchise science fiction or routine chainsaw horror could bear to read more than a handful of these pages; the reverse also tends to be true.

There Are Doors (1988) posits a literally alternative reality into which Visitors from our world can slip and return, often as lunatics. Mr. Green's hapless `happy fall' is into love with a woman of that other world, who chances to be an immortal goddess. Addicted to multiple disguises and personae, Lara is former mistress to a Kissinger-like political adviser whose pleasure it is to address Green as Herr Kay, a suitably Kafkaesque name in this demented, oppressively fevered confection. Its most unpleasant feature is to postulate that in Lara's world heterosexual intercourse is lethal for the male, put off as late as possible. Since people can slip back and forth between worlds, it is surmised that this accounts for the fear and hatred in our world of men for women. This is certainly the most grotesque excuse I have ever heard for sexist brutality, and it makes me wonder what the fluently mythic Wolfe thought he was getting at in his disturbing, uncanny fable. In case you think I am being ideologically hidebound (a.k.a. politically correct), I should mention that men in the other world can buy small compliant girl dolls. `Lara in miniature, ten inches high' (9). These dolls talk in a somewhat programmed fashion, and like to dress up. Don't look at me like that, I just work here, I'm as horrified as you.

What of the simple horror of death, and its ambiguous survival? Before Gene Wolfe began his immense labors charting the mythic future in three immense sf novel sequences *The Book of the New Sun, The Book of the Long*

Sun and *The Book of the Short Sun,* he created at least one perfect small enig-matic gem that still baffles and delights readers. *Peace* (1975) appears to be the extended written meditation of Alden Dennis Weer, ailing elderly Midwest gentleman and president of a fruit juice plant. Ewer's juice plant synthesizes orange juice out of potatoes, so successfully that Cassionsville and the Kanakessee Valley, its once-rich and various farmland surrounds, are blighted by monocropping, as its Irish settlers' homelands had been several centuries earlier. Wolfe has gone on record as saying that Den Weer more closely resembles the author than most critics have realized. Wolfe for years wrote professionally for, and edited, a magazine called `Plant Engineering' which dealt not with genetic botany but with industrial mechanical engineering.

The name of the narrator of Wolfe's *The Fifth Head of Cerberus* (1973), never given in that text, can be determined to be Gene Wolfe. A famous story by Wolfe is `The Hero as Werwolf'. This apparent spelling mistake is permitted by the dictionary, a volume Wolfe is not unacquainted with. It has been suggested that the lost `e' from `werwolf' lives at the end of the author's name. I instantly assumed that Alden Dennis Weer is, as it were, a weerwolfe.

The first line of the novel is this: `The elm tree planted by Eleanor Bold, the judge's daughter, fell last night' (1). What does not fall until page 193, in my 246-page copy, is the other shoe. Miss Bold, now married to one Porter, `wants to plant a tree on my grave when I'm gone. That's her hobby: she plants trees of endangered American species on the graves of her friends.' I had missed this absolutely fundamental revelation until Yvonne Rousseau explained it, and I felt sick with shame. Even so, at least I knew from the first paragraph that Weer was *probably* dead: `I was afraid I was going to have an attack, and then, fuzzily, thought that perhaps the heart attack had wakened me, and then that I might be dead . . . it seemed to me that the whole house was melting like the candle, going soft and running down into the lawn.' Yes indeed. The house is his skull, pierced by the roots of Eleanor Bold's now-ancient, vast and fallen elm.

Weer claims to have built a mnemonic house, each room the replica of one from his life. Alden does just this, in the chambered cavities of his skull. In a poignant quotation from the *Necronomicon,* that wicked book invented by Lovecraft and here re-invented by Wolfe, a man is called back from death. `His eyes were no more; their sockets seemed dark pits, save that there flickered behind them a point of light . . . I knew this spark for the soul of the dead man, seeking now in all the chambers under the vault of the skull its old resting places' (217).

Peace, then, is the peace of requiescat in pace.

The book is, to a quite unparalleled extent, a tissue of lies, or at least of substantial evasion. Lou Gold, Jewish refugee and rare book dealer, is, like one of Kurt Vonnegut's dubious saints, a fraud in search of deeper truths than mere veracity. If *Peace* is enlivened by many quoted voices, each distinct and agreeable, many of them are thrown by Gold's ventriloquial throat. Does this invalidate them? We cannot know. Gold tells Weer, and us, `The world shapes itself, I find, very fast, to what I write.' (And if to the writings of Gold the literary forger, so too, no doubt, to those of Wolfe the sf speculator.) `Or I write more than I know—perhaps all of us who do what I do' (215). It will surely occur to any suspicious reader at this point to wonder if *Peace* itself is a concoction of Gold's. I do not think it is—but perhaps, on the argument just given, it does not matter and could never be tested.

Certainly Wolfe writes more than *we* know, at least until we have done a fair bit of digging. Alden does some digging, looking for gold, which does not exist because his source is a fabrication of Gold's. I quickly speculated that he then finds the gold and kills the middle aged librarian who has led him to it (and become his lover). But is she dead? Does Weer become rich from this find? As well ask who killed Ewer's aunt Olivia, run down by a car while crossing the street in search of a little something from Dubarry's Bakery. Alden himself? Or one of aunt Vi's four suitors, Professor Peacock, a man whose laces drag like a small boy's, though he is agile enough; there is a clue concerning his ownership of a car. Certainly Alden, as a small boy, causes the lingering death of another child, Eleanor Bold's nephew (conceivably the first of those planted under a tree), and the death by freezing of a young workmate at the juice plant during a prank-gone-wrong.

Wolfe teases and provokes us, but only if we are on our toes. Gold's fraud uncovered, Ewer's potential denunciation is averted when Sherry, Gold's saucy 16-year-old daughter, unprotected against pregnancy, takes him to bed (204). Some 200 pages earlier, a little while later, Sherry Gold visits the doctor. `You seem to be putting on weight, Miss Gold,' Alden imagines the doctor telling her (11). A hairy dogman from a travelling carney writes Weer a letter about the pitiful death of Doris, a new girl with the show, `a kid that belonged to Mr. Mason,' Ewer's informant tells him, `(whoever he was—I myself never laid eyes on him . . .)' (222). Is Doris the bastard child of Weer and Sherry? There are reasons for doubting this (a mason is, of course, a worker in stone, of which more shortly), but nothing is certain or self-evident in this astonishing novel about identity and fabrication.

This theme of making, self-making and self-denying, is woven in a thousand threads. Three weeks after going to live with his aunt Vi, Weer read a portion of a fairy tale in a storybook. Because he nodded off before the end, and felt it `a sort of desecration to begin an evening's reading in the middle of a story,' he never finished it (61). A princess is wooed unsuccessfully by men of earth, sea and air; these are Vi's three principal suitors, as it eventuates, and the lucky (?) fourth, so soon to be widowered by the careless motorist who runs Vi down, is Julius Smart, pharmacist, and founder of the juice factory Alden first works for and finally owns. Julius tells an extraordinary Gothic tale of his patron, a paranoiac pharmacist whose concoctions turn people into freaks, including himself. The carney dogman is perhaps one of his productions; its mother, whose hands spring direct from her shoulders, seems to be a natural forerunner of those luckless victims of pharmacy, the Thalidomide babies. I suspect that the chemist's fatal disorder (though this is never explained in the book) is the fantastically rare genetic disease *myositis ossificans progressiva*, which turns ordinary tissue into bone (or `stone') so the entire body grows rigid, rather as a corpse does, before it liquefies. In short, natural and pharmacological causation is systematically and fiendishly confounded, to our confusion and delight.

As it chanced, I read and ferreted about in *Peace* at the same time I was gnawing on Omni's 1985 `world's hardest IQ test', which offered 48 nasty little puzzles requiring expertise ranging from Greek mythology to the theory of limits, etymology to the Periodic table of the elements. The two experiences were not dissimilar, although I certainly do not wish to reduce this complex and glowing book to a series of intellectual gags. In that year, I raised some of these points with Gene Wolfe, who confirmed my guess about `weerwolfe', which made me happy; agreed that Professor Peacock was indeed Aunt Vi's motorized killer, which made me chuckle and rub my hands together maniacally; and drew back in distress from my suggestion that Gold's invented `gold' actually came into existence as a result of his forged document, only to be retrieved by Alden. No, no, Wolfe said, pained; *Peace* is, on that level, a work of realism. Alden is rich because he is

Aunt Vi's heir, and therefore crabby old Julius Smart's.

We swapped gifts as we parted. I gave Wolfe a copy of my Australian anthology *Strange Attractors*, dedicated jointly to him and to Ursula Le Guin. He gave me, in return, a pleasing morsel. `What's the brand name of Julius's synthetic orange juice?' he asked. This hideous stuff is the fluid which flows like a phony alchemist's fake gold through the entire book; its name, never mentioned, was proposed by Aunt Vi, orientalist and wag. In fact I had spent some time brooding on this matter, but had to confess myself beaten. `Why,' said evil Gene Wolfe, `T'ang, of course.'[6]

[6] A useful *Peace Indexicon,* compiled in 2000 by Doug Eigsti, is available from Sirius Fiction, P.O. Box 6248, Albany CA 94706-0248, USA.

9: LIVING FOREVER

i

Nineteenth century poets, if my mother's old school anthology from the 1930s is to be trusted, got a retro buzz out of supposing themselves `in fealty to Apollo'.[7] Suitable enough for Keats, but it led me to wonder what Greek effigies sf fanciers might appropriate? Daedalus the Artificer was snaffled by Joycean modernists. Prometheus? Perhaps, with Mary Shelley's Ur-blessing. I prefer Mercury, trickster and messenger. In the first half of the twentieth century, his DNA caduceus and winged sandals stood high over various art deco mass media enterprises, and he still seems the right god for the age of the Internet, the epoch when the future jumped up and bit everyone on the ass.

One of the benefits of the net, for sf writers scribbling away in a corner, is the access it offers on the mysterious hearts and minds of their readership. It is a narrow slice, of course, mostly school and college kids and a virtual convention of programmers, sysops, engineers, astrophysicists, a few parents stuck at home with the baby. But on the net you can test that corner of the market, at least, you can listen to the unguarded confessions. `Every time I read an Aldiss book,' wailed one hapless soul on a Usenet list, `I find myself getting really angry at the book, the characters and the

---

[7] It's true, that is what it was called: *In Fealty to Apollo: An Anthology*, edited by A. A. Phillips and Ian Maxwell, Melbourne University Press, 1932. You have wonder what they thought they were doing.

author, for no easily discernible reason. His writing is reasonably good, and he doesn't put too many really objectionable elements into his books, but I always come away feeling dissatisfied, annoyed, and slightly . . . unclean.'

Remarkable. This was Brian W. Aldiss being dismissed and abused, Aldiss the finest stylist to enter science fiction in his generation, Aldiss the diverse, witty, knowing and magic master of the mode. Another fan critic, Richard Treitel, replied gently: `Possibly it's because they are so carefully made unheroic. If they achieve great things, it's by accident; if they are good, they're an everyday kind of good guy rather than a knight in shining armor. This has been known to grate on people.' Just so. Aldiss is an adult, most of the time, in fealty to Mercury, writing for adults. Little wonder his work and that of his peers makes many fans feel slightly . . . unclean. So sf still largely remains in the condition Thomas M. Disch long ago diagnosed: a branch of children's literature (Nicholls, ed., 1978, 142).

It is interesting that sf's prime theoretician-practitioner, Samuel R. Delany, chose to praise John Brunner precisely for his narrative realism: `There were vividly depicted men and women responding to problems, however grandiose, in remarkable and believable ways . . . Brunner has maintained an unbelievably high level of story-telling craft; and, more, he has demonstrated throughout that range the most humane concern with, insight into, and intelligence over the most pressing problems of our epoch' (1983, 27, 32). Both books examined in this chapter try to cope with adult life in a world skewed by the impact of science and tech-nology. Curiously enough, the one that comes closer to triumphant success is, in its rather ambitious, playful way, the gaudier. Children would not get much out of Raphael Carter's *The Fortunate Fall* (1997) even if it is, when all's said and done, a *faux* Russian/Czech/Polish novel of the kind we agonized over when we were 16 or 20, romantically defiant in our Kafka rags. But kids might get a bigger thrill out of James Halperin's *The First Immortal* (1998), especially if they have never read any thoughtful sf before.

In 1996, Halperin, a wealthy rare-coiner dealer, released a 1940s sort of novel about how the world would be changed to its roots by the arrival of a perfect lie detector. Not content with publishing it himself, following knockbacks from the usual suspects, he had posted it free in installments on the Internet, advertising it on various Usenet sf newsgroups (to the frequent anger of habitués), extra chunks accessible only after his readers answered an on-line poll. It was a truly klutzy move, everyone agreed. Then Halperin's site got 15,000 hits, and 10,000 survey responses, the book was taken up by Del Rey and published as *The Truth Machine*, and for a moment astute marketing made it the wowed topic (if you can believe the net hype) on everyone's lips. It was a foreshadowing of the success some years later of Cory Doctorow's internet sensation *Down and Out in the Magic Kingdom*, discussed below in chapter 23.

I looked Halperin's book out, eventually, with some dread, expecting some mildly diverting speculations wrapped in heavy sour dough. To my surprise I found an agreeable if crude revival of the early Heinlein utopia, told (in a clever move) by an artificial intelligence of confessedly limited narrative skills. Halperin's second novel, a promotional allegory for cryonics, followed much the same formula, but in third person narrated by the protagonist's great-grand son, Trip Crane (married to—*groan*—Stephanie Van Winkle). A family saga extending from the start of the 20th century to the close of the 21st, it was swiftly optioned for TV mini-series. The editor of Barnes & Noble's free sf promotional magazine was innocently beside himself: `I don't think I've ever read a book that has raised so many thought-provoking questions before'. And indeed it is not half bad as moderately conservative projections go, and given Halperin's limitations as a new novelist starting without any of the usual requisites.

Plainly he had read very little sf, and for that matter not much fiction. I thought I detected a tincture of Heinlein, not least in the names—his hero is Benjamin Franklin Smith—but felt sure he was ignorant of the sf canon, the usual reason for re-inventing the wheel. I asked him outright (using the Internet, of course). `I've never read anything by Heinlein,' he replied. `I read tons of nonfiction, and very little fiction. My three favorite sf novels are: *Ender's Game*, *The Sparrow* and *Snow Crash*. As an aside, I used to read EC comic books as a kid (*Weird Science*, *Tales from the Crypt*, etc.) and I still collect them. They were published in the 1950s . . . and remain, in my opinion, not only the most brilliant comic book stories ever written, but classics of American literature.'

The First Immortal is not a classic of any kind of literature, but it is somehow, against the odds, an engaging and heartfelt travelogue into an extropian future. Jaron Lanier, the VR guru, distinguishes between Steward and Extropian attitudes to the use of radical technology.[8] Stewards, cautious and backward-looking, wish to preserve and safeguard. Extropians—Lanier borrowed the term from Dr. Max More, who founded a whole philosophy on optimistic neophilia—embrace intelligent change, the wilder the better. Bring on the Vingean Singularity, that discontinuous moment when all the curves of technological advance cross the red line and go straight up the page! Freeze your head if, by bad luck, you die before immortality has been perfected, and sit out the wait in a Dewar flask! Upload your mind into silicon platforms and calve off xeroxes of your self to scour the galaxies for wonders! I recognized a whole lump of `dialogue' drawn without acknowledgment (although doubtless with permission) from posts on the extropian email list; the book is impressively researched. Halperin, like many sf dreamers not named J. G. Ballard, is an extropian at heart, although he is well aware of the risks of drastic change and conscious of the backlash to be expected from a frightened society and the sometimes malevolent ideologues it harbors.

The storyline is not terribly important, although Halperin clearly lavished a lot of pencil-licking attention on psychological themes and counterpoints, after the manner of, say, a Colleen McCulloch. Parents maim or encourage their children in broad-brush strokes; the generations strut and fret their way through the family drama—should we thaw Daddy's corpse and grab his freezer money?—only to be baffled, time and again, by new plot openings available only in the wonderful world of the future: nanotechnology, cloning your dead wife or parent, same sex marriages yielding gene-spliced children, rebirth and rejuvenation, hopeless addiction to VR fantasies. Sf readers know it all by heart, and every variation; have known it for decades. The mass market audience who will lap up *The First Immortal* on television will be agog, amazed that a human mind could dream up such outlandish wonders.

ii

The future in *The Fortunate Fall*, a fine first novel, is grievously out of touch with any plausible reality, because Raphael Carter insisted on grisly

---

[8] In a `special issue on the future' of SPIN magazine guested-edited by Jaron Lanier, November, 1995. See his homepage: http://www.well.com/Community/Jaron.Lanier/index.html

objective correlatives contrived to make our contemporary skins crawl: chips as big as your thumb socketed into the shaved scalp, interface devices for `moistdisk, opticube, dryROM' (11). `The chip was long and white, with many metal legs.' There are `five palm-sized holes drilled in my head, capped with black adapters . . . the Net-rune in my cheek, a scar of garish luminescence slashing down from eye to jaw in swoops and angles' (48). When you're Maya Tatyanichna Andreyeva (of News One hearth, a Camera), chasing down a disappeared genocide by the human swarm-mind Unanimous Army in Kazakhstan, that is the kind of cyber-kitsch your skull bristles with.

Except that it will not be, not by the 23rd century, despite disruptions in the rising curve of technology by the nasty Guardians and the horrific worse-than-the-disease solution of the Army. We really will require nanotechnology and advanced AI-mediated bio-engineering to get from here to there, and that will be a condition closer to Greg Bear's *Blood Music* (powerful smart microbes infesting your flesh) than to clunky old jack-in Gibsonian pre-personal computer cyberpunk. It is the difference between getting to the Moon by hooking up those swans and bottles of dew, and building the damned rockets and doing it according to the realistic laws of physics. In this case, righteous extrapolation looks more like magic than most sf has ever surmised. And in fact, Maya *is* infested by a `nano popula-tion' that requires refreshing now and then from a flask (21). In short, the implied technology is fatally inconsistent.

And yet this flaw does not damage Carter's deliciously written novel, because apparently it was *not* intended as a work of canonical sf—if one can trust the Library of Congress details on the indicia page:

1. Women journalists—Russia—Fiction. 2. Genocide—Russia Fiction. 3. Virtual reality—Fiction

I do not know who phrases such designations, but it is almost plausible that this authentic anchored-in-the-megatext sf novel might be read pref-erentially as a study of a woman journalist of the future, even if the Russia in question is a pretty strange locale in the Fusion of Historical Nations policed by the Emily Postcops (*very* polite and deadly if you breach their etiquette). Maya is also a lesbian, which her wildly diverse world inexpli-cably regards as a vile crime—but then so did ours, just as inexplicably, for centuries, and still does in plenty of places. (Raphael Carter's web site, as it happens, declares a passionate interest in androgyny as the way of the future, or perhaps just as an option that ought to have its ample space, and a certain tension in the substrate of the novel plainly derives from the author's own embattled endurance of bigotry.)

We are quickly drawn into the teasing but slightly sinister flirting between Maya, a telepresence Netcast journo, and her new `screener', Keishi Mirabara, a young Japanese Black émigré to judge from her VR image. This mysterious person stands between her unfiltered consciousness and the vast feedback ocean of the co-experiencing audience. Has Keishi known Maya before, in that decade-long blind-spot enforced in her memory by a patrolling chip? `You're a Postcop,' Maya speculates fearfully. `Or are you a Weaver?' (58). Paranoid and mind-scrambled, Maya, but no slouch. What is her relationship to Pavel Voskresenye, a revolutionary cyborged former victim of the Mengele-like author of the atrocity she studies? And how may the wrath of the deadly Weavers, virus-scouring denizens of grayspace, be avoided? And what gives with the snooty Africans, who have apparently gone through the Singularity, a hyper-hightech culture ruled or perhaps epitomized by the Unknown King and His Majesty-in-Chains and Only-A-Man and Its-Ethereal Highness? And what is it, exactly, that is very like a whale? You can pose these questions in the new languages Sapir or KRIOL if you would prefer.

Carter's brio and inventive spin on all the cyber tropes everyone else exhausted in the 1980s and early 1990s is fun, speedy, if never quite as wrenchingly moving as the writer clearly wishes it to be. Or maybe that is just an index of exposure to those very tropes. Naturally a mainstream reader, hunting for a novel on Women journalists—Russia—Fiction, would be baffled and infuriated by *The Fortunate Fall*. It takes knowing sf insiders to relish work this complex and detailed, which is itself a hazard for the author because if they know that much they are already immunized—not nearly to the extent that spoils a reader for the dogged advocacy of a Halperin, but some. Meanwhile, I am informed by computer scientist Paul-Michel Agapow's Internet review that the alife speculations are spot-on in their quicksilver detail: `Particularly noteworthy is a section that contains perhaps the most perceptive (and maybe the only decent) depiction of artificial life in sf [such as] a computational ecosystem in which a creature has evolved to blind its prey by flooding the system with millions of "look" requests.'[9]

The AI in Thomas Easton's *Silicon Karma* (1997) comments rather complacently, `You must have read Hans Moravec's *Mind Children*. It is a classic book, quite fascinating and prophetic. But . . . like most futurists, Moravec was far too conservative'(14). To the contrary: AI specialists such as the mercurial and brilliantly imaginative Moravec, especially in his *Robot: Mere Machine to Transcendent Mind* (1999) show all too easily how difficult it is for sf writers to imagine a rigorous future more startling, more amazing, more astounding, more fantastic than we can expect to find hurtling from the labs as we surge into this century's enigmatic Singularity, a topic to which we shall return, more than once, in the second half of this book. A visible convergence is upon us as emergent technologies such as genomic engineering, AI, and nanotechnology appear ready to sweep us in the direction of Vernor Vinge's Singularity.

That is the moment, recall, when the exponentially rising rates of change go so high so fast that even if those riding the curve manage to keep it under control, we here at the start of the twenty-first century simply cannot make head or tail of the thing. But science fiction has had a long, strange trip to that near apocalyptic prospect. Let us turn now and retrace some of mature sf's early footsteps, and then examine in greater detail several of the more interesting novels from the very close of the great century of sf and the opening of its fabled twenty-first.

[9] See
http://homepage.cs.latrobe.edu.au/agapow/Postviews/past_c-d.html#fortunatefall

PART II: THE TIMES OF OUR TIME

10: READING THE 1950S' GOLDEN AGE

·

`Don't stop.'

`"Don't stop,"' she repeats. `I've heard those words somewhere before.'
In fact, rarely has she ever heard the word `stop' *without* `don't'. Not from
a man. Not much from herself either. `I've always thought "don't stop"
was one word,' she says.

   Philip Roth, *The Human Stain* (2000, 231)

i

I wish I'd had Robert Silverberg's *Science Fiction 101* to read when I was 15
years old. Yet in a way I *did* have a large part of it, and read it closely, at
exactly that age and a little older, because its bulk is a gathering of thir-
teen stories from the true Golden Age of sf, the early and mid-1950s, and
eight or nine of those stories were near the heart of the municipal library
sf anthologies I devoured as a kid. The book's original and truer title was
Worlds of Wonder (1988), which places the emphasis correctly on the
reader's delight rather than its analytical appeal to the academy,
although it has that as well, at least to anyone intrigued by the techniques
specific to creating sf's distinctive textuality. What makes it entirely
special is Silverberg's candid autobiographical opening, `The Making of
a Science-Fiction Writer' (1-34), his careful, detailed commentaries on
the craft of each story, and the poignant intertwinings between the two

projects. Read it, certainly, for the intelligence, humor and honesty of his analysis. But read it, above all, for the agony and irony of the self-deception between the lines.

The intellectually gifted Robert Silverberg discovered sf pulp magazines at 11 or 12, in the late 1940s, and his account of the result is typical, even in its overwrought character:

> Their impact on me was overwhelming. I can still taste and feel the extraordinary sensations they awakened in me: it was a physiological thing, a distinct excitement, a certain metabolic quickening at the mere thought of handling them, let alone reading them. It must be like that for every new reader—apocalyptic thunderbolts and eerie unfamiliar music accompanying you as you lurch and stagger, awed and shaken, into a bewildering new world of images and ideas, which is exactly the place you've been hoping to find all your life. (3)

Not all victims of this exotic virus are so pleased to recall the fever of their infection. But for most fans, like *New York Review of Science Fiction* editor David Hartwell, besotted wonderment and a subsequent nostalgia for its impossible re-evocation are at the heart of science fiction, a heart that starts beating in early adolescence. `The Golden Age of Science Fiction Is Twelve', candidly declares the first chapter heading of Hartwell's wryly titled *Age of Wonders* (1985), a title echoed in Silverberg's own: `Immersed in science fiction. Bathing in it, drowning in it; for the adolescent who leans this way it can be better than sex' (Hartwell, 3).

Silverberg, too, discerns twelve as the year especially vulnerable to sf infection. This collection, he remarks, is `an affectionate gift to that 12-year-old kid with my name who set out, in Brooklyn long ago, to be a science-fiction writer. Look, kid, I'm trying to say: here are all those stories you loved so much, the ones you wished you could have written' (Silverberg, xii). Now as it chances, Bob Silverberg was 12 in 1948; only the earliest story in the book was published before then, the next earliest in 1950, while the modal date is 1953. He was a smart kid, no doubt about it (so were we all), but it is actually a stroke of luck for the reputation of the field that these stories which so powerfully branded his soul found Silverberg not at 12 but at 15 or 18, perhaps the earliest time when wonder passes into something closer to understanding.

H. L. Gold, fabled editor of *Galaxy* magazine, offered advice in 1956 that stung Silverberg then and should still disturb him (though he cites it with some complacency):

> ... Project your career 20 years into the future and see where you'll stand if you don't sweat over improving your style, handling of character and conflict, resourcefulness in story development. You'll simply be more facile at what you're doing right now, more glib, more skilled at invariably taking the easiest way out. (31-2)

A year later, Gold tightened the screw:

> ... I'm appalled and outraged that a talent should be *encouraged* to stay small, so that the least effort and maximum glibness will sell the most literary yard goods ... and the hell with whether you grow as a writer. ... I've seen too many aged hacks, Bob, and damned if I want to help even one person join that pathetic ragged crowd. (32)

Chastened finally, Silverberg tells us that he pulled up his socks and knuckled down, becoming in the process the writer who emerged in the late 1960s. For a different opinion, we might look at a heart-on-sleeve review by the late John Brunner—another high-production sf machine who never managed to become Ursula Le Guin or Brian Aldiss or John Crowley or Geoff Ryman—of Silverberg's 1991 *The Face of the Waters*:

> ... I can't keep my mind on it. Every few pages I start reminiscing to myself about when and where I first ran across this, that or the other element of the plot. ... To my dismay, it turned out to be effectively inter-changeable with the sort of thing I used to write myself about a quarter of a century past.

What had happened? Here is Brunner's explanation, drawn upon his own soul-destroying experience in sf publishing:

> ... even though I have in mind stories that, I'm sure, would prove as notable as the Big Books I wrote in the '60s and '70s, in a different way ... I simply cannot persuade an editor—any editor—to pay me an economic advance for what I think of as my *modern* stuff ... or less than shopworn, at any rate.

On the strength of this book, I conclude Silverbob must be a victim of the same phenomenon. (1992)

An assessment from the academy would reach an even harsher conclusion on the basis of *all* Silverberg's novels, even the interesting failure *Dying Inside*. (And it is worth noting, in passing, what a devastating admission it is that one will not write one's best because there is not enough money in it. As George Turner used to insist, you can always get a job cleaning the streets. What is at stake is how much you value your art over your comforts. A more persuasive complaint might be that, once written, challenging sf simply cannot gain publication or meaningful distribution, given the realities of today's mass market, which is not at all the same thing and perhaps not true, though Australian Terry Dowling—despite rave reviews in *Locus*—evidently cannot get into print in the USA, and I—despite the odd national and international award—seem to have lost what small charm I held for readers outside my own small country.)

It is not just that Silverberg, like Brunner and many other professionals, learned well the lesson of how to turn out those `literary yard goods' with smooth and consistent polish, but that he showed no evidence in his work of knowing what makes fiction deeply moving, memorable, powerful, subtle, adult. He learned how to punch the tale along, how to churn out the expectedly unexpected variations on alien life forms and cultures, how to daub in the `surprising' colors and moods, how to echo with a certain graduate school knowingness the tropes of canonical art (an urbane thematic reference to Conrad here, a citation from Kafka there) which is embodied, horrifyingly, in the degenerating parasitical life of his protagonist in *Dying Inside*, who writes and hawks university essays for illiterate jocks. But, alas, some sensitive inner portion of Silverberg's brain (or heart) seemed blocked off from the slick left-brain segment dedicated to his word processor.

In his extremely interesting analysis of James Blish's `Common Time' (1953), he tells us that Kenneth Burke's notion of `the tragic rhythm' gave him an early clue to structures of art. In essence, the formula is *Purpose, Passion, Perception*. `Of all the formulas for constructing fiction that I have heard, this seems the most useful' (187). Curiously, in this sinuous and insightful unraveling of Blish's `marvelous story' (as Silverberg justly dubs it), he closes with what I think is a perverse misreading of its end. You

will have to follow the logic by re-reading story and critique for your-
selves, but Silverberg insists that Garrard the star pilot `realizes, once he is
safely back on Earth, that he will not go' back to the Centaurian
clinesterton beademung `with all of love' (189). Blish's single technical
failure, Silverberg tells us, was to skimp the motivational contrast which
might have intensified the `renunciation of star travel' by formerly
space-mad Garrard. Yet the story plainly shows that Garrard does decide
to return, a decision thwarted and betrayed by his mission controllers.
`Don't move' is the haunting reprise in this story, the dictum which saves
Garrard when subjective time plays dangerous tricks on him. Its utterance
at the finale is not Garrard's secret self speaking a loss of resolve or drive; it
is *society* speaking on its own behalf, for the time being, a (much slower)
time-scale drastically out of synch with an individual's. How much more
preferable, how much closer to the voluptuous heart of non-pap science
fiction, is Philip Roth's robustly sexual `Don't stop.'

And so yes, one must ask if this interpretative error reveals something
bitterly frustrated in Silverberg's own reading: that in embracing the
common time of commercial readership, in accepting `don't move' as the
principle of sf's evolution, too many sf writers blunt their own perception,
squander their passion, and lose their deepest artistic purpose.

ii

Most of the stories in the collection are exemplary, even if they creak a
little after all this time (which tells us, happily, that the genre, the mode,
has lifted its narrative game in the meanwhile). They are not necessarily
the stories I would have chosen, but for obvious reasons everyone has his
or her own `age of wonder' favorites—and, of course, any Golden Age
gleaning undertaken in the '80s or '90s followed upon a multitude of
predecessors, some by Silverberg himself, which have already collected
the period's very best sf.

Silverberg chose C. L. Moore's `No Woman Born' (1944), Cordwainer
Smith's `Scanners Live In Vain' (1950), Cyril Kornbluth's `The Little Black
Bag' (1950), Jack Vance's `The New Prime' (1951), Damon Knight's `Four
in One' (1953), Henry Kuttner's `Home is the Hunter' (1953), Robert
Sheckley's `The Monsters' (1953), James Blish's `Common Time' (1953),

Phil Dick's `Colony' (1953)—that fabulous year!—Alfred Bester's `Fondly Fahrenheit' (1954), Brian Aldiss's `Hothouse' (1960), Bob Shaw's `Light of Other Days' (1966) and Fred Pohl's `Day Million' (1966).

The least of them, for me, are `The New Prime', `Home is the Hunter' and `Colony'. `Scanners' is the Smith piece everyone of a certain age falls about over, but for me it lacks the dreamy, idiosyncratic mythos of the core Instrumentality tales: I prefer Smith's `The Ballad of Lost C'Mell' (1962) or—a bit primitive these days, granted—`The Game of Rat and Dragon' (1955) or `Alpha Ralpha Boulevard' (1961) or `The Burning of the Brain' (1958), critic John Foyster's choice for just such a book. I would leave Kuttner out, turning instead to Theodore Sturgeon: `The Touch of Your Hand' (1953), say, or `The Skills of Xanadu' (1956, and, admittedly, seen in every other classic anthology), or `The Other Man' (1956), with their charming if reductionist cognitive psychology. The Aldiss selection is a bit too winsome, but so are mine: `Old Hundredth' (1960) and `A Kind of Artistry' (1962). On the whole, though, these are outstanding choices, and the editor's part-analytic, part-nostalgic readings are enthralling in their own right. And yet what comes through, again and again, is a heart-breaking blend of envy and admiration, wistfulness and slightly unconvinced boastfulness.

iii

A study of these pieces, and others of their caliber, could perhaps tell us what went wrong with sf, as well as what went right with it. Silverberg's own summary is this: `To think well, and to write well: those are the minimum requirements for writing great science fiction. High demands; but those who choose science fiction as the center of their writing lives accept those requirements unresentfully' (348). Well, but they don't, not often. And note the absence of *to feel well*, although we are assured that `technique is merely a means to an end, and in this case the end is to convey understanding in the guise of entertainment' (33-4). George Turner was not alone in berating most sf writers for avoiding hard thought, for playing children's games with adult perceptions and passions and purposes. If the best commercial sf writing today generally has a finer finish than we find in these stories of half a century past, I am still not at all persuaded that most of it could be described as `written well'.

And yet— It is not simple greed or laziness that holds sf back (assuming you agree that it *is* being held back, rather than standing proudly where many fans still place it, at the steely pinnacle of world art to date). `By a rough calculation,' Silverberg remarks, `I find that the writing careers of everyone in this book aggregate a total of nearly five hundred years. That's a long time for fourteen people to spend wrestling with the phantoms of the far reaches of time and space' (348).

This can be taken at face value. These stylistic pioneers, these children of primitive sf, these parents of today's speculative writing, they were undoubtedly driven by a kind of artistry, a search for the skills of xanadu. They could have made more money, back in the 1950s and 1960s, writing ad copy (as some of them did, to keep steak on the table). It was the comradeship of fandom, I expect (except for Dr. Linebarger—`Cordwainer Smith'—gulping hydrochloric acid to contain some terrible gastric revolt and dreaming the psychological conquest of more worlds than one),[10] the fever of that shared, funny, nerdish, clever, knowledgeable, profoundly genre-shaped (*mutually*-shaped) company. That social vortex has never truly been known in backwaters such as Australia, my homeland, where the 1985 World SF Convention could gather together barely enough writers of international standing that, when I whinged and complained of the absence of a Science Fiction Writers of America suite, Bob Silverberg could twist his lips and suggest, in the driest possible voice, `An SFWA *booth*, perhaps?' *Worlds of Wonder* takes us into a booth of sf writers from another time and space, and it is well worth the visit, but at the end of the day I was left wondering if we sf readers are not just the victims of a plague, as our irritated mothers warned us so long ago, confiscating the gaudy magazines, but not before infection had worked its way deep into the heart and head, where fancy, after all, is bred.

iv

In a special number of *Science Fiction Commentary*, 51, editor Bruce Gillespie arranged a Silverberg Forum. It was striking how exactly the several contributors (each working at his own level of insight or stupidity)

---

[10] See Arthur Burns, `Paul Linebarger' [1967] in the `Cordwainer Smith Revisited' issue of *Australian Science Fiction Review (Second Series)*, 21 Vol 4, 4, 10-12.

betrayed a consensus of estimate of Silverberg's work. George Turner: `. . . interesting stuff but still muddle . . . ' Stanislaw Lem: ` . . . an interesting phenomenon.' Van Ikin: ` . . . Silverberg's career has taken some interesting turns lately.' Gillespie: `The interesting question is . . . ' Gillam: `*The Cube Root of Uncertainty* is interesting because . . . ' Derrick Ashby: ` . . . Silverberg is one of the most interesting . . . ' Gillespie again, hacking straight in to it: `You must admit that Bob Silverberg is a clever bloke.'

And that, alas, seemed the highest pitch of response which Silverberg's work was capable of eliciting. It is . . . interesting. Inescapably and probably fatally, Robert Silverberg made himself a laboratory preparation, a paradigm of pain we scarcely register as a poignant human burden but increasingly as the demonstration of a theorem. John Brunner, who died after a heart attack at the world science fiction convention in 1995, was another of the same species. It is easy enough to get brittle about this, harder and crueler to speak the truth. In an access of drunken sentimentality, I stood close to Silverberg's then-wife Barbara at the 1975 World SF Convention in Melbourne, Australia, and gestured inarticulately toward her doleful spouse. `If only I could express to you,' I said stumblingly, `how much I want to go to that man—but by what right? on the basis of a reader's imagined intimacy, and self-serving projection?—and put my arm about him, and tell him how much I love him as a human in pain.' So Barbara said, `Why don't you? If only people would.' Words to that effect.

But I couldn't, of course, because I could not say that much without also telling him that his life's work seemed to me worthless, the refinement of woeful slick technique in the service of interesting cleverness, of a perception so guarded that its real or apparent shallowness made *Dying Inside*, his best book, read precisely like the prodigious accomplishment of a brilliant 15-year-old who would never grow up to equal Malamud or Bellow or Roth.

The impression was never stronger than during the excruciating minutes, a day or so later, when Silverberg read from *Son of Man* (1971) after declaring it his finest achievement. My sympathy drained away. What could you do with a fellow like this? *Son of Man* seemed to me the apotheosis of all that is ersatz, shoddy, dishonest and mechanical in his work. Unreadable in the way the worst pseudo-philosophy is unreadable—built up out of dreary abstractions that repudiate no alternatives, words cemented by proximity with no image of sense or reason generated from their concatenation, the dead mockery of imagination, rows of trained neural monkeys cranking out sentences singular only for their tawdry adherence to some Principle of Concerted Nominal Incompatibility. And, as always, the pulp cliches for sexuality: the globes, the spheres of milky flesh. George Turner and others critics continued to hail Silverberg's alleged virtuosity, his technical bravura. What I saw, and it broke my heart, was mechanism, affectless banality, the inane, arid contrivances of despair of *The Stochastic Man* (1975), the self-loathing comic-strip sardonics of *Shadrach in the Furnace* (1976), the endless soapy saga of Marjipoor.

But still I want Silverberg—in his seventies if it comes to that, and in agony—to become a true writer (youthful by Bellow's standard); I want it of all the skilled technicians who became only reliable sf writers, ingenious graduates of Science Fiction 101.

11:1939-1975: THERE AND BACK AGAIN

Three In Space: Classic Novels of Space Travel:
The Voyage of the Space Beagle, A. E. van Vogt; *Galaxies*, Barry Malzberg;
The Enemy Stars, Poul Anderson (White Wolf, 1997)

i

Sf's stylistic trajectory, as mapped by this odd troika, echoes shocks of change and repetition, from the start of global war to the end of the Vietnam conflict. Its span stretches from six years before the first atomic bomb to six years after the first moon landing. Each of these remarkable but utterly disparate novels is introduced by an sf connoisseur, after a fore-word by Arthur C. Clarke—plus two afterwords to *Galaxies*, one a 1980 retrospective appreciation from Marta Randall, the other Malzberg's despairing reflections, in 1997, on *Galaxies*: `What a remarkable novel this is: of life and science fiction it says nothing but of its thirty-five-year-old author it says as was meant nearly everything. BUT IT DOESN'T SAY WHAT THE AUTHOR THOUGHT HE WAS SAYING' (431). Certainly each of these books was significant in my own life.

The book's compilers, Dann, Sargent and Zebrowski, upmarket deni-zens of sf's generic ecology, retain a warm fondness for the wonderful pulp dreams incubated by generations of John W. Campbell's famous magazine, *Astounding Science Fiction*. In the shadow of World War Two and without anyone noticing, modern science fiction burst into squalling life. In 1939, Robert Heinlein, Isaac Asimov and A. E. van Vogt published their first stories there. Van Vogt, chosen 1995 Grand Master by the Science Fiction and Fantasy Writers of America, was the last to die—and perhaps the least known, out of fashion. Yet his influence remains visible everywhere, from *Star Trek* and *Star Wars* to the most surrealist slipstream sf. His first stories, `Black Destroyer' and `Discord in Scarlet', became the closely reworked heart of his classic *Space Beagle* fix-up novel (the *locus classicus* of that narrative patchwork device, and van Vogt's own term, adopted by Nicholls and Clute in their *SF Encyclopedia*).

The very language of each novel tells us a great deal about these consecutive generations of wonder-weavers. Van Vogt's space opera is as primal and menacing as any *Alien* movie: `On and on Coeurl prowled. The black, moonless, almost starless night yielded reluctantly before a grim reddish dawn that crept up from his left' (22). By turns, four terrifying aliens disrupt this intergalactic expedition: Coeurl, the hypnotic birdlike Riim, terrifying Ixtl who lays eggs in human bellies (van Vogt won $50,000 recompense from the makers of *Alien*), and a vast gas intelligence, the Anabis, that infests our neighboring Andromeda galaxy. Gluing the episodes together is the patient missionary work of Elliott Grosvenor, the ship's Nexialist, an interdisciplinary holistic thinker and forerunner of van Vogt's classic supermen and perhaps L. Ron Hubbard's dianetics and scientology. As a credulous child, I gulped down van Vogt's wonderful novel, and dreamed of being a Nexialist.

ii

Two decades after that tale of an almost indestructible alien loose among scientists on a starship eerily like the *Enterprise*, a second generation of Campbell's *Astounding Science Fiction* children was peaking, more fluent and often better trained in the sciences. Poul Anderson, 1997's Grand Master and writing until his death in 2002, offered a poignant hard-sf novel about the quest for knowledge—knowledge of the human heart, and of a dark star that smashes an expedition but yields first contact with alien minds. Serialized under the haunting title *We Have Fed Our Sea*, it closes this volume, its physics revised in 1979, as, thuddingly, *The Enemy Stars*. (I wish Poul had taken the chance to reinstate the title borrowed from Kipling.)

In the era of Sputnik and the other early satellites, Anderson was more solemn than van Vogt, confident yet incantatory: `They named her *Southern Cross* and launched her on the road whose end they would never see' (443). After ruinous wars, space exploration is renewed. Mattercasting allows crew and supplies to be teleported instantly by tachyon beam, but a receiver must await them. Starships plunge into the void at nearly the speed of light, temporary shells for international technicians who watch over them during short tours of duty. A remnant black sun, not quite a black hole, smashes *Southern Cross*'s engines and 'caster web, and the aghast crew must struggle to rebuild their link to Earth. What they find is the price in blood of admiralty, and community with a people utterly unlike themselves. Anderson's melancholy, stodgy, somewhat sexist poetry moved me deeply in my late teens.

iii

Tucked between is a text tagged sf only by twisting the genre's definition to breaking point, as its audacious author surely intended. At the limit of this 36-year narrative arc, Malzberg is shamelessly in-your-face: `To define terms at the outset, this will not be a novel so much as a series of notes toward one. Nevertheless pay attention, for it will cease to become a novel exactly at the point where it seems to be at last gathering force' (257). Clearly this was not a story serialized by John W. Campbell, who would have detested it. Ironically, though, its source was several Campbell *Analog* articles about black holes, as it tells us almost at once, but Malzberg folds, spindles and mutilates every fact and surmise he found there.

Galaxies seems no less radical today, in its taunting, metafictional way. In 1975, six months after Joanna Russ's equally transgressive feminist novel *The Female Man* finally appeared, it marked an end to innocent sf tale-telling. The book brandishes its contrivances, forces us to slog through Malzberg's own mocking meltdown as a highly self-aware artist toiling in the humus of a medium he genially despises, satirizes without mercy, and perhaps loves.

Solo pilot Lena and her cargo of 515 Dante-esque frozen dead plunge into a black hole (variously and characteristically misidentified as a `white dwarf', `neutron star', and `galaxy') and torment themselves with elegant futility, fetching up at last in Ridgefield Park, New Jersey, 1975. This journey and its recounting sounds as much fun as a bowel re-section, yet Malzberg's bleak realism about life and text deconstructs sf's melodrama into something vehement, painful, extraordinary. In maturity, Malzberg teased and confronted me with mysteries of narrative deeper, in their way, than deepest space. His narrator observes: `A writer who could combine the techniques of modern fiction with a genuine command of science could be at the top of this field in no more than a few years' (269). Malzberg himself has now fallen almost silent, but two decades on, writers such as Kim Stanley Robinson and Greg Egan and Greg Benford and Greg Bear and Paul McAuley have proved him right, even if in his `Epilogue Again' he declared bleakly that since *Galaxies* appeared `twenty-three wonderful years have come and (almost) gone and the work seems to have survived not only the state of science fiction which motivated its composition but science fiction itself' (430).

iv

What possessed Dann, Sargent and Zebrowski to yoke these quite different texts into a single volume? They had previously produced *Three In Time* (1997), an effective omnibus containing novels at once less famous and formally less confronting than these: Anderson's *There Will Be Time*, Wilson Tucker's rather dated *The Year of the Quiet Sun* and anthropologist Chad Oliver's *The Winds of Time*. Their brief, according to the back jacket, was to bring `enduring classics of science fiction to a new generation of readers', which presumably accounts for the explanatory apparatus fore and aft—that, and the obdurate taste of sf enthusiasts for camp-fire gossiping, time-binding memorials in a culture where memory is shockingly fleeting and the constituency in ceaseless flux. Malzberg might be right: if science fiction is a sub-culture built on the foundation of books such as these, and their active engagement, perhaps it has already passed away. `Who killed sf?' is a theme, after all, regularly rehearsed in sf critical journals.

Let us say that White Wolf and the editors were at least trying their damnedest to pummel the dying creature's breast, shouting its name in its Walkman-plugged ear. I do not think happy campers in Franchise-land will embrace Malzberg's chilly pomo demolition of tropes already sublimed (one way or another) in the hot media sun, especially not jammed between van Vogt's gaudy oneiric sleepwalking into genre bliss and Anderson's glum epiphanies of duty in chill heaven. Better, perhaps, to have preserved the chronological arc. But such a natural conclusion must have seemed altogether too minatory. White Wolf wished to sell more anthologies, after all, so they could hardly send away their young readers bruised, wandering eyeless in Gaza. But I might be wrong about that. People do not always start at the front and trudge or bound onward to the back cover. The street has its own uses for rediscovered history.

12: 1997: SPARES,
MICHAEL MARSHALL SMITH

Spares, eh? Before opening the covers we knowing sf knowers know
something of what we will meet. Cloned copies of the rich and famous,
kept on ice or otherwise quiet, culled in emergencies for their
histocompatible organs (protected against immediate immune system
attack by the recipient). Like zombies they will rise, taking their
revenge as Other against the smug, hegemonic Self. Or they will be set
free (as they are in Lois McMaster Bujold's *Mirror Dance* [1997]) against
their own ferocious and indignant, or just muddled, opposition. All of
this, inevitable as it is, constitutes a category mistake, a congeries of
dumb errors, so blatant and infuriating that you wish the author had a
dozen cloned necks, that he might be hanged more than once for his
crimes.

Spares is all this and worse, but also more than this, and strikingly better,
here and there, in bricolaged patches that peel off like organs stitched
together without much concern for their mutual coding. That kind of
audacity is fun. You can be reading some conventional evocation of
visceral horror—`Vinaldi and I stopped running, our chests suddenly
filled with liquid fire. I reeled off into the bushes and vomited uncontrolla-
bly'—and lurch right into Martin Amis trade-marked wry: `Bodies are
great, and I wouldn't go anywhere without mine, but sometimes they're so
disappointing. If we mistreated them as badly as we do our minds then
everyone would be dead, and yet there they go, complaining all the time.

Someone needs to get all our bodies, sit them down, and give them a good talking to' (220).

But this is not really a Robert Sheckley knockoff, so whimsy carries it only so far. Its generic cut-ups echo a certain non-stop hallucinogenic whirlpool which is the narrator's Rapt-ruined brain—Rapt is a *deus ex machina* psycholytic drug—but the central seriousness (I suppose it is) gets compromised again and again by cheap theatrics, or bleugh yuck Barkeresque set-pieces, or *Hitchhiker's Guide* frolics, and those dumb, dumb, truly stupid trope snowcrashes.

Here is a Douglas Adams bit: Our guys (ragged breathing, bang bang the guns at their backs) slam into an xPress elevator and Jack Randall, our main guy, lights up. The elevator's droid halts between floors and delivers a tiresome health lecture. Jack is not going to be stalled by a politically correct machine.

> `Where are your cognitive centers stored?' I asked, racking a shell into the barrel of my gun . . . `And can the elevator function without them?'
>
> `Yes it can,' the elevator said, with an air of slight puzzlement . . .
>
> `Because,' I said, `if you don't shut the fuck up I'm going to blow you to shit and then spend the rest of the journey smoking in comfort. I may even have a cigar.' (135-6)

Fun-*ny*, as Homer Simpson would say appreciatively. But in the context of a story set in the 22nd century, we are being told that nobody in a century or more has ever before scammed an AI, or if they did nobody reported the fault, or if they reported it nobody worked out how to fix the glitch. And why are they still using cathode ray tube monitors (20)? Am I being too dully earnest here? After all, the story is set in New Richmond, which is a city that grew out of a five-mile square aerial shopping Mall whose engines failed one day. It is a sort of Blishean Cities-Not-In-Flight, a kind of Ballardian Really-High-Rise, a merry gag that never quite takes off because it is stuck on the ground to begin with.

I was once sent a feminist woman's sf novel entitled, unpromisingly, *Wingwomen of Hera: Book One of the Cosmic Botanists Trilogy* (1987). It started with some astronomy, perhaps of the school of Velikovsky:

> Two planets hung in a quiet corner of space, revolving in leisurely orbits around their two suns . . .

[A] comet fell between the two planets, coming so close to the second that all landgrowths spontaneously burst into flames and the seas boiled at the same moment. But not close enough to pull either planet into its lethal embrace.

As its tail lashed them, both planets were pulled away from their comfortable orbits, reeling crazily until they found and settled into new paths of destiny.

The first planet now swung in a slow figure eight around both of the suns (1-2)

and so on and so forth. I did not read any further.

Was it unfair of me to be offended by such culpable ignorance, such `poetic' tosh? The author, one Sandi Hall, and her publisher, Spinsters/Aunt Lute, of San Francisco, might have felt that I was being unduly severe. But I did not care. Ms. Hall was playing, as Gregory Benford might say, without the net up. `Robert Frost remarked that free verse was like playing tennis with the net down . . . Hard sf plays with the net of scientific fact up and strung as tight as the story allows' (Benford, 1994a, 8). Indeed, I doubt she had ever heard of the net. I am pretty sure Mr. Smith, too, was innocent of that informal contract which binds us to *make sense* in science fiction, even when the high point of our novel is peeling off a child's face and sticking it on the front of the television set.

The big problem, the one that will not sink down and go away nicely, is the Spares, of course. They live in horrid humid tunnels, the Farm, where bruised Jack has wandered after barely surviving the Vietnam War, sorry, the Gap War, where they went into the jungle and killed and raped the uncomprehending, incomprehensibly violent villagers and children (`often used by the villagers to carry mines') who lived in the North, appearing and disappearing through a confusion of military-industrial quantities of drugs. Jack, reduced by a domestic horror that we finally meet on page 116 and a military atrocity on page 278 (`He had his cock out, and was thrusting it in and out of a gash which had been cut across the throat of the five-year-old girl who was being held down in front of him . . . She was still alive'), oversees and tends the mindless Spares who blunder in the Farm's tunnels, until he takes upon himself the redemptive task of teaching them to be human.

These are teenagers who have never had the least socializing, and who are regularly mined for organs, limbs and other portions of their persons, and beaten and raped between times. There is a word for such unfortunates: `wolf-children'. In the real world wolf-children are, and remain, mute, barely human, even when they are caught young and treated with great care. Jack teaches some of them to read. Then he cracks his most apt students out of the Farm and takes them on a ruinous saga, blundering forward in a path that reflects, unless I am mistaken, the author's anguished real-time search for a plot.

I will not try to explain the plot Smith stitched up, because that would not be fair and because it doesn't matter a hoot. There are mock-Lacanian essays in explanation:

> ... the fucking Gap ... It's making people think things that aren't true.'
> I told him that it *was* true now. That it was seepage, stuff that should be unconscious become conscious. The planet's dreams, seeping through the wall like hallucinations on the edge of sleep. (164)

You can get a long way with an explanatory device like that. But once you have got there, where have you got?

> I believe The Gap is made up of all the places where no one is, of all the sights which no one sees. It comes from silence, and lack, and the deleted and unread; it is the gap between what you want and what you have ... (211)

Desire as absence, as Lack. Well, yes, ho hum.

What I Lacked, dragging myself unwillingly though a book I had agreed to review, was some explanation for how Smith thought he could get away with the fundamental dumbness of his titular idea. What he was trying to blend is schlock horror and genuine science, casting aside the guidance of fifty years of cloning as a well-plumbed, highly developed sf trope. I am not blaming him for going off on his own. I am complaining because of where he went. Look at the logic of the thing.

Against the law, one gathers (not that there is much, for this is a crude police state where the rich and lofty own the police), rich people have set up reserves of genetically identical copies of their children, a year or two younger. Evidently they have no feelings of kinship for these twins. And only one copy per donor, apparently, but maybe there is some redundancy, for there is more than one Farm. At any rate, the rich have gone to the trouble of cloning their kids, lest something awful happen to these scions. Yet this is the condition of their ambulatory organ-banks:

> Twice a day, a medic drone checks vital responses and gives each spare a carefully designed package of foodstuffs to ensure that it grows and develops in tandem with its twin. [!] Sometimes the droids'll get them to move around a bit, so their muscles don't atrophy. [!!] Apart from that, all the spares know is one long endless twilight of blue heat . . . The doctors find the right spare, cut off what they need, and then shove it back in the tunnel. There it lies, and rolls, and persists, until they need it again.'
>
> [M]angled and dissected bodies stumped around them, clapping hands with no fingers together, rubbing their faces against the walls and letting shit run down their legs. (46-7).

Yes, no doubt that would be the optimum way to ensure that your medical back-up is in peak condition for the rare disaster when you will require a graft or organ transplant. But wait a minute—*rare* disaster? The SafetyNet Farms are less than 20 years old. A clone is useless to anyone except the original donor. So what are these hapless creatures doing with no fingers, or missing limbs or eyes? Even at my advanced age I do not know anyone who needs a compatible major body part. True, given the amount of feckless gun-play reported in the novel, these people are careless with their fleshy parts. But *this* careless?

Even Michael Marshall Smith is embarrassed by the absurdity. He mumbles a bit as he mentions the exemplary case of Steven Two and his `brother out in the big room' who was `a real piece of work'. Steven Prime crushed one hand in a car door at 10. `A little discomfort for a while, some tiresome physio sessions, but he ended up whole again.' I wonder if Smith has ever broken a major bone, or had eye surgery. You would not be eager to go through that again. But Steve was such a rotter that at age 17 his face was scalded by a woman scorned, so the doctors `took his brother's face away' (46). That would be the way to do it. Just peel it off, I suppose, and pop it on the scraped surface.

And the SafetyNet doctors have a strangely defective idea of the impact of stress on the human body. `The operations on the spares were never made under anesthetic, [just] muscle paralyzer . . . ' (59-60).

In other words, we have here *Grand Guignol* under the pretence of medical science, and it doesn't stand still for an instant when you pay it the mildest scrutiny.

It would have made more sense to kludge the science more boldly, as others have done before. Solve the rejection problem, and a single body-shop spare can be mined by numerous purchasers. That way you can whittle down your victims without making a complete fool of the reader. Even so, it is hard to make sense of the economics of `spare hands [with] no fingernails left, only ragged and bleeding tips, when internal organs were found to be so bruised they were barely usable, when spares' skins showed evidence of cuts and burns which did not tally with any official activity' (56). Smith makes some sort of attempt to rationalize these atrocities, and their acceptance by those who pay to sustain their children's spares (it is the pathology of The Gap, you see, poisoning everyone it touched).

By that stage, though, we are not just playing with the net down. We have abandoned our racquets and balls.

13: 1999: FINITY, JOHN BARNES

John Barnes is the turn-of-millennium equivalent to those reliable craftsmen (and a few women) at the end of the Campbell Golden Age of sf and the mid-century: an entertainer who hardly ever lets you down, a writer with literary ambitions beyond the confines of genre restrictions but happy to work at their boundaries, schooled in at least the elements of the sciences and prepared to do the hard slogging needed to get it right within the limits of the game, blessed as well with an edge of humor and that mysterious bubbling imagination which flows across the terrain of formula and renews it, if only for a moment, while leaving it formulaic. Think of Poul Anderson in the '50s and early '60s, or Harry Harrison, perhaps even Sturgeon and Heinlein, inexhaustible, various, often delightful, sometimes just cranking the pages out to pay the bills. Of course, because those fortunate writers worked the seam when it had just been opened up, their work carried an additional frisson of shock, novelty, unrepeatable pleasure.

We cannot get that any longer, half a century on. We have to make do with the pleasures of repetition and recombination, with John Varley's deliciously exfoliating Eight Worlds and Heinlein remixes (*The Golden Globe* [1998] with its astonishingly rich, detailed tapestry in themes out of Heinlein's *Double Star* and the psychotic heroism which ends his *The Puppet Masters*: `the free men are coming to kill you! Death and destruction!' [1950/1969, 219]), with Jack Vance striking endlessly variant droll postures in the pastures and canyons and sourly suspicious marketplaces of the sky, with John Barnes and his pleasing engagements on fields long since surveyed and pegged by pioneers: here, Fritz Leiber's *The Big Time* (1961/1979) and Keith Laumer's *Worlds of the Imperium* (1962) and all the other warriors sidewise in the big time, stretched out and echoed in every possible variant across the probability landscapes of the Many Worlds hypothesis like a metaphor of sf's burden of memory and repetition.

Finity has the look to me of a confection built on the run, if that makes any sense, ingredients grabbed from whatever shelf comes to hand, stirred and heated and cooled as the winds of chance carry the chef one way and another, in the confidence (Barnes is a professional; he can keep his nerve even when a scarf flies up and covers his eyes) that the tale will evolve to a good-enough conclusion, that the telling itself is where we find our satisfaction. Not that he did not set out with a nifty notion or two. I have the suspicion that this one struck him one day after the third dickhead incapable of reading eight or nine numerals in a row called his phone in error and hung up in his ear. Where are those wrong numbers coming from? Can the world really be so stupid? What if—

A lovely and satisfying part of *Finity*, for a certain kind of reader (there might not be many of us around, though), is Barnes's borrowing of what is known technically as the logic of abduction, a topic explored by the great American semiotician and pragmatist Charles Sanders Peirce.[11] Abduction, or retrodiction, was his stab at an explanation for how, when faced with startling facts, we crystallize some single hypothesis out of the myriad possible. Peirce hoped it would take its place in the armamentarium of logic, alongside syllogistic deduction and empirical induction. In the event, Karl Popper arrived to throw induction out the door as well, although it seems to be creeping back in again lately. Abduction never really gained acceptance, perhaps because its method is impossibly hard to specify; it is not unlike Delany's imaginary modular calculus, described in chapter one. I suspect that what Peirce mistook for the activity of an abductive logic is actually one or more inherited cognitive templates kicking in at a level inaccessible to scrutiny, the kind of painfully evolved filter that matches up language's universal grammar to those observed aspects of the world salient to human survival.

Barnes gives a charming account of the idea, which makes his bland protagonist Lyle Peripart special; he is an abduction theorist and New

---

[11] That's pronounced `Purse', by the way.

Zealand US expatriate, in a 2062 world partitioned a century earlier after the victory of the German Reich. So at once we have a pleasing conjunction: the trope of parallel worlds (or `counterfactuals,' as they are termed modishly today in an academy ignorant of sf's exhaustive exploitation of the idea) and a logic of seizing or constructing a true description out of the infinite seething combinations of the world's plenty.

Can Barnes carry off this narrative abduction, to our insight and gratification? Can his cast of miscast operators, abducted from any secure premises, carry the tale forward to some happy syllogistic conclusion? That is his modest goal, curiously enough, declared in advance: `Just once,' a loyal reader asked him, `would it kill you to write an adventure story, with a reasonably happy ending, only a little weird?' (prefatory note). A sophisticated and witty fellow, Barnes does just that in a suitably unexpected way. Weirdness drenches his tale, but by the standards of a Phil Dick dislocation it is only a little weird after all. Perhaps sf has suffered too many torsions by now, perhaps the demands of excess have spoiled its infinite possibilities.

Still, there is a cozy enjoyment to be had in the remixing. And Barnes does have a neat gadget for stirring up the Many Worlds, for shoehorning you out of one reality and into its neighbor. If anything, the gadget is too neat, and the insights at the narrative's heart too grand, for the implied weight of the shocking stuff we fetch up in or surf across. `Shocking' only in a rather remote intellectual sense, however. The only event to ruffle a maiden aunt is a scene of don't-hurt-me-I-love-it rough sex that recalls Barnes's taste, which worries me a bit, for sadistic infliction in his parallel worlds template series *Timeline Wars*, started with *Patton's Spaceship* (1997). The same defect of narrative disproportion somewhat spoiled Greg Egan's far more spectacular novels *Quarantine* (1992) and *Distress* (1995), where moral choice and cosmological grandeur/grandiosity crunch into the final pages with an inevitable and dizzyingly paradoxical sense of cheated disappointment: is That all there is?

It would be improper to reveal much about the plot (where has America gone? why can't I remember the question I just asked?), because the propulsion of the book is confusion, bumbling accommodation, hugger-mugger, moments of tenderness, lots of talk, lots of action (of an effective if routine kind). The bond between Peripart and his gal, a historian with the oddly similar name Helen Perdida, has something of the pleasing asperity and fondness of the best Heinlein couples. The fate of this team is a rebus of the fate of the novel. The book will do, in the way of a solid H. Beam Piper or Murray Leinster serial in *Astounding*, but I am holding out for another *Mother of Storms* (1994), Barnes's study of a self-bootstrapping super-consciousness.

14: 2000: DISTANCE HAZE, JAMIL NASIR

I so much enjoyed Jamil Nasir's delicious fourth novel *Distance Haze* that I was plunged into self-doubt about its virtues—the problem you get with Dali's consummate but somehow troublingly facile, almost airbrushed paintings. Is the pleasure of the text, however unexpected and delightful, somehow too easy? Or is that a stupidly puritan question? The novel trembles in the phase space between Douglas Hofstadter's *Gödel, Escher, Bach*, Oliver Sacks's *An Anthropologist on Mars* or maybe Dennis Overbye's *Lonely Hearts of the Cosmos*, and *Buffy the Vampire Slayer*. I could not prevent myself from reading out long passages to a new friend, and although I am not especially adept at reading aloud, the words flowed like honey, with just enough grains of pepper to gravel the tongue; it is a book for the ear, and perhaps for the inner eye (although, as I can't do that part, I tended to confuse subordinate characters, at least to the extent that they speak like generic scientists).

And I suspect that I missed some hidden payoffs. In places, epiphany falters to graceful hand-waving. Certain mystical/oneiric episodes are either authentically savvy or delusions fostered by grief, thwarted pain and ambition and love, and perhaps the concealed machineries of one or more of those Evil Brain Scientists whom Daniel Dennett likes to adduce in his merry cognitive science philosophy thought-experiments. Nothing much is as it seems. It is arguable that Nasir himself did not know ahead of time where the narrative arc would come to rest, had sent the arc careening into several alternative superposed trajectories that together create a kind of mutually constructing and self-deconstructing curve drawn sparkling inside the Cloud Chamber of Unknowing. He even risked the suspicious irritation that strikes most readers as they put down Thomas M. Disch's wondrous but all too science-fictional tour de force *Camp Concentration* (1968): here we were, supposing we had been teased by some just-out-of-reach evocation of the numinous, and the damned thing plops itself down on its tail and turns into an Eric Frank Russell jape where the Earthman defeats the thumb-fingered alien empire with a blaster made out of two bent spoons and the elastic from an old sock—that sort of thing. Nothing quite so jolting occurs in the climax of *Distance Haze*; indeed, the resolution pleased me with its Eganesque reasons to be cheerful. Still, the design palpably has . . . designs . . . upon us, always a risk when a novel plays with, you know, the Meaning of Life and Death.

Sf writer Wayne Dolan, something of a dud after five books (success with his first two, the next flopped, his marriage crumbling, his child lost to him), visits the lavishly endowed Deriwelle Institute for the Electrical Study of Religion. He will reignite his flagging career with a popular science account of loony-tunes but enthrallingly New Agey doings at the Institute, where Nobel laureates and workaday drudges seek the spirit in labs that combine something close to the real world Dr. Michael Persinger's research into electromagnetic influence on the brain, current parapsychology work at Princeton University using random number generators, fMRI scanners probing the active mindscape, and genome research into DNA codes for religious sensibility. Dolan plans a book akin to recent bestsellers about the Santa Fe Institute, and is driven in doing so to examine the murk in the depths of his own self-damaging and dissatisfied soul. He might be a little like Nasir, but less exotic; he is certainly a little like a Rudy Rucker transrealist character, or one of my own. So I was bound to enjoy his portrait, wincing as I did so. It helps to be the target. (I have never met Mr. Nasir—son of a `Palestine refugee father and [grand-child of] the inventor of the fork-lift truck . . . started college at age 14 . . . law degree in 1983 . . . meditates three hours a day'—and I swiftly sought out his earlier novels.)

The key feature of *Distance Haze* is that, like quite a few good current sf books, it strongly resembles a, forgive me, real novel. The fluent sentences convince you quickly that this fellow is not working the vein opened by `Doc' Smith, van Vogt, or even Heinlein, despite clear reverberations from key works by these last two. Nasir's concerns do not arise from within the sf megatext's main track. Wayne Dolan is dying inside, but unlike David

Selig, in Silverberg's *Dying Inside,* he comes close to convincing you that he might be the real thing. That is quite an impressive achievement, since the storyline itself is a string of silly pranks, one tasty absurdity mounted on another. Dolan dreams repeatedly that an oracular Indian requests payment of $5000 into a numbered bank account in exchange for insight. Fair enough, too; better than beads and mirrors. Does Dolan get smoke and mirrors back? I cannot say, but it must be apparent already that the crazy man actually does make the deposit, and it is not as if he is especially flush.

Nasir's near-science postulate is based on genuine recent work in neuroscience. Reputable scientists do claim to have located a `god module' in a specific region of the brain: a portion of specialized temporal lobe circuitry that lights up preferentially during religious experiences. It is also true that lesions near this region can precipitate `hyper-religiosity,' a clinical disorder. And that Persinger and others have learned, in a rough and ready but ever more precise way, to stimulate activity in such regions by bathing a subject in fields of a particular frequency and intensity. It is not at all a stretch that certain determinate sequences of the genome encode these modules, and might in future be switched on or off in the brain of a developing child. What then? Might a person mature without any intrinsic, evolved bent for faith? If so, would he or she be cruelly impaired, hurled into inconsolable Sartrean nausea and meaninglessness, or liberated from programmed illusion to an unprecedented degree? It is a topic that has been explored lately by Greg Egan, the current master of this sort of speculation. But Nasir writes more joyously and hurtingly than Egan. Could such a transformation be worked on the brain of an adult? The mind hums with the science fictional/literary possibilities: Flowers for Ecclesiastes . . .

Theodore Sturgeon or Daniel Keyes, or just possibly Roger Zelazny, if he had ever escaped his mythic gridlock, might have done something outstanding with this premise. Nasir comes close to making it work successfully because he is ready to put his character through comic pain:

> . . . he had reasoned that out there somewhere must be a girl beautiful and young and educated that would love him, blonde with silken skin who unclothed was all catlike languor and fire . . . They sat in a quaint cafe and talked about Emily Brontë and Shakespeare, Doyne Farmer and God, complexity and love and the structure of the universe, their eyes locked together, until he could feel the earth turning about him, the blood

rushing in his veins, time bringing the sun to light the flowers in the window boxes, the rain to water them . . .

But where to go? A singles bar? The idea both repelled and tantalized him. He holding a drink and sliding through air-conditioned dimness toward a half-seen hairdo in the smoke, which would probably conceal a drunk dental hygienist or secretary who, smelling his fear and uncertainty, would sneer at him in her stupid vocabulary and bad grammar. He didn't know where any singles bars were, and anyway even if he managed to pick someone up he would have nowhere to take her but his smelly, disheveled apartment. (4–5)

The fatuous but heartbreakingly elegiac, the callously cruel but self-laceratingly candid . . . none of this is remotely new to the mainstream, but it remains rare in an sf novel. What you might not find in a `literary' novel, outside Updike, is Nasir's easy confidence with the rhetoric of scientists in full flight, notably in a concerted scene with a Francis Crick–like genetics Nobelist, Dr. Raymond Hall:

`Do you think scientists are immune from the lure, the seduction of higher meaning? . . . Science began as a religious exercise: it was believed that the study of nature would reveal the hand of the Creator and hints as to His divine plan. It was never suspected that no sign of a God would ever be found at all, that deep, rigorous study of nature over hundreds of years using incredibly sophisticated techniques would turn up not one iota of evidence—not *one*, anywhere—that God exists. . . . This isn't some whim or premature conclusion or philosophical sleight of hand. It is the result of five hundred years of concentrated study by thousands of the best minds of every generation . . . all of which has been gone over again and again by people of all backgrounds and biases, but most of whom, the vast majority of whom would much rather have concluded that there was a higher meaning. If there had been one there to find, we would have found it, we would have fallen on our knees before it, we to whom meaning, pattern is everything.' (178–186)

As it happens, I tend to agree with this nicely wrought summary; as it happens, Jamil Nasir might not, and Rudy Rucker and Philip K. Dick, those other god-snaring transrealists, almost certainly would not. What counts here is Nasir's scrupulous annotation of a worldview rarely seen in the mainstream, and often just assumed as background in sf. When the epiphanies tumble down, as they inevitably do (most blatantly, surprise surprise, in the exact middle of the book, pages 136–140), their sweetness is only slightly cloying, since we know in our bones that awful reverses lurk deep within such narratives of redemption and illumination. The only question is, which redemption will be unmasked as villainous error: the probing scientific meliorism with its inevitable thalidomide risks, or the Zenish post-illusioned elevation of the ordinary? Nasir's answers are ... thought-provoking. So how was this fine novel received by the sf readership and its critical elite? I expected it to be a strong runner for the Philip K. Dick award (as was Nasir's previous novel, *Tower of Dreams* in 1999), or the Campbell Memorial award. It was not even a nominee.

15: 2000: THE COLLAPSIUM,
WIL MCCARTHY

When we and science fiction were young and silly and giddy with the rapturous possibilities of all things large and waiting to be done (rather than young and banalized or strip-mined or breakfast-cerealized, as now, all too often), E. E. `Doc' Smith took the emerging genre on a marvelous ride. *The Skylark of Space* (1928) was a fairytale with alleged superscience in place of magic, its heroes at once wizards and boy's-own plucky adventurers. To my chagrin, that is the only Doc Smith novel I have ever been able to read all the way through, because I missed Smith during the adolescent window of forgiving opportunity. Luckily, his galactic-scale space opera *mise en scène* and *modus operandi* were at once adaptations of earlier breakneck commercial forms (and so hardly restricted to his work) and immensely influential on later storytellers, comic strip artists, movie and TV scenarists, a few of them at least a little more sophisticated.

So I know some pale shadow of the excitement that must have raged in the blood of children and young adults 60 and 70 years ago, when the sf world was for the first time wide open and expanding (like the real universe, as it turned out), when your guys could cobble up an inertialess space drive out of odds and ends in the mansion's home lab and before the tale was done transit faster than light to the worlds of distant stars and engage in righteous battle, using the ravening energy weapons worked up during the trip, to best the evil of the cosmos.

But you can't do that any longer, can you? For one thing, science keeps shutting down the wilder possibilities even as the fabric of the universe is seen in wonderfully greater fractal detail. No superluminal travel (too many toxic paradoxes, and anyway Einstein forbade it), no simple tele-portation devices (the data demands of transmission would be insanely hungry), no cheap transmutation of elements, certainly no breezy aboli-tion of inertia, and, above all, no backyard superscience, since we all know to our cost that major science and technology are the fruit of vast industrial projects, thousands of driven specialists working according to tempera-ment like lunatics or bureaucrats in a planet-wide college of knowledge and commercial application. There will be no Promethean or rather van Vogtian secret genius building artificial intelligence on a home computer, let alone inventing a faster-than-light space drive and then going out to the garage and fitting it into the car for a quick test run around the Solar System and then to Andromeda.

Then again . . . everything we accept as given might be about to change drastically and discontinuously in the next fifty years, or (more cautiously) the next few hundred. Will humans become gods, able to do all things, not in the year One Million but before the end of the century? Or might we, instead, poison our world in a gale of unforeseen lethal conse-quences to our Faustian knowledge? Or, indeed, provide our own replace-ments: gene-modified posthumans, or AIs so powerful and self-enhancing that they represent a leap in understanding as far above ours as human is to insect or bacterium? If so, science fiction (putting aside for a moment the *gravitas* of our shivery real-world prospects) is here and now flummoxed, drowned in an embarrassment of riches. Because in such a world, everything foolish and grandiose in 1930s space opera is back on the table, in spades. With vast Banksian Minds at work in our world, who would be so presumptuous as to deny the possibility that science's para-digms will bulge and buckle and birth fresh insights to underwrite those Clarkean god-intelligences whose technology will be indistinguishable from magic?

But accepting that premise, as Greg Egan understands, tears away the flooring from beneath a conscientious sf writer. You cannot assume that your characters will be remotely human, that their interests and impulses will look much like ours, that they will even inhabit the same universe. Although truly conscientious sf writers will not wish to invent arbitrary breaches in the rules of known science, they will feel confident that fresh knowledge will open astonishing possibilities. The trick is to find them, and then to convey them in tales that do not repel us (as Egan's brave *Schild's Ladder* [2002] comes close to doing). Despite coy anthropomorphic Disney movies, adults do not relish fiction about the inner lives of insects or dinosaurs or, for that matter, incomprehensible AIs.

One way around this roadblock is to find a challenging scholium (in James Blish's wonderfully portentous phrase) that stands outside the current science paradigm without entirely tumbling into pseudo-science. *Astounding/Analog* editor John W. Campbell's advocacy of parapsychology was perhaps such an attempt, although in practice it was rarely more than a slick way to repackage the thrills and terrors of magic tales. Still, one could propose certain principles that might underwrite mysterious abilities familiar from thousands of years of folklore. By applying some measure of rigor and constraint, mind reading and levitation and the rest of the arcanum might be construed as a form of technology, and vivid new stories created that respected the habit and form of science while opening the door to monsters from the Id.

Blish himself played rhetorically with this sort of narrative device, explaining his faster than light spindizzies and psi-powered supermen by reference to Milne's non-Einsteinian cosmology (in *Cities in Flight* [1955-62]), or cunningly tweaking Planck's constant (in *Jack of Eagles* [1949/1975]), thereby getting a quantum handle on plenty of larger aspects of the world. Can that be done again today? After all, each month brings us more astonishing news (An accelerating universe driven by dark energy! Macro-scale observations of quantum superpositions! The human genome sequenced!) that just seems to anchor current informed opinion the more solidly.

One alternative scholium that has been doing the rounds for some years, but has not got much of a run in sf world creation, is the zero-point field interpretation of physical interactions. While canonical physics tries in its multibillion dollar experiments to test supersymmetric models that squeeze the four known forces into a single majestic Ur-force, the inventive proponents of the zpf theory say it is all just electromagnetism after all. The nineteenth-century guys were right, if you spruce up their ballistics with some Lorentz invariance. Gravity and inertia are side-effects of pushing through the energetic vacuum. It sounds like a re-invention of the Aether, but then so can the Higgs field, beloved of canonical unified physics mavens. The devisers of this wonderful model (which, incidentally, seems to allow for extraction of unlimited amounts of free energy from the vacuum field if you do it just right) are Bernhard Haisch of the Lockheed Martin Solar and Astrophysics Lab, and colleagues A. Rueda and Hal E. Puthoff. A blue-skies man, Dr. Puthoff is a former parapsychologist who worked on the classified but now dismantled government program in psychic `remote viewing.' (Did he use precognition to catch a glimpse of tomorrow's physics paradigms? He is not telling.)

Wil McCarthy's previous five books gained him a reputation for stylistic diversity and hard scientific rigor blended with panache and striking imagination. He worked at Lockheed for a decade as a rocket engineer, and presumably got to know Haisch there. In *The Collapsium* and its sequel *The Wellstone* (2003), he borrows the zpf model as the armature of his twenty-fifth or maybe twenty-sixth century future Ruritanian solar monarchy complete with super-genius inventor, twisted evil genius foe, and the most delicious superscience since Larry Niven's Ringworld and Stephen Baxter's Xeelee universe-builders.

The Collapsium looks like a fix-up, although McCarthy insists it is not. It is made of three parts, `Once upon a Matter Crushed' (*SF Age*, July 1999), and two previously unpublished parts replete with irritating info dump backgrounders that harp on what we just read a few pages back, `Twice upon a Star Imperiled' and `Thrice upon a Schemer's Plotting,' which swallows half the book and is the most interesting section. But wait, there's more: Appendix A, where eight chunks of fascinating technical discussion have been banished, to spare the neophyte or ignorant reader; Appendix B, a useful lexicon; and Appendix C, `Technical Notes' on the theory of zero-point fields, complete with URLs to papers in such journals as *Speculations in Science and Technology* and *Phys. Review A*. So the novel, while plainly a fairytale, is not just the confection it might be taken for. It would be fair to call it an Entertainment, in Graham Greene's sense. While McCarthy works hard to draw out pathos and character development, it is hard to get too involved in the inward journeying of a man who (with the help of nanocomputers and robots, it's true) builds his own small planet in the Kuiper belt after first assembling thousands of miniature black holes, devises the fax (teleportation) setup for the Solar System, and then in a fit of urgency invents the principles behind an ertial (inertialess) space drive, builds a small spaceship shell to embody it, and flies off to rescue the Sun from imminent destruction. This is a wonderful hoot, of course, and the presence of a genuinely exciting scholium that just might be true adds luster and frisson. But it is not a novel, not really. That should not spoil anyone's enjoyment.

Bruno de Towaji is one of Queen Tamra's Declarant-Philanders, or consorts. A beautiful former Tongan princess (one gains the impression that she lacks the traditional *avoirdupois*, but then it is easy to stay young, healthy, and beautiful when a trip through the fax can edit or reset your body and even your mind), Tamra has been elected by the citizens of the solar system to fulfill the deep-stamped monkey urge humans share (McCarthy assures us) for obeisance to a striking leader. Despite this, she has no real power beyond the immense affection of her subjects. She is Princess Di, then, so one awaits her fated doom. But then this is a fairy story, where perhaps doom is always averted, or made good.

Bruno's genius is coupled with a powerful aversion to society, fashion, triviality: he is a nerd, but a passionate one, driven by his ambition to construct an *arc de fin*, a vast gadget that will open a portal into the end of cosmological time and feed his relentless hunger for total knowledge. Meanwhile, far from his self-imposed exile at the boundaries of the system, immense artificial structures are being built near the Sun, designed to create a supervacuum within which the velocity of light will be a hell of a lot faster than plodding c. Here is the Ring Collapsiter, and Bruno's ironic consciousness:

> Imagine a universe of stars reaching up to infinity above you, pinpoint splashes of light filtering through and around the collapsium. Imagine Sol beneath your feet, swollen and huge but eclipsed by a disc . . . invisible but for the effect of its light echoing through the arch rising high above you.
>
> *Like choir music through the rafters of heaven*, Bruno de Towaji would later write, to be quoted out of context for tens of thousands of years. In truth the passage continues, *It was grand, enormous, an absurdity of unprecedented scale and scope. A glimpse of heaven, yes, but as we dream it, beach monkeys fond of glitter. If it's God we hope to impress, I daresay a tower of socks would serve as well.* (25)

And that is just the opening. The scale of immensity and change and invention and peril and horror and an intriguing cast (a police Commandant-Inspector embodied as her own girlhood body due to a faxing gaffe, the inevitable irritating environmentalist poet, a poignant robot, the queen herself) and the Solar System at stake several times and awards ceremonies and the admiring gasps of billions and even death, true death without fax reconstitution, and heroism and getting stuck in a supraluminal realm and the poignant cost of being the finest mind in the history of the species, all this and more. It *is* a confection, after all, but a mighty tasty one, and stuffed with nutritious alternative physics that might even, who knows, turn out to be true. But if it does, and if the Singularity takes a form anything remotely like McCarthy's alarming but engaging future, then they will not be quoting Bruno for tens of thousands of years because our history will be a puff of wind in the fan-forced furnace of the true history that only a working *arc de fin* could show us.

16: 2000: GENESIS, POUL ANDERSON

i

Stanislaw Lem, the great Polish polymath and sf writer/critic, published *Fantastyka i Futurologia* in Cracow in 1970. Lem noted almost in passing that repeated total regressions in technological progress, back to medieval ignorance or the Stone Age, are implausible. Such regressions, he suggested, are added to science fiction for a literary motive only: that taking into account the measure of change we can genuinely expect would make it impossible to write an sf novel like Stapleton's *Last and First Men* or *Star Maker*. Lem noted:

> Another vision, in which . . . there would be some continuity in the current of civilizational transformations—would have made it impossible to write the book. For the ascent that follows exponentially from this premise would surpass the capacities of any artist's imagination. . . . [T]he existence of future generations totally transformed from ours would remain an incomprehensible puzzle for us, even if we could express it. (285–7)[12]

[12] Parts of this work were translated [via Hungarian] by Istvan Csicsery-Ronay, Jr, and published in 1986 in *Science-Fiction Studies*, Vol 13, 272–91.

Vernor Vinge would independently rediscover the Singularity more than a decade later (in his *Marooned in Real-Time*, 1986), eventually postulating a partitioned or Zoned universe, in *A Fire Upon the Deep* (1991) and *A Deepness in the Sky* (1999), that allowed certain restrictions on routine and swift technological transcendence. It allowed him, as well, to create a rip-snorting yet principled space opera. Lem preempted Vinge's metaphor of an event horizon of prediction: `[Olaf Stapledon] has invalidated the real factors of exponential growth, which obstruct all long-range predictions; we can't see anything from the present moment beyond the horizon of the twenty-first century' (287).

No less remarkably, perhaps, Lem made a cognitive leap still seldom seen in most futurism. There are reasons to doubt his Fermi paradox conclusion, but it is an impressive leap of connective imagination:

> Predictions beyond 80 or 100 years inevitably fail. Beyond that range lies the impenetrable darkness of the future, and above it, a single definite sign indecipherable, but impinging on us all the more: the Silence of the Universe. The universe has not yielded to the radiance of civilizations; it does not scintillate with brilliant astro-technical works—although that is how it should be, if the law of psychozoic beings were an aspect of the exponential ortho-evolution of instrumentality in cosmic dimension. (288)

Must we assume that cosmic superintelligences, whether AI or augmented organic beings, future human or past alien, would place their stamp detectably on the physical universe? In Arthur C. Clarke's *The City and the Stars* (1956), advanced Intelligences reposition seven differently colored stars to form a ring in the heavens. They might not be so modest.

ii

One of the late Poul Anderson's final novels made an interesting attempt to confront that basic and almost insurmountable fact about the far future, that technological time will be neither an arrow nor a cycle (in Stephen Jay Gould's phrase), but an upwardly accelerating curve. It will pass through a Vingean Singularity, what I call the Spike (Broderick, 1997, 2001). Unless self-inflicted disaster inevitably reduces intelligence to ruin and global death, explaining the Fermi paradox of the absence of ETs, it is plausible that intelligent consciousness once evolved must proliferate on a galactic scale, mutating and extending its own capacities, perhaps replacing its very substrates. It might relocate itself, for example, from limited organic bodies to very much more adaptable synthetic forms (Moravec, 1999). Poul Anderson, like Fred Pohl and other sf writers steeped in the ever-revised history of the future, was familiar with Moravec's extrapolations, and built them gracefully into his own saga of a galaxy a billion or more years farther off into deep time.

An earlier version of *Genesis*, a 100-odd page novella, appeared in Gregory Benford's uneven anthology *Far Futures* (1995). Anderson's tale was perhaps overshadowed at the time by Greg Egan's extraordinary 'Wang's Carpets' in a competing volume, Greg Bear's anthology *New Legends* (1995): a post-Singularity story so uncompromising that it seeded his remarkable novel *Diaspora* (1997), probably the most rigorous posthuman sf work yet published. Anderson subsequently extended his story of Gaia's plans for ancestral Earth threatened by a swelling, terminal Sun. The vast, immanent AI custodian and consciousness of the world, Gaia rather frighteningly wishes to allow the world to perish in final flame rather than disrupt the 'natural' astrophysical trajectory. Other mighty Minds throughout the galaxy, and to the 'shores of the Andromeda,' find this plan perverse. One such godlike node, Alpha, hives off a sub-mind (still Olympian by our standards), and sends Wayfarer to Earth to investigate and intervene. A still more diminished aspect or agent of this fragment, a reconstruction of the early upload engineer Christian Brannock (merely a human-scale genius), visits the planet as his larger self communes and debates with Gaia. What he finds, inevitably, is baffling yet emotionally moving (in its constrained way), recalling those Norse sagas Anderson loved so well.

And all of this impossibly remote story is told to us as myth, as repeatedly distanced construct. We are informed again and again that what we read is nothing like the vast reality (as of course must be so, given the premises of ruthlessly projected futurism). 'All is myth and metaphor, beginning with this absurd nomenclature [Alpha, Wayfarer]. Beings like these had no names. They had identities, instantly recognizable by others of their kind. They did not speak together, they did not go through discussion or explanation of any sort, they were not yet "they." But imagine it' (112).

And we do, for we have been here before. This is the grand proleptic mythology of Stapledon himself, of Roger Zelazny's 'For a Breath I Tarry'

(1966)—in which Machine remakes Man, but then bows before Him (which is absurd and sadly farcical, however much we loved that story in the 1960s). In this revised version of his myth, Anderson eases our entry to allegory via several well-formed episodes from the comparatively near future: a boy's epiphany beneath starry heaven, in our Earth; Christian's empathy with his robotic telefactor extension on Mercury, prelude to his own status as an uploaded and finally multiply-copied personality; English bureaucrat Laurinda Ashcroft who plans the first millennial salvation of Earth from the brute assaults of a heedless cosmos; a small, neat parable of rigid, gorgeous clan rivalries held in check and paralysis, finally, by the emerging Mind of Gaia. These are Anderson's antinomies again (and perhaps American sf's): the sacred autonomy of the self, the craving for transcendence in something larger; personal responsibility, and its terrible limits in a world linked, defined, by a billion threads.

Returned to Earth, Wayfarer's Brannock and Gaia's Laurinda tarry in *faux*-eighteenth-century civility, falling in love (of course), driven together and apart by a series of visitations to simulated histories as dense and real and tormented and doomed as the `real world.' Their own personalities are no less constructed (of course), however rooted in some small early reality, and so the poignancy of their dilemma is the greater. But for us, knowing that we read a fiction, and fetched in a kind of postmodern gesture again and again by Poul Anderson from our comfortable readerly illusion, these figures and their worlds run the risk of all allegory: can we care?

It is the great artistic problem for any form of art predicated upon utter disruption and dislocation. Religious art faced it long ago, and clad its transcendent message in parable, majestic song—and quietness, sacralized domesticity, anguish transformed at the graveside. These are territories Poul Anderson trod in all his work, more so, perhaps, than did any of his peers. Confronting the Singularity, reaching for these well-honed tools to give himself voice and range, perhaps he succeeded as well as anyone can manage—given that the task is impossible. I suspect he did not truly succeed, however. It might not be his fault, if so: it might be that it takes an entire culture to sustain such a mythos. Sf has begun to grow the mythos, but meanwhile the world's culture turns technological runaway into jingles and plastic toys. It will be interesting to see how the genre, the mode, of sf responds to this immense new perspective, into the pitiless depths of which Poul Anderson, not long before his death, made his brave foray.

17: 2001: *A SHORTAGE OF ENGINEERS*, ROBERT GROSSBACH

Engineers, we understand, toil in the boiler room of the ship of fools. High above them, in the brilliant light of gleaming chandeliers, wealthy heedless fools dance, gorge, quaff. Men in sharp uniforms issue orders urging the ship to its inevitable doom. When the ship founders, do the engineers pour into the sea to perish with the rest? Do they sink with the holed hull? In the real world, it is the passengers and crew, often enough, who dance heedlessly on, while the rats and engineers feed their sea.

Grossbach's comic purgatorio, not his first set among the accursed of the aerospace industry, is by Thomas Pynchon out of Joseph Heller, with Dante waving in the background, Horatio Alger drowning, and Archaean sailors in every mythic doomed voyage making up the complement. Pynchon, luckily, conferring descent, praised Grossbach's first satire, *Easy and Hard Ways Out* (1974), as having `captured perfectly the eerie ambience of the aerospace business with remarkable skill, humor and compassion.' Pynchon had worked there too, as a technical writer for Boeing, but as with John Sladek, master of superb parables of industrial purgatory, you do not need to have been there to recognize the horrid truth. Well, except that what I kept stubbing my toe on was not truth but pastiche and hommage.

Young wet-behind-the-ears electronics nerd Zachary Zaremba, freshly graduated from the University of Michigan and not, as his benign, kindly, uninterested dentist father had wished, Michigan State (the family alma mater), enters the mad rationality of International Instruments late in 1989, anticipating `eight hours in the concrete blockhouse,' followed by `45 yrs. x 240 working days/yr., 10,800 days under the pale fluorescents, while outside the sun shone' (2). This drab, soul-sucking prospect is enlivened, up to a point, by a cast of ne'er-do-wells with funny names: Shopper Jim (cynical, knowing, in Hell's Angel beard and snakeskin boots, he has no loyalty to anything, we are given to misunderstand, poised always to leap to the next favorable job opening), Asians such as The Boy Named Hsu, Gung Ho, Meee, Yu (imagine the Catch-22 hilarity possible with those two!), Wonderboy, Medieval Man, Mr. Softy. Zach finds it hard to laugh, though, in a world where you cannot order without order forms, but if you have run out of order forms you cannot have any more unless you order them on order forms, and where a presentation to the Air Force of their current hopelessly fucked-up project has an audience filled out with `thirty black people I'd never seen', there to soothe the feelings of the black contract administrator who made it known `how distressed he was to look out into a company audience and see hardly any people of color ... ' (82). That mandatory jab at euphemism and political correctness might make you wince and smile, but I suspect this one just leaves a sour taste:

> `Tell ya, what I wouldn't give right now for a decent paraplegic ... ' He held up a folder. `State human rights people, all over us. You miss the quota by one or two minorities, short a couple of cripples, and right away they're up your ass! Had a microcephalic quit in Shipping—imagine! Guy with a two-inch head gets a better offer—and five days later I get a notice in the mail ... Just crazy. Now I gotta hire three minorities just to make up for one retard.' (234)

All-but-virginal Zach, for the opening stanzas, assuages his tedium in the toilets detachedly observing the varieties of pissing styles (Dribbler, Delayed Responder, One-Hander, Faker, Girlie-Man Retreater) while brewing coffee, since you are not allowed to make it at your desk and the installed vending machines just steal your coins. He falls madly in love with programmer Lilah Li, and who can blame him:

> Kushner and I were in the cashier's line at the cafeteria, he with his bean salad and small yogurt, me with my chicken sandwich, absolutely plain, when she came toward us. She was wearing a thigh-high,

body-clinging orange dress, sheer black stockings, heels, and an ocher ribbon in her hair that tied the ebony strands back into a short bun. For a moment, on her way, she twisted sideways to acknowledge someone behind her, so that the bulbous outlines of her breasts and ass strained and stretched the knitted material. (64)

Just so, although this is surely 1971 not 1989, and who can blame Zach and his hapless, doomed pal Kushner for coming in their pants? You know that matters cannot rest here, that Zach, with his sit-up strengthened abs, will aspire to Lilah, fly high, crash and burn, or something along those lines. It is a credit to Grossbach that Zach's relations with Lilah (and her six year old son Kevin, whose unexpected presence enriches a die-stamped narrative arc, or maybe just provides some saccharine, it is hard to tell with a book like this) develop some real lust and at least competently faked complexity, if you can have complexity in a spoof-come-parable. The truth is, for such a gossamer, such a soufflé, I had to drag myself through the first quarter or half of *A Shortage of Engineers*, slowly warming to its ironies and schematic revelations and occasional genuine prickle, and only did so because it was apparent from the start that this book about an engineer designing military-spec equipment written by a man who has spent decades manufacturing military-spec components (it says on the jacket) was an instance of . . . transrealist fiction.

Grossbach's fourth novel is a fable tilting over into transrealism, or maybe that is an illusion formed by its familiar settings: the Pynchonesque, Rucker-world transforms of postindustrial fluorescent wage-slave cum classified military hell. Really I doubt that Zach and his terrible, sometimes funny microcosm have enough density to be persuasive, even at the level of man-who-learns-better farce. If so, perhaps it is better to read the novel through another filter after all. In some odd way, it reminds me of those stories John W. Campbell used to delight in, during the 1950s and 1960s: the put-upon, hard-working competent radio shack engineers and nuclear technicians besieged and hounded by bureaucrats, military popinjays, pompous politicians, pests of every kind from the World Out There. Usually there was a satisfying pay-off, when despite all the needless obstacles your guy Got It Done. His reward, it has to be admitted, was rarely that `she opened her lips and our tongues intertwined and our salivas mingled and every bit of blood in my brain and body ran down toward my penis and I just about blacked out' (129). But then that is not the true reward here, either. Zach's joy is the sublime engineer's moment, as his subterranean Daedalus-like mentor has promised him, when he `began to feel something not quite describable, a *lightness*, a chill, a certain *quietness*' (276). The great work is in the alembic, heating toward to the glorious moment, against every rule and meta-rule of the balky cosmos, of . . . actually *working*. Meeting the spec.

Forget pay, promotion, job security—what counts, finally, as we learn from the Old Man in the Back, the secret Daedalus at the heart of the irrational enterprise, is that `when you make something *work* . . . *that* is beautiful. You created something. You did something no one else ever did. And in that moment, and it doesn't last long, that's where you take your pleasure' (253). Does Grossbach's novel work? Does it do something no one else ever did? Although I have been gesturing at all the other people who already did it, that is true of every work of fiction. So yes, in a way, I guess, it does. Engineers and writers, god bless us, every one.

18: 2002: SWIFT THOUGHTS, GEORGE ZEBROWSKI

A plaintive note is struck more than once in the Author Notes to George Zebrowski's handsome small press collection, with its Bob Eggleton cover and laudatory Gregory Benford introduction, of twenty-four short stories published between 1973 and 2001. `The *Locus* reviewer surprised me,' he remarks a little tactlessly of the response to his title story, with `the pleasant realization that I was in danger of being understood' (133).

During a third of a century—his first story appeared in 1970—Zebrowski has gained praise and recognition as one of the philosopher-poets of science fiction. The long novel *Macrolife* (1979) carried humankind in swarming space habitats from a dying Earth to the final transcendental Omega Point collapse of the cosmos; the usual adjective is `Stapledonian', but companion work such as *Cave of Stars* (1999) pays more attention than Stapledon did to the people involved in his own immense future history.

At 25, Zebrowski became editor of the *SFWA Bulletin* for six years, then again with his sf writer partner Pamela Sargent in 1983-91, and now knows everyone in the field. He has a large body of short work, young adult and other novels, some in collaboration, has edited anthologies, even published *Star Trek* franchise books of more than usual ambition, and in 1999 won the prestigious Campbell Memorial jury award for *Brute Orbits*, an uncompromisingly bleak exploration of future penal theory and practice. Yet in today's epoch where *sci-fi* has become the wildly lucrative common currency of mass entertainment, he struggles to make a living from his much-praised writing, or so one senses; it is a common paradox and misery among the exacting in the genre.

One clue to his lack of broad commercial success might be a feature found repeatedly in these formally quite diverse stories: a reviewer called them 'outrageously didactic', and they are often that—although rarely *only* that. Nor is this an accident, a failure to master fundamental pleasing narrative arts ('Show, don't tell', you know the sort of thing). Zebrowski has adamantly chosen this path, these several parallel paths, convinced, it seems, that only in such an austere program will he find the purity of intention and construction suited to his self-imposed task. Which is? Why, to push at what Kant called the antinomies, what deconstructors called aporias: those knotted aspects of brute cosmos and luminous mind where we hit the end of our tether and are brought up short, choking, fearful, confused, blinded by light too dazzling for our locally adapted eyes or plunged into darkness too terrible for mortal thoughts to comprehend. There, only our successors—enhanced humans or artificial minds—with their swift, post-mortal thoughts, may tread with any confidence. Perhaps, though, carried on wings of uncompromising, unblinking judgment, we may tarry there even now, if only for a breath, if only for the span of a short story.

The theory is plausible, overlapping with the minimalism of much fine art twentieth century fiction, and also with postmodern refusals of 'readerly' satisfactions (in Roland Barthes's terminology, contrasting such low pleasures with the 'writerly' bliss of a text seamed with gaps, traps, false lures, hints, holes to be filled by the strenuous cooperation of the engaged reader). Zebrowski admits this partial filiation in his closing dalliance with pomo forms. Even the titles—'The Last Science Fiction Story of the 20th Century' and 'Catch the Sleep Ship: The First Science Fiction Story of the 21st Century'—are candid.

Their Author Note boasts that 'If one views these stories as postmodern in technique, then they say everything about themselves in the text—including that I also subvert postmodernism in favor of explanatory narrative, in which one tells the truth about one's characters and how they got that way, in a fiction that is by definition a lie necessary to the task' (307). This is to misread the postmodern program, though, which asserts that *all* texts speak exclusively within their own frames, whether they explain themselves or prance deviously. Wrapping a tale's jagged edges in pomo motley might not be the best justification for a mode of telling that often eschews dramatization in favor of explication. You can see the attractions, though. All this time people have been complaining about the chilly didacticism, but wait a minute, this was just postmodernism *avant la lettre* and auto-deconstructed in advance! (I am not claiming bad faith here, just an understandable touch of spin.)

Certainly the typical tale here is less sf than *conte philosophique*, the kind of fanciful ludic *jeu* we associate with Stanislaw Lem or Ian Watson, and which can be traced back at least to Voltaire. You start by freely postulating cats in pajamas, let your thoughts run loose as swiftly as they might, and in a couple of uproarious moves (boom boom) you are probing the axiological status of haberdashery and its relationship to Being and Nothingness. It is no accident, then, that the collection is dedicated to Watson—`Conteur Splendide'—and that Polish-American Zebrowski has always admired and promoted Lem's often weirdly funny if abstruse paraliterary games.

The opening piece, `The Word Sweep' (with its somewhat misleading bow in the direction of J. G. Ballard's `The Sound Sweep'), is just the first of five inventions featuring an ensemble cast of Felix, Bruno and June. Unlike classical templates from the 1940s and 1950s—comic duos in space by Campbell, Asimov, Sheckley, say—these recurrent names denote new characters each time, in wildly different Lewis Carroll (or Rudy Rucker) worlds, yet retain a certain glum continuity. Bruno, practical and, of course, bear-like, assists and frustrates infelicitous Felix; it is no real surprise that one of these tales features a visiting alien impersonating Curly from the Three Stooges, with showboat astronomers Carl Sagan and Robert Jastrow in Stooge drag interrogating him on a mock-up of the Johnny Carson show. Maybe my total lack of exposure to the Stooges (and indeed Carson) prevents me from rolling about hooting with laughter; certainly the notion is a cute set-up, and not without its potential for poignancy.

Inevitably, perhaps, the early stories are the least satisfying (although this was not the case with Roger Zelazny, say). In a revealing on-line interview with Kilian Melloy,[13] we learn that `Rope of Glass' (1973), together with `Bridge of Silence' (1986), were salvaged by editor Marty

---

[13] www.infinityplus.co.uk/nonfiction/intzebrowski.htm

Halpern—'one of the most meticulous, respectful, insightful editors I have ever worked with'—against the author's initial prejudice. I wish he'd stuck to his guns. The ideational spark in both is tempting, but its narrative embodiment is unforgivably lumpish:

> Suddenly Andrews swung at the gun, kicking it from Sam's hand. It clattered in the rubble. Andrews crawled, half leaped onto Sam, reaching for his face. Sam tried to kick but fell backward, the sharp debris pushing into his back. Andrews grasped him tightly around the middle and pulled himself into a sitting position on top of Sam's chest. (186)

And so on. Contrast this with the smoother, terribly persuasive tale told in an alternative Stalin's voice, 'Lenin in Odessa'(1989) and the even more disturbing 'The Eichmann Variations' (1984), perhaps Zebrowski's most celebrated story; neither is without its expository gristle yet each serves to convey something chilling of the men who speak to us.

A kind of rapprochement is attained between the readerly and the preacherly, or rather philosophic, investigative impulses in two 'History machine' tales. In 'The Number of the Sand' (1991), a historian with benefit of cliometricon (and we, over his shoulder) views Carthaginian Hannibal's meeting with Roman Scipio before battle in the valley of Zama. The history machine tells more than the simple truth, however; it reveals as many of the infinite alternative outcomes as a historian can bear to trace. In the Eichmann variations, the tragedy is that character is stamped so deep that endless xeroxed copies cannot deviate from their *faux* history. In the Hannibal variations, circumstances alter everything, even the man himself as he learns different lessons from his local history. What of the historian (and us), looking over his shoulder at those yet to be born who will gaze at him in their own past? He

> yearns for the closure that would end the dismay of infinities, the final, firm place to stand, from which there is no one to glance back to, where all perspectives converge into the sleepless eternity of perfect knowing that would never belong to him. He would never awake from the dream of history in which he was embedded and see it whole. (239)

And why must that be so? Because 'Being was adding to itself endlessly, an infinite growing thing, branching, probing through a greater infinity of probability, springing from no soil and obeying no tropism . . . ' (239). It is a view of the world almost universally denied, even among scientists, and if it is perhaps hyperbolic (is the universe *truly* infinite, or just incomprehensibly large?) nonetheless this is the horizon within which honest human minds must today   cower—or reach out as resolutely as we might, knowing our limitations. Yet those limits might be temporary, or at least less stringent than those we suppose. Zebrowski speaks to us directly in his final Author's Note:

> Every age, as Dickens noted, seems to be a transition to somewhere else. Our last 500 years may well be viewed as a Dark Age, with its corporate and political doings being little better than criminal, and our last mortal human generations the magnificent bodies over the wire before the true awakening of reason and justice. (307)

That utopian projection of our posthuman possibilities, with its hope for some future redemption fused with tragic acknowledgment of our present limits, finds explicit expression in the best stories in this volume. Few provide an ameliorative, comforting embrace; Zebrowski is a grown-up writing for other adults, and knows that the world is a place of pain as well as joy. The temporarily enhanced grasp on reality loaned to the narrator of the title story is painful in its glory, taking the legacy code of a human brain to the ruinous edge of an illumination it cannot sustain, no more than the frozen leopard could sustain the high cold of Hemingway's Kilimanjaro.

For all that, perhaps the most satisfying story in the book is the most conventional, `In the Distance, and Ahead in Time' (1993), one of the sequence derived from *Macrolife*. Settlers on a somewhat Earthlike world are restricted to a single lofty plateau, rid of its poisonous native life after the starship fell into ruin, gradually eroding as human culture falls back into a kind of complacent, hard-working Luddism. An arriving asteroid ship offers escape, its crew indeed urging that the colonists abandon their dead and the fruit of their toil because `Planets should not be invaded . . . They have their own lives to fulfil' (195). Perhaps, after all, other species tremble on the verge of awakening into consciousness, and human presence will thwart this fresh flowering.

What is fascinating about Zebrowski's treatment is the genuinely mature, modest approach by these technogaians from space. They do not

179

march the settlers away at the point of a blaster (although they could). They do not rail and bluster. When a few depart with them and the remainder stay behind, some visitors remain as well, discontented with their roaming life among the stars. As Zebrowski notes, these tales descend from James Blish and his immortalist spindizzy `cities in flight', and like Blish's tales the characters tend more to the functional than the fully rounded—yet here Zebrowski comes closest, I think, to creating figures we care about, can believe in, can hurt for. There are no simply bad people in this story, no wrestling for guns. If you find a copy of this book—only 3000 copies have been printed—I recommend starting here. After such knowledge, one might then more satisfyingly consider the painful forgiveness in `Wound the Wind' (2001), which approaches the lucid balance of a Le Guin parable.

19: 2002: THE GOLDEN AGE: A ROMANCE OF THE FAR FUTURE, JOHN C. WRIGHT

Pastiche? *Hommage? Sfumato*, perhaps? (That is the Renaissance technique of layering paint, so that light gleams through each thickness of oil, like echoes of plainchant in a cathedral.) And that is how science fiction textuality works now, after a century in which—to change the figure—the ground was broken open, aerated, watered, planted, torn up, built upon, power lines and sewers added, malled, high-rised, urban renewed, solar-celled . . . Or more exactly, this being the future *today* (three chairs, no waiting), nanoteched, AI'd, lifespan-extended, brain-chipped. Thus, the influence of the megatext, that shadowy background infusing everything we write and read, enriching our guesses at tomorrow's trajectories, teasing us with ironies and missed chances, lending us those vocabularies out of which we make these fantastic yet powerfully resilient *faux*-realities, these worlds out of words.

John C. Wright arrives in our midst apparently from nowhere (aside from a few recent short stories), in his mid-forties, with an immensely detailed far future romance, instantly fluent in sf's tongues of fire. Well, perhaps fluent is putting it a little too strongly. Despite the overheated enthusiasm of several early reviewers (`magniloquence', etc), Wright is not yet a master of prose; he is often clunky, the opening book of his far future trilogy stomps along manfully but, except in certain especially effective Pre-Raphaelite set pieces, fails to dance. Consider this expository passage:

Wheel-of-Life was a Cerebelline ecoperformer of the Decentral Spirit School, as well as trustee for all the copyrighted biotechnology based on the Five Golden Rings mathematics. She appeared as a matron of serene beauty and grave demeanor, seated on a throne of living flowers, grass and hedge, in which a dozen species of birds and insects nested. (36)

It is typical of Wright's method, which is an attempt to create conviction by inundation. Such generosity of detail is impressive, even over-whelming; it suggests that here we have a writer who (like John Varley) has lain awake in agonies of insomnia devising all these wheels within wheels and their special designations. But a defter writer might have named some of those birds, plants and blooms, picked out their color and scent; Poul Anderson, say, would have done so by reflex.

Yet what Wright does palpably grows from long immersion in the megatext, and for all the abundance of wheels there's very little wheel-inventing here. A lengthy and useful interview with Nick Gevers, one of the best informed of sf's new critics, offers frank witness to his grateful borrowings:

A. E. Van Vogt formed my childhood picture of what a hero was. Van Vogt portrayed a man who was more sane, more rational, than his foes, was able to overcome them. No other writer's works fill me with the sense of awe and wonder as does Van Vogt.

Jack Vance and Gene Wolfe are masters of style, and I filch from them without a twinge of remorse.[14]

The clearest influence on Wright's voice, and a welcome one except that he cannot yet quite carry it off convincingly, is Jack Vance. Here is Wright in typically Vancian mocking dialogue:

`Now we have heard him speak; and our open-mindedness is rewarded; for we now learn that [he] believes that what he does is to benefit mankind, and to spread our civilization, which he claims to love. A fine discovery! The conflict here can be resolved without further ado.' (291)

---

[14] At http://www.sfsite.com/05a/jcw127.htm

Wright introduces his own novelties, but the most conspicuous is a regrettable tyro usage that marks disbelieving anger thus: `You blame the solar disaster on Helion?!' His copy-editor was either absurdly indulgent or asleep at the stick (this jarring solecism recurs throughout, and the book is littered with such literals as `where' for `were', not to mention `Apha Centauri' and `Bernard's Star'). Will ?! be extirpated from the sequels?! I hope so!!!

Elsewhere, he recalls the impact of van Vogt's sf on him, `the sense of wonder that the grand . . . tradition of space opera embraces. I am trying to write a space opera in his style, so I never have a super-starship ten kilometers long when a ship one hundred kilometers long will do; I never blow up a city when I can blow up a planet.' So Wright is the latest of the recent, and ambitious, deep future space opera boom—David Zindell, Steve Baxter, Paul McAuley, Iain M. Banks, Peter Hamilton, Alastair Reynolds, Wil McCarthy. As a long-time fan of this mode I rejoiced to read his Prologue, `Celebrations of the Immortals', which in about 350 words sketches a truly wondrous carnival of beings gathered for the Golden Oecumene's millennial High Transcendence. All human and posthuman neuroforms are represented, fictional as well as real, high transhumans returned briefly to earthly estate from their calculational realms, projected future descendants, `languid-eyed lamia from morbid unrealized alternatives' (11). It is a beguiling pageant, an instance of what Paul Witcover has dubbed `posthuman space opera' (*NYRSF*, 167, 12).

In this feverish, abundant, user-pays utopia, foppish Phaethon of Rhadamanthus House finds himself inexplicably ill at ease. Before the book is done (and it is only the first third of the sequence: *The Phoenix Exultant* and *The Golden Transcendence* appeared in 2003), this flawed sun god will test the very nature of his identity and that of his beloved wife Daphne, a natural human and former Warlock of the Cataleptic Oneiromancer School and now builder of fantastic VR worlds, of his clone father Helion (another solar name, for an engineer who works literally in the bowels of the Sun like an escapee from Charles Harness's *The Paradox Men*), contest with artificial minds thousands of times more potent than his own, spar with human variants collective and modified, and test his nerve in a puzzling challenge that combines the curse of Orpheus with the temptation of Pandora.

Is this libertarian Golden Age truly one, with all its immense wealth, cruelty, absolute responsibility to and for self? A certain hard-luck case complains, to comic effect, `You are wealthy people. You can afford to have emotions. Some of us cannot afford the glands or midbrain complexes required' (294). Or might it be a Golden Cage, penned shut by the caution of immortals within a Solar System that can be reshaped (the Moon brought closer, Venus relocated farther from the Sun, the Sun's chaos itself tamed) but not escaped. There are no aliens in this future, no superluminal physics, no time machines, and apparently the single extrasolar expedition failed long ago. (Our suspicions on this score pay off in the second volume.) Who attacks Phaethon with such determination, guile and ferocity? Are there alien invaders after all? Or perhaps Sophotechs (AIs) gone to the bad, which is to say become as self-interested as their charges? Or is Phaethon, like many of sf's amnesiac supermen, a terrifying rogue force about to reduce order to ruin if his self-inflicted shackles are opened, or carry all into some transcendence beyond the year's festive High Transcendence?

The book is on one level a travelogue, and Phaethon's misadventures a pretext to display spectacular scenery. In this case, though, the spectacle is rarely as simple as a catalogue of advanced technology (although there is lots of that, and rather nice it is, too), or dazzling settlings (one poor man is obliged to trudge downstairs all the way from geosynchronous orbit, a 40,000 kilometer trudge, compiling his food and drink from air and wastes as he descends a space elevator's core, a ludicrous but enviably crazed plot move). No, the spectacle shares something with the posthuman cognitive explorations of Walter Jon Williams (*Aristoi*, discussed above) and Greg Egan. Tens of thousands of years hence—Wright says millions in an interview, but that cannot be right—these people differ in mentality as much as in flesh or chip, or so we are told; this is rarely enacted satisfactorily, perhaps because it would exceed our capacity to grasp, and Wright's to imagine. Still, it is enchanting to consider the segmented and spliced levels of Phaethon's own consciousness, the ways in which his inward construction of the world can be tweaked, betrayed, filtered, manipulated, clarified, the profusion of people in the Golden Age: the Hundred-mind near the kindled star of Jupiter, the gelid frozen brains of Neptune with their envious designs for good or ill, the idealized computer eidolons of the Aeonite School, Warlock neuroforms with intuitive skills derived from non-standard neural links between brain modules, Invariants with a unicameral brain immune to filtering and hence dwelling within an utterly stark *Weltbild*—hideously deprived, not unlike our own current condition yet perhaps saner. On and on it goes, in a sort of extended commentary, from the right, on Olaf Stapledon's classic, minatory, marxist *Last and First Men: A Story of the Near and Far Future*. (Brian Aldiss called its successor, *Star Maker*, the `one great grey book of science fiction' [1986, 199].) How successful that argument proved one could not know until all three volumes are in print. The first third of the trip was clearly worth taking.

If all this sounds boringly didactic, it is not, just. (Certainly it can get weirdly stretched out; Phaethon is asked a question on page 280 and apparently answers it, instantly, on page 286, with an outburst aimed at somebody else in a simultaneous accelerated conversation.) Wright has a quirky sense of humor—Wells's Martian pops in for a guest appearance— perhaps alarmingly manifested in the names of his own sons, Orville and Wilbur. Reading this in his biography, one seriously starts to wonder if perhaps he was really a composite invention himself, dreamed up in an idle afternoon by Bruce Sterling and some Texan pals. Actually I doubt it; Mr. Wright's rather ramrod young fogy sense of propriety—he deplores the louche way sf editors and writers freely address each other by their first names—lent an eerie patina of conviction. And his characters are not wholly given to mighty projects, although Phaethon, it is true, unblush- ingly craves `deeds of renown without peer' (183); one AI likes to manifest in the collective virtual world as a penguin, fishy-breathed but able to fly so fast he leaves a vapor contrail (52).

The writer I found myself thinking of quite often—aside from the obvious begetters, Stapledon, E. R. Eddison, David Lindsay, Jack Vance (*Emphyrio* and all the rest), Charles Harness, Michael Moorcock (*The Dancers at the End of Time*), Felix Gotschalk (*Growing Up in Tier 3000*)—was Ian Wallace, a quirky psychologist who briefly flared with *Croyd* (1967), *Dr. Orpheus* (1968) and several other tales of superhuman razzmatazz before fizzling into the backwaters of DAW books. That fate is not for Mr. Wright, we can be sure. But I did have one jolting thought, at about page 70: Oh, dear God, this is the *Ralph 124C41+* of the early 21st century. It is better written and thought-out than Gernsback's dreadful prophetic classic, of course, because it stands on the shoulders of giants (as do we all, luckily), nor do I mean to imply that Wright has read his scientifictional predecessor. In fact, it reminded me more closely of accounts of a lost masterpiece or oddity I've never had the chance to read,

Curme Gray's *Murder in Millennium VI* (1951). Damon Knight extolled Gray's `audacity and stubbornness', noting that while the tale is set thousands of years hence, in a society whose customs and technology are utterly unlike ours, `there is not a word in the book that might not logically have been written by the narrator for the edification of his own posterity' (*In Search of Wonder*, 183). That is Campbell's and Heinlein's `lived-in future' taken to the ultimate. I felt Wright was trying for the same goal, perhaps by similar methods, and was pleased to find hidden on his website, among other sf writers' names and characters from his book, `curme grayphoenix exultant'. Oddly, Wright denies knowledge of the book.[15] Similar spookiness (literally) attends the name of one among Phaethon's jury of Hortators, guardians of tradition: Casper Halfhuman Tinkersmith of the Parliament of Ghosts. `He was a writer of educational matrixes famous for his cold logic when he was in his human body, and for his unusually vivid passion and drive when he was downloaded into an electrophotonic matrix' (305-6). That should be `uploaded', but it sounds more than a little like the late Dr. Paul Linebarger, CIA spook and psychological warfare authority, yet hallucinatory creator of the Underpeople and the Instrumentality as Cordwainer Smith. A `cordwainer' is a shoemaker, not a million miles from the tinker's craft. All this is coincidence, Mr. Wright informs me. Ah well. Such are the perils of the megatext.

What we have then, in *The Golden Age*, is part of an enormous future history that takes for granted many of the narrative devices that are, for our time, what rockets, robots and television sets were to sf's golden age. What it appeared to dodge was the ghost at every deep future feast today: the absent Singularity. A recent rec.arts.sf.written thread on Wright's novel even had the telling subject line: `Domesticating the Singularity'. You cannot do that, of course. All you can manage is to duck and weave, as Vinge himself, and Banks and Zindell and others (me, too) have been doing. In the interstices between the human present, the transhuman prospect and the radically posthuman future, there remain localities to set superb fiction, as Bruce Sterling showed with *Holy Fire* (1996). Can one leap ahead millennia to the High Transcendence and retell Vance's *To Live Forever* (1956/1987) or battle Stapledon ideologically, and get away

[15] Personal email.

with it? Not really. But then, by definition, the Singularity or Spike stands hidden from us by its own appalling upward curve toward infinity, or some sublunary approximation. So in the meantime all we can do, perhaps, is build as well as we might fables decorated with ingenuity, density, wit, sly comedy and, it is to be hoped, some passion. Wright does not do half bad at that.

20: 2002: *APPLESEED*, JOHN CLUTE

Once I dedicated a book of theory thus: *For John Clute, the world's finest science fiction critic.* But what has he done for us lately? An sf novel, that's what. Not many notable sf critics have dared attempt it, not unless, like Brian Aldiss, Gregory Benford, James Blish, Algis Budrys, Samuel Delany, Gwyneth Jones, Damon Knight, Ursula Le Guin, Stanislaw Lem, Joanna Russ, a handful more, they started out as fiction writers. George Turner is the only one who comes immediately to mind. He would have detested *Appleseed*.

i: A Modest Proposal in a Time of Singularity.

Science aspires to the condition of deicide.
Technology aspires to the condition of theogenesis.
Science fiction aspires to the condition of theophany.

ii: Why, This is the Megatext, nor am I out of It!

Like any really good sf novel written by an intelligent author at the peak of his craft, *Appleseed* is a byte dance and sorting of all the sf protocols we are likely to call up from memory. In an afterword, Clute acknowledges various predecessors on whom he has done, in echo of his deicidal, theogenic, theophanous book, Oedipal riffs—John Crowley, Thomas M. Disch, L. Frank Baum, Jorge Luis Borges, Rudyard Kipling, Arthur C. Clarke, Gene Wolfe, Roger Zelazny—and he could have mentioned quite a few more, Samuel R. Delany and Dan Simmons, to name two, but perhaps there is no real need to be explicit, for the book is radiant with the language and moves of the genre-edge and all the way back to the deep center; and the thrill of the thing lies in the sense of new things transfiguring the old.[16]

It is a tale fetched up from the Ocean of Story; arguably, it *is* the story of the Ocean of Story, which is us, is all.

iii:
Of the Origin of Narrative Species

Storytellers once spun out their inventions by the hour with rhythm, bold colors, engaging or horrid characters: simple tricks. Then they took up pens. After fiction and journalism parted company, manner swiftly put out a thousand blooms. Matter grew baroque. On the tables of the languid, grand operatic works groaned unread.

Future shock put a brutal stop to that. Bullrings and blood and short hard words.

The kids of those kids went to school and studied fine art, high culture, and the sentences went lacy again, and irony caught every word in a trap. Who knew how to read?

Some of those without reading accreditation did it anyway, with factory fairytales. They built bigger muscles in fourteen days or had their money back. Sf was anti-mandarin. Punched like a rivet. It was, as well, magic out of a whirling adolescent heart: it sang incantatory romance.

Finally the thing went decadent with over-use. Sf risked expiring in this terminal generation of embroidery on ideas which once . . . blazed. Still,

---

[16] This paragraph, as keen observers of Clute will recognize, is an appreciative if inevitably ironic appropriation of his own comments (in Clute, *Look at the Evidence: Essays & Reviews*, 1995, 350) on an admirable novel by Michael Swanwick, *Stations of the Tide* (1990).

opportunities arise in a decadent art-form. As in a retirement village or a jail, everyone knows the narrative shorthand. You can write whole novels in the number of words it once took to get the spaceship out of the lab.

Then, it seems, it changed again, somewhat. Exfoliation happened. In the first 63 pages of *Appleseed* what happens is that the chicken crosses the road, ornately, or rather gets part of the way to the other side, then goes back. That is all, really. What happens in the second chapter shows that this estimate was too hopeful. In fact, the chicken does not get back from attempting the curb until page 84, the end of the chapter, a quarter of the way in. Later we learn that we have misunderstood the chicken, have seriously undervalued and misidentified this baffled but plucky fowl. In fact, the chicken (Nathaniel Freer, than whom nobody is, or is less than: O paradox!) and his wife (named Ferocity Monthly-Niece, whom hereafter we might be tempted to call PMT for short) will be the rulers of the sevagram. I bet you expected that.

iv: Clute For Dummies

It is an involuted ocean, this Ocean of Story. The inside, as so often in canonical sf, is larger than the outside. Wormholes eat at the core of the apple, which is the world, which is Trantor, which is the Yggdrasil, which is the Omphalos of the Pleroma, and so on, yet they do not so much *eat* it as *constitute* it, spiraling inward and outward like choirs of angels. Certainly we can add Dante to that list above, and perhaps Geoff Ryman. Perhaps you think I am being irritatingly obscure or roundabout, but reading Clute does that to you. Be prepared to work like buggery at this novel. Persist, reader, there is treasure to be had.

I think I could tell you the plot, but then half the fun is gone, because really there *is* no plot, just a revelation space in the core of the tumble and burnished blazing array of verbal icons telling a story of God as plural cannibal shit-eater (shit here called `plaque') and the necessary revolt against themselves. Killing God is not very shocking these days, it being the escape artistry theme of the century we have left behind, not when Philip Pullman can place it at the hinge of his rather good children's trilogy (something earnest librarians urging kiddies to try *His Dark Materials* have not noticed, apparently—but wait for the plaque to hit the wall when they do). *Appleseed* is a puzzle palace, a memory palace, a cryptic crossword, a map of the world carved up into small absurd pieces and scattered, so that its gestalt recovery in the mind's eye urges theophany, or its simulation. You do not get that from looking up the answers in the back of the book, not even if the book is *The Dark Night of the Soul* or *Morte D'Arthur*. That was a hint: it really is the Matter of Britain on a cosmic as well as the classic Glastonbury cosmogonic scale. Maybe that is not surprising from a Canadian who has lived much of his adult and intensely book-drenched life in England.

v: Matière de Bretagne on Mars

`Stinky' Freer is hired, or so he supposes, to convey in his starship *Tile Dance*—which is laminated with Janus-faced tiles, congealed minds—a cargo of nanoforges from the planet Trencher, where he is nearly eaten, to the unknown planet Eolhxir, but he doesn't need to know where it is because his pilot is a parthenogenic tree named Mamselle Cunning Earth Link (and I do not *think* it is a pun on cunnilingus, but what else can it be?) which proves pregnant with the once and future king who is named, I kid you not, as such: Arturus Quondam Captain Future. You might find this almost unbearably whimsical and recursively knowing, but then Quondam's Mom apparently learned her English from Alfred Bester's fabulous temporal beachcomber, tall, gaunt, sprightly, bitter Mr. Aquila (from `5,271,009', half a century ago):

> `Shivering with anxious joy, behold me, sure! O enormous masculine sophont of dead Earth,' she continued, `bucking the bronco sigillum into badlands . . . Agog with flush was I, you can altogether bet! Seeing you in the skin that wears those mighty bones! That was scrumptious! That was lagniappe! But reck you, O striking figure of a man, that such solace of the senses was my purpose down below? Nix!' (92)

That's charming, that's lagniappe, and it goes on for pages, wonderfully sustained, you can get hungry for its return in these densely wrought pages; there were stretches, elsewhere, I could hardly bear to get through more than a page and a half at a time. Freer buys and wakens an ancient AI battle bot called Uncle Sam (later revealed to be SammSabaoth, Sammael plus Sabaoth):

—Uncle? said Freer into Teardrop.

The archaic eyes of the truculent Uncle Sam glared at him, rimmed by flaming grooves, which shifted and flowed and became the image of an open fist, a fist appaumy, an heraldic warrior fist apparently aflame. The face of the Uncle Sam was at one and the same time a face and a hand, a hand which was a weapon, a weapon which raised a palm of peace, but a palm clenched. (26)

And on and on. `Appaumy', I learn from the web (it's not in my fat dictionary) is simply heraldic jargon for `palm outward', as advertised. The citation below is niftier, but there's page after tens of pages of this *Forbidden Planet*/Delanyesque/Gibsonish stuff as Freer gets from his spaceship (in orbit) down to (?) the planet Trencher (`Bite me!' as it were), like the chicken and road joke indefinitely extended:

The braid did a loop-the-loop, gathering stray capillaries in like knitting, and exited docking country, passing through walls of rock and into a central intersection, seemingly roofed with glass, where bilateral and non-bilateral networks linked briefly, where Trencher opened downwards and up like the veined inner atrium of a dream of cities; vast artificial suns and moons and discs flickered through luminescent cupolas miles above Freer's head downwards through vertical arcades lined with mirrors. The float skidded through terrifyingly open air, freefell down a spidery frond curling for hundreds of yards over an abyss that dived downwards to magma. They hurtled into darkness shot by fireflies which turned out to be argosies ferrying homo sapiens upwards, perhaps heading towards an ark and the deepest of senior-citizen sleeps. There were a dozen of them; more. The inside of the world was churning.

—Is this normal?

—Aye aye, said the Uncle Sam.

They continued down, through a great shaft of light, dazzled, sigillated by photonic data flows cascading downwards from far above, perhaps ultimately from orbit, where the great Care Consortia arks shot perpetually their perfume and their honeytrap slogans into the apertures of the planet. Most of the data streams displayed the Insort Geront logo, the fiery three-snake caduceus almost too bright to read, the marque of the vastest of the godzillas—a ancient Human Earth term for any corporation, whether snail or trad dotcom or seeded nous cube, which having gone rogue was no longer subject to the rule of law of any individual state or planet or system—prating `Enkyklios Paedia' incessantly, boring its mantra deep into the bone of the planet. (31-2)

And boring not just its mantra, I fear. This is overload in the service of bedazzlement, but it keeps going wrong: godzilla is parochial enough, but dotcom was dead before the book came out, and I doubt they'd have knitting in this remote future. There's an explanation for the explanation, of sorts: Freer's viewpoint is geared to ours, since our time is his selected `era of empathy choice' (94) on Human Earth, the ancestral world of pheromone stenchy, sex-obsessed bipedals now swallowed up, one gathers, like much of the universe, by encrustations of plaque, corrupted legacy data shit: Malacandra, as C. S. Lewis told us long ago it was, and is (82).

All space opera aspires to the condition of Quest. *Appleseed* has more grails than you can shake a lance at. Johnny Appleseed, a scabrous rogue, wears one upside down upon his hairy head, like a tin pot, as in Vachel Lindsay's folkloric poem (`The apple allied to the thorn/Child of the rose') which is quoted *in extenso* in several places. He scatters his seed, we might suppose, across the galaxy. All Quest aspires to the condition of Tantra, delayed gratification to the max, unendurable pleasure indefinitely prolonged. Still, novels have climaxes, and Clute does not blink: as in several Norman Spinrad space operas where captains literally fuck their way through hyperspace (*The Void Captain's Tale*, 1983; *Child of Fortune*, 1985), Freer and Ferocity screw the world back into place, screw the inscrutable, as their ancient Predecessor starship, secret hero of the tale, fucks the world back to heaven. Sort of thing.

vi: Holiest Communion

Appleseed is a consummately Catholic novel. It's a God-eat-dog world, and vice versa. In the hollowed fecundities of its grails lie lenses, hosts which focus Eucharistic haecceity. They are, finally, eaten; almost everything is. A malign triune godthing named Opsophagous of the Harpe (a harpe is a scythe)—sons born endlessly in the dying bellies of fathers, which they munch—deliriously and continuously eats its own flesh in a Clutean rapture of disgust. Luckily for the galaxy, it's a dog-fuck-dog world too. Humans are, famously, on heat all round the clock. They can do it face to face, looking scandalously into each others' eyes, but in this unbuckled honest Darwinian future, 5000 years hence, reeking and leaking with sex day and night, they start it doggie fashion, sniffing and licking and mounting to heaven:

> Her body glowed with sweat . . .
> `Shall we fuck slow?'
> `No,' said Ferocity. `No, I don't think I can.'
> She leaped toward him.
> He shifted sideways, slipped his hand between her legs, and they fell through the light gravity on to the floating bed, hardly noticing as it rose into the cupola, where windows real and universal gave them to the world. They burrowed into position, as was the normal habit of homo sapiens anywhere after the loss of Human Earth, lowering their heads to each other's orifices, sniffing, touching tongues to the pomace of sweat and juices. It was as though they were checking passports. (232-3)

Those windows are for seeing through. The Predecessors, we learn, `were epithalamial . . . Anything an excuse for a marriage' (202), and everyone loves to watch. It is a robustly binary universe, which aspires to the condition of unitarity (down there in the quantum foam, here in the human heart, the wedding of Möbius), of dialectical sublation, and gets it, for a while. This is not surprising to devotees of Clute's emergent theoretics. He has been telling us for some years that the secret heart and driver of sf's mode is *exogamy* (for example, Clute, 1993, 1).

vii: Tell me a story

All art, all science, aspires to the condition of story. In the Ocean of Story, which is the world, liturgy tells the world into being and sustains it. In the liturgy of science fiction, new thing upon the face of history, liturgy not only repeats, it insists upon the *novum*. In *Appleseed*, here is the mantra refrain, universally acknowledged, before which all fall silent and listen, or tell:

`Tell us a story . . . Sacred is the new.' (94).

In *Appleseed*'s world, the world is written on the face of words, but also tucked away inside, doubled, mirrored, counter-braced, upended. Freer, we learn, wears the face of Jim Thorpe, Indian, finest American athlete of the first half of the last century. (So?) On Trencher, Freer's ancient starship buys him those two Made Minds, bound to service, warbot Uncle Sam (or SammSabaoth) and absolute navigator Vipassana, which Clute does not tell us is the Buddhist term for clear insight, the Art of Mindfulness; this is a book of ironies. Stinky's angel at the helm of *Tile Dance* or more truly *Ynis Gutrin* (which is Glastonbury, cathedral of the Grail) is she/he quantum KathKirtt, wedded Kirttimukha and his bride. Now Kirttimukha, as everyone surely knows and so Clute need not tell us, and does not, is the horned, leonine `face of glory' from Indian myth, but what of Kath? Here is my guess: she is Kathapitha or Katha Sarit Sagara, from the same Sanskrit writings: Ocean of, of course, Story.

That sundered Möbius world they knit up and make new, reprieving its Waste Land wound, echoing `that great wound all homo sapiens bore, as though their heads had been torn off, and harlequin masks substituted for real faces' (238), is Klavier, reality's birth canal, perhaps, the cosmic bicameral brain, all that, and in Klavier, of course, the condition of all things aspires to the condition of music, Beethovian thunder, glory, molten light. *Appleseed* is the fall of seed into fertile soil, kenosis, Clute tells us: incarnation of `the divine into the progeria of mortal flesh' (86). That, at least, is the opinion of `the theophrasts of the inner stars', but the novel insists that the theophrasts are wrong. For all that, the machine angels of the world `found it strangely thrilling to spreadeagle themselves on the rack of time: to gape through the peepshow eyes of their chosen faces at the meat faces of the mortals to whom they gave suck' (86). These faces are dual: flyte and jack, out and in, you'll find out, or won't. The narrative blows in the winds, the gales of time. It winds in gyres. It closes in theophany and deicide, as space opera ought.

21: 2003: DOWN AND OUT IN THE MAGIC KINGDOM, CORY DOCTOROW

Call it `blogpunk'.

I know, I winced too, but it seems terrifyingly apt. Worse, we might regard the characters in Doctorow's 47,350 word novella-plus as `blogketeers': halfway between rocketeers and Mouseketeers, maturity-arrested cast members in a future Disneyworld retirement village neurotopia. Money and paid work are gone, by 2130 or thereabouts, replaced by what the book engagingly dubs `Whuffie' (pronounced woo-fee, not wuh-fee): instantly updated tallies of peer esteem, reputation, online bloggy buzz. Whuffie registers how much you are being the opposite of dissed, and Doctorow builds the distribution arm of his nanofacture economy on it. The world, the solar system, is itself the magic kingdom, fueled and fed and entertained for free by self-replicating molecular machines running napsterishly downloadable programs. The Whuffie-busted are down and out but not dead, or if dead at least revivable: you can queue at any of the makers around town and eat or drink without charge. `The number of low-esteem individuals at large was significant, and they got along just fine, hanging out in parks, arguing, reading, staging plays, playing music' (156-7).

The disgruntled kids aren't writing virus or worms any more; they are competing for potlatch and what sf fans traditionally dub egoboo but more negotiable, earning the respect of their Bitchun Society peers (*tout le monde*, effectively, for the past century) and making a good living at it while doing their fourth doctorate. Bitchun Society. Really. That is what these wannabe hip, cool, disastrously nerdish nitwit ancients call their culture. If this had been hippiepunk, 30, 35 years back, they'd call it the Spliff, or Loveworld, or the Wow Man Society. Same as, really.

So Doctorow is taking the piss, right? Well, it's hard to say. This little book enacts itself. It is building up humungous gusts of whuffie for blogmeister Cory, a hyper energetic web presence at boingboing.net. Before the print book was released, it was festooned with encomiums from the great and near great of the wired and retired worlds. Mitch Kapor figured it `captures and defines the spirit of a turning point in human history'. Rudy Rucker, who has been writing versions of this future forever (*Software*, 1982, *Wetware*, 1988, and so on), asserts that Doctorow `starts out at the point where older sf writers' speculations end'. Bruce Sterling sparkled, fizzed and backflipped in his enthusiasm. Cory's blog quotes Paul Di Filippo claiming that `*Down and Out in the Magic Kingdom* is some kind of transgenic supergoat whose milk is full of spidersilk proteins and nutraceuticals.' The *New York Times* liked it. I was eager to read on, because you could feel that righteous Whuffie gusting and swirling up a storm.

And that was the thing of it. It was not the book's merits as fiction or as futurism or as satire; it had become, in a clever marketing move, a whuffie magnet. They were giving it away free! You could download the text in a dozen convenient and various formats: PDF, for printing to look like a book, or HTML for the screen, or .txt for ease, or your choice of hand held. Then if you liked it and couldn't be without your own hard printed copy, you could dial up amazon.com or trot to the bookstore and buy the hard-cover from Tor. Whuffie! Cory Doctorow's meter was spinning, lights were flashing, the machine was binging and dinging, it was awesome: *twenty thousand free downloads in the first two days!* This was blogpower. This was blogpunk, working the global room, sparkling, fizzing and backflipping, anything but down and out.

But in the novel, poor Julius the narrator, dismal prat that he is, has to fall. It's a narrative arc, d00D. It's a fortunate fall, Felix. First they kill him, then he bounces back, because we are dealing here with early postmortal posthumanity. Then they give him enough rope and he strangles himself, and he doesn't even get off on it. But it all turns out okay in the end, except of course that in an early posthuman novel the end never comes, except that when it does, when the heat death of the universe rolls along in 10^{100} years, someone is gonna be deadheading in hibernation toward it (we learn on the opening page), waking just often enough to take its temperature and roll on toward the End.

Now that last item was enough to throw a reader in 2003 up and out of the book. Is there going to *be* a heat death of the universe? Didn't they just show that the cosmological constant is pushing everything apart faster and faster, so that the light cone, the boundary of Everything, will cut the cosmos into dreadful detached chunks long before that old close of the 19th century doom comes upon us? It was difficult keeping up, even when you were doing blogpunk in a post-Singularity 22nd century. Yet Paul Di Filippo thought that was the setting:

> what we have here is a rare example of post-Singularity fiction. The Singularity, or Spike, is deemed to be that moment at which mankind emerges into transhuman existence, with or without the help or hindrance of strong AI. (Doctorow eschews the AI, for the most part.)

I, too, am assuming that the *mise-en-scène* actually *is* edge of Singularity, since mind back-up and other effortless advanced tech here deployed requires the vast computational grunt to get you there. But you *cannot* eschew artificial intelligence and still have a singularity, not really, not as late as the middle of the 22nd century. Not without a mighty good argument you can't, and there is no trace of an argument in the book, just *parti pris.* Arguably that is a point in its favor, since a healthy lived-in future should just plunk us down (punk us down) in the magic kingdom and let the crafty ride take us into its invented reality on the wings of discourse and the pre-established iconography of the megatext. But Doctorow did not eschew datadumps. Julius, his narrator, is endlessly chewing over the facts of the world with his old buddy Keep A-movin' Dan, who argues happily with a man who's died and been recompiled more than once that

> ` . . . you're not really an atom-for-atom copy. You're a clone, with a copied *brain*—that's not the same thing as quantum destruction.'
> `Very nice thing to say to someone who's just been murdered, pal. You got a problem with clones?'
> And we were off and running. (42)

I don't *think* so, d00D. Not after a century and more of this stuff being as utterly ordinary as opening the car door and slipping behind the wheel. So this is not a datadump, it could not be, no writer, no Campbell Award winner, was that clunky in 2003. Julius explains it away for us:

> I knew what he was doing, distracting me with one of our old fights, but I couldn't resist the bait, and as I marshaled my arguments, it actually helped calm me down some. (41)

Still not convinced, sorry. Doctorow is far more effective when he just drops the floating sf signifiers into the story, as one does these days (since about 1953): Free Energy, ad-hocracy, HUDs (wait—they still use CAPS to indicate head-up displays? they still *have* head-up displays?), Whuffie itself. Sexy engineered gals lollop in with double knee joints and fur, all the rage among the kids. People cavort in sexy musical orbital bubbles, naked and disinhibited; it is the kind of thing Spider Robinson could never have invented 20 years ago. Oh wait, Spider *did* invent it 20 years ago. And those Disneyworld riffs, and downloads into clones after you have been killed, and web connects inside your head—wouldn't John Varley have bitten his lip to think that if only he had tried harder he could have told these stories 25 years ago. Oh wait—

Now it would be unkind to complain that Cory Doctorow had rein-vented all these wheels, instead of recombining them with a certain blogpunk zest, if it were not for all the retired and wired great and good shouting so loudly that he was *the next New Thing*, gather round and marvel! No, in fact his sometime-collaborator Charlie Stross was the Next Big Thing, or at any rate the Now Big Thing. Charlie writes like a bastard, rips off your limbs and then tears off your head. Still, loads of Whuffie were being shoveled to the man with the bright, the inevitable idea of blogpunking his little book through the pores of the net. Is whuffie a non-zero sum commodity? Hard to be sure just yet. As an act of olde worlde Canadian Marshall McLuhan medium messaging, Doctorow's gambit was welcome and interesting to watch.

But what about as a *novel*?

What about as a now-moment science fiction novel?

What about as a post-Singularity novel?

Sorry, my dears, it doesn't really cut the mustard. The whole is less than the sum of several intriguing parts that Doctorow and others will surely develop more interestingly in other fiction and non-fiction. My own reac-tion, as a sample and unrepresentative non-American reader, is skewed by not having much of an advance clue about the Magic Kingdom; it give me zero throat-choking, eye-watering nostalgia. I have heard of Florida's Disneyworld, and that's it. Doctorow does not bother describing his setting, at least not in detail, because (I guess) he assumes it is universally known and loved. Maybe 99.2 percent of US readers will thrill to the familiar invocation of those lovable settings, the Haunted Mansion and Liberty Square and the Hall of Presidents and the House of Something or other, with their ancient animatronic dignitaries and spooky ghosts and child-thrilling rides, but it is all empty signifiers to me, d00D, you have really got to pump some more elbow-grease into the keyboard. (For the Florida and even the Alaska locals, perhaps this admission is almost incomprehensibly dull and dumb of me.) But the trouble does not stop with the locale hand-waving.

The story is simplicity itself. Julius and his local affinity group are besottedly devoted to one part of ancient heritage Disneyworld, and beaver away to keep its legacy equipment and rides gleaming. Visitors pay in dollops of esteem, but only as long as they keep coming through the turnstiles. Meanwhile, Debra and her competing ad-hocs run another concession but they are not content with maintenance and micro-tweaking; these shocking radicals with no respect for the eternal verities want to 'tear down every marvelous rube goldberg in the Park and replace them with pristine white sim boxes on giant, articulated servos' (28). When Julius is shot to death mysteriously and rebooted, he's livid, certain but without proof that this was Debra's work (like children, they have only first names), meant to bollix his own team and pave the way for its ouster. He fights back with a stunning new idea: offsite visitors could port into robot bodies and become part of the show! Nobody has ever thought of such a daring scheme during the past century or so, but it is doomed unless the vile plans of the sim box claque are defeated, and meanwhile they are fighting dirty, maneuvering poor Julius permanently offline and outta touch with the happening world. Meanwhile, Dan and Lil betray him sexually and in other ways. The jig is up for the Haunted Mansion. Or so it seems. But Jules pulls his chestnuts out the fire in the nick of time and goes on his way, down and out for now, but in the chastened expectation of plentiful whuffie once he gets his new symphony done.

So this is not one of those rousing pre-Golden Age space operas with a silver-clad hero saving the universe, let alone a Greg Egan novel where entire ontological realms are at stake. There is much to be said for such comic cosmic deflation. But—

None of the technology hangs together. These people can do perfect back-ups of their brains in a few minutes at the handy corner facility. They can flash-bake whole VR lives of the great and the dead into punters passing through hoopy rides, rich with sensory conviction and replete with historical information. They read each other's minds, in effect, with their embedded web systems, and google the world via their HUDs. Meanwhile, they enter data with . . .

. . . keyboards, real or virtual, air-typing their code and reading the results on their HUDs. This is roughly the equivalent of a blogger entering the news of the day by chiseling it into rock.

I do not think that is just an accidental oversight, or a concession to the bloggers with their own keyboards and hell-lit laser mice; it cuts to the core of what is fux0red in this future. True, the corner of the future inhabited by Julius and his screwdriver-savvy grrlfriend Lil, 15 percent of his 120 years old, and Debra his vicious strategic antagonist and old farts Tom and Rita, Lil's absconded deadheading parents, and all the Disney groupies, it is a convenient narrative aperture for us early XXI readers to watch through. Even bloggers need a helping hand with the *mise-en-scène*. But you get the feeling that the rest of this world, too, is trapped in some kind of endlessly recycled Ricky & Lucy dreaming (which is, ostensibly, the problematic at the heart of evil Debra's plans to upgrade the sacred traditions of Walt's Kingdom, which makes her the secret hero by neophilic sf convention; well, except that most beloved sf is recuperative, whenever possible stabilizing and restoring the status quo). But it cannot be, because there is easy offworld travel, `mortality rate at zero and the birthrate at nonzero' (8), so that `the world was inexorably accreting a dense carpet of people, even with the migratory and deadhead drains on the populations'. Resistance is futile, because by the nature of the thing Luddites who resist die at the traditional age while the adopters blithely live on. It is hard to believe that all the world's historical trajectories would lock down into Disneyland (I know they don't, but that is the metaphysic the book's myopic focus insinuates), even given the ceaseless plotting and seething of competed ad-hocs that provide the semblance of a plot. I wanted to see at least the rest of the novel, the next 47,350 words, once our guys were free of the compulsion to repeat. Maybe that will be Doctorow's next move, at this crux. But then maybe that itself would be, fatally, to repeat. Sadly, today's sf mostly gets major whuffie by repeating, and very little for innovating.

22: FAR FUTURE FICTION

> In some way yet to be determined, a genuine historicity is possible only on condition this illusion of an absolute present can be done away with, and the present opened up again to the drift from the other ends of time. This is, once again, why the work of art is in this context a privileged object of study . . .
>
> Fredric Jameson, *The Prison-House of Language* (187)

i

If a millennium is only the ticking of an arbitrary clock, still, that is a clock with consequences to those who watch its face for frowns, nods, smiles. But it is only by a very modest clock that a thousand years is so large an interval. The stars exhale their light by a seasonal chronology a thousand thousand times as long. Planets follow the same calendar until they crisp and cool.

Is it cynical or hubristic to test our aspirations, our doubts, against such a sundial? Skepticism, even cynicism, is not absent from sf's fictions (its parables) of the far future, but mostly they reach out and touch us in a different register. Fetched up from the shallows of lost time, they stand as a kind of distillation of everything elegiac, like the music of Debussy, Ravel, Elgar, in the romantic melancholy of adolescence and young adult-hood—and simultaneously as the first attempts of a mature civilization to reach forward into the deeps of time.

We could easily wonder if humankind, as a species, is yet grown beyond the blaring and wistfulness of adolescence. If some of the rich are at last lowering the fuel settings on their pleasure-domes (a change that might be, as yet, more wishful than real), the poor of the earth continue to rot and die young, in their billions, effectively powerless in their exhaustion or furious rage. At the start of a millennium during which all the statistical curves will cut through the red lines and smash or soar with an exponential on-rush of technological change (unless we take change into our charge or least ride it with grace and courage), there is something to be said for turning back to the imaginative guesses from the end of childhood, and forward to the close of childhood's end. Recall the most famous of all journeys to the end of time, the mournful expedition of H. G. Wells's Time Traveler. The Earth has slowed, dragged by tidal forces, until one hemisphere eternally faces the sullen red heat of the exhausted sun:

> The sky was no longer blue. North-eastward it was inky black, and out of the blackness shone brightly and steadily the pale white stars. Overhead it was a deep Indian red and starless, and south-eastward it grew brighter to a glowing scarlet where, cut by the horizon, lay the huge hull of the sun, red and motionless . . . There were no breakers and no waves, for not a breath of wind was stirring. Only a slight oily swell rose and fell like a gentle breathing, and showed that the eternal sea was still moving and living . . .
>
> Far away up the desolate slope I heard a harsh scream, and saw a thing like a huge white butterfly go slanting and fluttering up into the sky . . .
>
> I cannot convey the sense of abominable desolation that hung over the world. (*The Time Machine*, [1895], 1983, 305-7)

Thus, an early evolutionary perspective on deep time, shocking and titillating its Victorian readership. Wells, in a way, wrote us into that very future even as he sought to divert the current of history from its all-but-inevitable misery. By contrast, regard the persistent doctrine of text and self at the opening of the third millennium: we write what we are written, and we are written by what we have read and been and are—which is to say, by what we have written. It is a circular interpretation at once ample, enameled with paradox and conceit, yet intolerably constricted (being, after all, fashionable opinion in an academy increasingly removed from the true levers of power), edgy with internal fractures eager to crump and crumble.

Suppose that text is a calendar, and the calendar is running out?

Not immediately, not by any means. I am not raising yet again the tedious apocalyptic fantasies of those who expect the world's end at any moment (as in the tedious and absurdly succesful *Left Behind* sequence of fundamentalist pot-boilers), with a judgmental trumpet blast. Still, the end of the world, and perhaps of the universe entire, finally *will* come: that much is just scientific knowledge, no longer myth. So do we possess fictions, other than ancient myth, answering to those truths uncovered by scientists with their telescopes, scanners, brilliantly probing theories? Luckily, yes. And very enjoyable fictions, at that, if never quite adequate to the (impossible?) task.

The end of time! The close of all life on Earth, packed away like a bazaar on some long, calm, mournfully bereft Sunday afternoon! Yet the occlusion of our own blue and white world, we now know, need not spell the end of all life and mind, far from it. Our seed will spill outward into the heavens, during the millennia and billions of years that remain before the galaxies drown in the blackness of everlasting night.

Out of the dreams of such strange stories something pure shines. I found it myself when I was a child of perhaps 12 or 14, the age at which, as we have seen, many science fiction readers stumble on this treasure-trove of dragon-haunted, star-strewn futures. I must have been 14 when I picked up the late John Brunner's tale of the deep future, `Earth is but a Star' (1958) in the British magazine *Science Fantasy*, and rushed eagerly into its rococo depths. Soon I found Jack Vance, true begetter of the dying Earth, and his predecessors—Wells, Olaf Stapledon with his stark vistas of the Last Men and the Star Maker, John W. Campbell, cloaking his poeticisms under the pen-name Don A. Stuart, Arthur C. Clarke with his ancient city of the future, Diaspar—and those who follow even to this day: Gene Wolfe with his magisterial, bottomless *Book of the New Sun*, Paul McAuley's *Confluence* trilogy, Stephen Baxter's Stapledonian spacetime voids.

ii

We are not dealing, in far future stories, with any future we might expect to live in, even if tomorrow turns out very differently from currently advertised models. This is especially so in an epoch such as

Michael Moorcock's romantic future, in this quotation from his imagined *High History of the Runestaff*: `Then the Earth grew old, its landscapes mellowing and showing signs of age, its ways becoming whimsical and strange in the manner of a man in his last years' (1967, 7). Most of these fanciful dying Earths are lit by Wells's baleful red glare, or perhaps a guttering lamp looming dim across half the horizon with its feeble crimson flickering: the dying Sun. Here is Jack Vance, from *The Dying Earth* (1950), in typical mood:

> `Earth,' mused Pandelume. `A dim place, ancient beyond knowledge. Once it was a tall world of cloudy mountains and bright rivers, and the sun was a white blazing ball. Ages of rain and wind have beaten and rounded the granite, and the sun is feeble and red. The continents have sunk and risen. A million cities have lifted towers, have fallen to dust. In place of the old peoples, a few thousand strange souls live. There is evil on Earth, evil distilled by time . . . Earth is dying and in its twilight . . . ' He paused.
>
> T'sais said doubtfully: `Yet I have heard Earth is a place of beauty, and I would know beauty, even though I die. (1950/1972, 38-9)

Wouldn't we all?

In reality, the true story of life in the solar system (as we currently understand it) is this: the Sun ignited some five billion years ago, and has been brightening ever since, by about an extra fifth to date. Its orbiting worlds, not least our own, have therefore warmed and will eventually swelter, and cook. There will be no great, dully glowing coal in heaven.

In another four or five thousand million years, the nuclear hydrogen fusion within our local star will shift gear to helium burning, in a ghastly few seconds of `helium flash'. Restabilized, the Sun will be a core of blazing helium surrounded by a shell of hot hydrogen, and beyond that a vast hot outer envelope. While this red giant phase of the Sun will fail to swallow the Earth (as old fashioned science fiction often imagined), it will blaze for a further billion years . . . and then go out. Nuclear fires extinguished, the Sun collapses into a white dwarf, and then an all-but-invisible black dwarf star (not to be mistaken for a black hole, which needs a star much larger than our Sun as its progenitor.) The Earth, surface charred during the red giant phase, will chill in the blackness, air and water lost, crust locked into eternal night.[17]

And that doleful fate is only a step or two away, no farther into tomorrow than the solar system's genesis was, looking backward. True, it is an inconceivably great distance from our annual round, but by cosmic measure just a decade or two. Other stars have passed already through this great cycle: born in a shock-wave compression of thin interstellar gasses, spinning down, throwing off worlds, some of them surely growing life of some kind, burning for billions of years (the universe has been here for at least 13 billion), flaring, scalding in red fury, gasping, gone. And their life with them, unless that life has found passage away from its doom.

Perhaps our descendants will find that escape route as well. Perhaps, indeed, by the time death comes to our Sun and Earth we shall have seeded all the sky. If so, many of sf's earliest tales of the deep future were just fairy-stories told by lost children, fearful of the night, crouched about a sparking fire in the eerie dark woods.

But far future tales were not written, of course, as scientific prophecy, nor to be read by the strangely altered children and adults of the far future. They speak to us here and now, as all myth and poetry speaks: in metaphor and metonymy, as figuration of today's dreads and aspirations. If we cast ourselves headlong into the mortal ends of time, it is in the hope, surely, that we find something secret, mysterious and revelatory awaiting us there, some part of ourselves usually hidden out of the bright light of daytime scrutiny. Coaxing timid voices from the silence is difficult but rewarding work. So, too, is listening patiently to their stories, or, indeed, with a measure of skepticism and hermeneutic suspicion. Just how do such tales work, what are their declared and hidden ambitions and mechanisms, what do they obscure (the number of women writing in this mode has been noticeably low, for example; why?) and what do they divulge? They touch readers with a peculiar sidelong appeal, their striking evocation of a tonality most contemporary fiction has abandoned, or lost: the elegiac, the haunted, the dying fall, and yet, paradoxically, the odd pleasure that comes from confronting a chilling truth. Brian Aldiss once referred to Thomas M. Disch's `bracing despair', a candor rare in this literature of hi-tech consolation. That is an apt description of the mood of many dying Earth tales, for they know that all flesh is grass, that all grass will

[17] For a summary of this long future history, even to the ends of time in an ever-expanding open universe, see Adams and Laughlin, 1999.

burn in that final fire and then be seen no more. In many of these tales, however, what we read goes well beyond despair to a kind of rapture: perhaps we shall attain powers and knowledge in those final days equal to the undoing even of cosmic nightfall. Consider this exultant passage from a surprising writer:

Deep Time: 1,000,000 mega-years. I saw the Milky Way, a wheeling carousel of fire, and Earth's remote descendants, countless races inhabiting every stellar system in the galaxy. The dark intervals between the stars were a continuously flickering field of light, a gigantic phosphorescent ocean, filled with the vibrating pulses of electromagnetic communication pathways.

To cross the enormous voids between the stars they have progressively slowed their physiological time, first ten, then a hundred-fold, so accelerating stellar and galactic time . . . [T]he slow majestic rotation of the universe itself is at last visible.

Deep Time: . . . Now they have left the Milky Way . . . have extended their physiological dependence upon electronic memory banks which store the atomic and molecular patterns within their bodies, transmit them outward at the speed of light, and later re-assemble them.

Deep time: . . . Now, too, they have finally shed their organic forms and are composed of radiating electromagnetic fields, the primary energy sub-stratum of the universe, complex networks of multiple dimensions, alive with the constant tremor of the sentient messages they carry, bearing the life-ways of the race.

To power these fields, they have harnessed entire galaxies riding the wave-fronts of the stellar explosions out toward the terminal helixes of the universe.

Deep Time: . . . They are beginning to dictate the form and dimensions of the universe . . . The universe is now almost filled by the great vibrating mantle of ideation, a vast shimmering harp which has completely translated itself into pure wave form, independent of any generating source.

As the universe pulses slowly, its own energy vortices flexing and dilating, so the force-fields of the ideation mantle flex and dilate in sympathy, growing like an embryo within the womb of the cosmos, a child which will soon fill and consume its parent.

Despite intimations of a Star child embryo, this is not Arthur C. Clarke in *2001* mode, nor his great canonical novel of the remote future, *The City and the Stars*. No, it is a passage from that famously `pessimistic' and stylishly contemporary British New Wave writer, J. G. Ballard, from his story `The Waiting Grounds' ([1960], in Ballard, 1967, 77-9), published over four decades ago. Indeed, US editor Gardner Dozois asked in his recent gathering of far future fiction, *The Furthest Horizon* (2000), why it is that `so *many* Britons write far-future stories'; he adds another question that puzzled me too: `and why so *few* women do, way out of proportion demographically in both cases'. Dozois chose to leave these topics `for wiser critics. . . to try to puzzle out' (xi). Certainly fewer women than men have written reflectively on this topic. Those who do tended to find metaphors of the deep future in texts closer to home than the literal death-pangs of the sun. Consider that much-anthologized, irreplaceable feminist reading of time's end beside a kitchen-sink, Pamela Zoline's heartbreaking `The Heat Death of the Universe' (1967). Can it be that the very far future lends itself too readily to whimsical escape or transcendence, to evasion of the daily, insistent, politically urgent realities many women find themselves closer to than men? Carolyn Cherryh's significantly-titled *Sunfall* (1981) is palpably a dying Earth story, yet its Paris and other cities are those we almost know.

iii

A range of dreamers has visited this locale. A 19th century view of last days is French astronomer Camille Flammarion's *Omega*. Sir Arthur Clarke (1949) and Poul Anderson (1954) wrote early, haunting tales of an Earth abandoned by vigorous humanity. Often Earth in the extremity of time is mired in ennui, that Pre-Raphaelite mood brought early to perfection in Jack Vance's Dying Earth and a little later in the core oeuvre of Cordwainer Smith, the `Rediscovery of Man', which built for us a genuinely alien yet embracing distance that seems very remote despite ostensibly being set a mere 15,000 years hence. By contrast to these sidelong approaches, Brian W. Aldiss plunged profoundly and comically into the long afternoon of earth in *Hothouse* (1962). Much more recently, Gene Wolfe has created a truly vast, almost Proustian interpretation of deep time in his three linked sequences of novels, using, like Vance earlier, special linguistic apparatus discussed ingeniously by Michael

Andre-Driussi in his scholarly *Lexicon Urthus* (1994). George Zebrowski has written several major far-future works, notably *Macrolife*. Equally ambitious is David Zindell's sequence of four novels (*Neverness* [1989], *The Broken God* [1994], *The Wild* [1996] and *War in Heaven* [1998]), set in a future where humanity and our altered offspring have spread across the heavens, occasioning war and insight and, indeed, the creation of gods, fulfilling Ballard's sketchy conspectus. (Why so many people with a special interest in the terminal future have names from the far end of the alphabet is another mystery.) Wolfe's far future plainly paved the way for the heroic skyscape of Paul McAuley's *magnum opus, The Books of Confluence.* McAuley's fellow countryman Stephen Baxter has almost trade-marked the deep future in a series of stories and novels about the war of humans against Xeelee and other foes.

And if finally the immense vistas of Stapledon, Ballard and Zindell seem too close to the religious or grandiose, we may instead release ourselves in baroque, imagined adventure, or happily laugh at the preposterous things we and all mindkind choose to believe to comfort ourselves as evening closes in, if close in it must. Or, ambitiously, with the Singularitarians, look rather to a posthuman future without limits. And if not that, why then, with Pamela Zoline's tormented artist/housewife, perhaps at the very least we can burst free of the entropic trap of that damned kitchen sink.[18]

---

[18] This chapter is adapted from the introduction to my anthology of far future fiction and essays by various critics, *Earth is But a Star: Excursions Through Science Fiction to the Far Future*, Perth: University of Western Australia Press, 2001. See that volume for an elaborate intertwined conversation among exemplary texts, fiction and critical, especially Brian Stableford's definitive history `Far Futures' (pp. 47-76).

APPENDIX: AUSTRALIAN SF

i

The stars dusted on the Australian sky, as you gaze up into the great southern darkness, are not the constellations known by most humans throughout history, the hundred millennia of pre-history. High in the southern sky, invisible from London or St Petersburg or Chicago, two bright stars point to the five comprising a slightly dented Southern Cross. Australia's flag shows that cross, plus one of the pointers—the less interesting one, oddly enough. The brighter of the Pointers, farther from the Cross, is actually not one star but three, locked in mutual orbit: Sun-like Alpha Centauri A and B, and dim red Proxima, closest to our world of all suns except the Sun.

To grow up under the light of the nearest stars is . . . *science fictional!*

Alpha Centauri, that bright composite light, has other names. Few know that, though once the secret knowledge of stars was hugged to the breast of all who stood watch on cold nights. Aborigines, with their hundreds of separate tongues, use many names for the nearest star. For the Boorung people (from the south-eastern part of the nation, the rich farm-land that white people choose to call Victoria) Cross and Pointers are Tchingal and Bunya, an emu and possum from the spirit Dreaming. If science fiction myth-makers tell different tales, perhaps those are poten-tially no less resonant for the new composite culture of 20 million people that has taken command of the continent, and is in the process of being reshaped by its immense, austere power.

It has been called the last continent—or the second-last, if we count Antarctica, under all that ice and snow. But Australia was by no means the most recent great expanse of sovereign land found and inhabited by humans walking out of Africa. They did so 50 thousand years ago at least, perhaps more, tens of millennia before humans trudged into the Americas. By that calendar, European settlement of the southern continent—some call it invasion, and certainly the native peoples were trampled, infected and murdered in dreadful numbers—was the merest blip in the past. Whites have re-made the rediscovered continent in little more than two centuries—but it has re-made them in turn.

It is notorious that the first European painters who tried to render the intractable Australian landscape uttered curious chimeras: soft, decid-uous dales and gentle woolly skies, complete with half-remembered Grecian ruins. Nothing could be farther from the experience of the outback, the numinous hard blue heavens, the hot sun, the lashing down-pours, animals that hop and bear their young in pouches, snakes and insects that sicken or kill with venom so poisonous it seems like a Biblical retribution. The same kinds of perceptual blunders happened for a long time in writing produced by English-speaking Australians. Writers and readers in the 'last continent' are denizens of two worlds, and only slowly is Australia's fiction bringing the two into meaningful conjunction. For a long time it has seemed that Jewish intellectual New York, say, or whitebread rollerblading Los Angeles, are more vividly recognizable and germane than Sydney or the bush.

ii

Unlike the ancient teachings and songs of the first peoples, sf is not much more than a century old. H. G. Wells called his pioneering efforts 'scientific romances', still a good name, and his wonderfully fecund *The Time Machine* and *War of the Worlds* were published as late as 1895 and 1898. So Australia as a Europeanized nation—it became a Federation, a unified nation, as recently as 1901—is even younger than this 'space age' genre. If you push sf's birth back to Mary Shelley's *Frankenstein* in 1818, it coincides with white settlement. Time enough, you might think, to grow plenty of Aussie sf.

In fact, though, it has seemed rather thin on the ground. In 1982, Dr. Van Ikin gathered a swag of futuristic, Lemurian, satirical and utopian tales from 1845 to 1947, and placed them (in his landmark anthology *Australian Science Fiction)* side by side with a selection of more recent generic sf and fringe surreal fiction. Ikin argued at length for this inclusive eclecticism, perhaps not persuasively. Science fiction is hardly achieved by the simple act of supposing that the world differs slightly from the consensus version. Many of the early candidates were crudely wrought and depressingly racist, with titles like *The Yellow Wave* (1895) and *The Coloured Conquest* (1904). Erle Cox's *Out of the Silence* (serialized in a newspaper in 1919) *is* authentic sf, and troublingly nasty: a farmer finds a beautiful white superwoman from an earlier civilization, preserved underground in suspended animation as `lower races' wrought ruin upon her ancient world. On the other hand, feminist utopias suggested new paths: Mary Ann Moore-Bentley, in 1901, adventured with *A Woman of Mars, or Australia's Enfranchised Women.* Despite some controversial highlights and flurries—notably, *Tomorrow and Tomorrow* (1947) by M. Barnard Eldershaw (actually Marjorie Barnard and Flora Eldershaw), politically censored for subversive views—most of the twentieth century saw little sf from Australians, and most of that derivative and third-rate. The population was very small, and access to publication extremely limited.

In the last couple of decades, Australia has seen a burst of talented activity in both sf proper and commercial fantasy (usually fat novels or trilogies set in a variant of Middle Earth, with dashing derring-do among semi-divine characters enacting mythic themes). Still, you could easily get the impression than Australians do not care to dream about the stars and the strange inhabitants of alien worlds—unless those aliens speak in American accents, in which case Aussies eagerly gulp down *X-Files, Star Wars, Star Trek, The Matrix,* a hundred gaudy movies, a thousand imported paperbacks.

It comes as some surprise, therefore, that Australians are at least notable sf *critics*—not just carping complainers, either, but astute anatomists and cataloguers of these strange new literary fruit. The first major *Encyclopedia of Science Fiction and Fantasy,* in three parts (1974, 1978, 1983), was written by a Tasmanian amateur scholar, Don Tuck. Indeed, Tuck gained the 1984 Hugo, sf's premier award, chosen by its fans assembled in their thousands at the World SF Convention—held, of course, as usual, in one of the large cities of the United States. The field's most important critical volume, *The Encyclopedia of Science Fiction,* was also the brainchild of an Australian, Peter Nicholls, who got a Hugo in 1980 and then in 1995 shared another with John Clute, for its even more impressive revision. (But, Australia being a provincial little universe, Nicholls failed to be nominated for the equivalent local award for sf criticism—an award named, in an inevitable irony, for the *nom-de-plume* of pioneering American sf critic James Blish, who wielded his sharp scalpel as William Atheling, Jr.) A comprehensive study of Aussie sf from the earliest days is *Strange Constellations* (1999), by Russell Blackford, Van Ikin, and Sean McMullen. Melbourne University Press published an entire, if not entirely reliable or complete, *Encyclopaedia of Australian Science Fiction & Fantasy* (1998), edited by Paul Collins, Steven Paulsen and Sean McMullen.

Australia's science fiction at its best (which admittedly is seldom) is among the finest ever written in any country: Greg Egan's *oeuvre* is proof enough of that. This should not be surprising. Australians no longer live under what historian Geoffrey Blainey memorably dubbed the `tyranny of distance'. It costs a little more to freight books and magazines across the vast oceans, to airmail stories out to the metropolitan centers of the world, but it can be done with only an extra week's lag. Today, of course, even that rupture is healing, as instantaneous everywhere-at-once is made real by the Internet and email. A vivid local sf magazine like *Eidolon*, where some of Egan's first stories were published by editors Jonathan Strahan and Jeremy Byrne, could be sampled on the World Wide Web, and subscriptions were no harder to arrange than those for *Asimov's* and *F&SF* in the USA or *Interzone* in Britain. (Unfortunately, too few readers took that opportunity; *Eidolon* is no more.) Australians travel prodigiously, and are as likely to meet by accident in a small town outside Boston or in a pub in London as in their home suburb. Australia is *big*, and the locals find it almost as easy and cheap to fly to Portugal or Madras as to cross their own red-desert nation's heartland from one green coastal patch to another thousands of kilometers distant. The late, very funny sf fan Roger Weddall had no difficulty convincing those he met overseas that it is a legal requirement, like military conscription, for all young Australians to leave the country for two years.

Still, the names of the writers of Australia's science fiction are perhaps still not known well to most of the greater world's sf enthusiasts. Egan, of course, is a wonderful exception, the *wunderkind* who startled US and UK audiences so acutely that for a time *Year's Best* anthologies were incomplete without *two* stories apiece by him. For a time I considered him the most important sf writer in the world. More recently, Sean Williams and

Shane Dix, and Sean McMullen, have placed well-received series in the USA; Kate Orman has gained acclaim for her *Doctor Who* novels. At a quite different angle, Peter Carey is another exception, much admired by literary readers, from his earlier fabulations that borrowed sf tropes to his parabolic allohistory, *The Unusual History of Tristan Smith* (1994). One can conscript Gerald Murnane (*The Plains*, 1982), Peter Goldsworthy (*Honk if You Are Jesus*, 1992) and James Bradley (*The Deep Field*, 1999) for `slip-stream' fiction. Other authors have made a mark, more often among sf's specialist critics than with mass readerships. George Turner came to sf late, at 62, after middling success as a mainstream novelist of manners (he shared the 1963 Miles Franklin Award, a distinguished mainstream prize). *Beloved Son* (1978) made a powerful impression, and 1987's *The Sea and Summer* won the Arthur Clarke award and was in the running for the Commonwealth Prize. Before his death in 1997, he produced a body of mature work that is still finding a world-wide audience comparable with, say, Stanislaw Lem's.

Frank Bryning, attracted to sf around the time of World War One, had published a notable series of tales about a Commonwealth Space Station, and sf that introduced Aboriginal characters. Lee Harding, John Baxter and David Rome (David Boutland) virtually colonized John Carnell's English magazines *New Worlds* and *Science Fantasy*, and his original anthology series *New Writings in SF*, in the early to mid 1960s, but later moved to other genres, or fell silent. Jack Wodhams' dementedly inventive and popular japes appeared regularly while he had the tutelage of John Campbell at *Analog*, but with the great editor's death his work sprawled into indiscipline and near-illiteracy (a sorry fact I shall illustrate shortly). The late Wynne Whiteford sold his first sf stories in the USA to *Amazing* and *Fantastic Universe* in the early 1950s, and in the 1980s returned to form with a number of routine adventure novels.

And of course the most well-known Aussie sf writer of all was merchant navy Captain A. Bertram Chandler, known confusingly as `Jack' to his wife and friends and `Bert' to the sf fans. Guest of Honor at the Chicago World Science Fiction Convention, and several times at Japanese conventions, he was the only Australian member of that Golden Age generation who got their start in John W. Campbell's famous *Astounding Science Fiction*. Or is that a misleading claim? After all, Chandler was 44 years old when he emigrated from Britain in 1956, and his most famous stories (such as the much anthologized `Giant Killer', from 1945) were sold *before* he moved to Australia. By comparison, Arthur C. Clarke became a resident of Colombo in the same year Chandler settled in Australia; one might doubt that Clarke is known as the finest *Sri Lankan* sf writer.

By the same token, should we regard Nevile Shute, author of the most famous after-the-bomb novel (surely an sf theme, even though *On the Beach*, 1957, is hardly sf), as an Aussie writer? He arrived in 1950 and left a decade later. John Brosnan, born in Australia, has been expatriate (like Baxter) for more than 30 years. Cherry Wilder, a fine writer represented in many Aussie anthologies, was actually a New Zealander who lived in Australia for 22 years of her young adulthood before moving with her husband Horst Grimm to Germany, returning to her birthplace to die. Call her an honorary Aussie. Jack Dann, Aussie sf's most illustrious adopted son, arrived as recently as 1993, aged 48, married an Australian, holds dual residency, and is as purely an upstate New York writer as the world will ever see.

David Lake, however, clearly *is* best seen as an Australian sf writer, although his career was brief. An academic raised in India, he settled in 1967 at the age of 38, becoming an Australian citizen. Victor Kelleher lived for the early years of his maturity in Africa, settling in Australia at 37, in 1976; like Lake's, his work was written in his adoptive homeland. At the farthest extreme, consider the odd case of Dr. Paul Myron Anthony Linebarger, godson of Sun Yat-sen, psychological warrior, and author under the name Cordwainer Smith of the most memorable science fiction short story sequence ever conceived. Smith lived in Canberra, the Australian capital, for extended periods during several stints at the Australian National University, and his Instrumentality tales, with their refrains from the planet Old North Australia, stand near the heart of world science fiction mythology. It would not be realistic, alas, to conscript Smith to the roster of local talent.

Terry Dowling is among the best-loved local writers and most-awarded in and out of Australia, a writer who stubbornly hews his own path (one mapped ahead, it is true, by Cordwainer Smith, J. G. Ballard and Jack Vance), no doubt to the detriment of his appeal to the larger commercial audience. My own novels and stories have sold modestly and gained awards in Australia and the USA.

In the late 1990s, newer writers were exploding into existence. Some of them, finally, were women, although successful Australian women fantasists including Sara Douglass, Rosaleen Love, Isobelle Carmody, Lucy

Sussex, Leanne Frahm, Jane Routley, Kim Wilkins, Kate Forsyth, Beverley Macdonald and Shannah Jay (Sherry-Ann Jacobs) have tended to prefer varieties of Gothicized or satiric or heroic fantasy (the latter favored by Keith Taylor, Garth Nix, Dirk Strasser and several other male writers), ghost stories or the uncanny. Other women of considerable gifts have written little, regrettably: these include the superb Philippa Maddern, Yvonne Rousseau, Petrina Smith. The many indigenous Australian Aboriginal or Koori cultures are drenched in a complex mythos known as the Dreaming, yet few black writers have emerged as fantasy or sf writers in English; three who have are Sam Watson, Archie Weller and Eric Willmot. Mudrooroo Nyoongah, formerly Colin Johnson, apparently not of Aboriginal descent but accepted by tribal elders as one of their number, has published important fiction on the margins of these genres, as has B. Wongar, the alias of Sreten Bozic, a Yugoslav immigrant also accepted among tribal Kooris.

Among the best of the sf newcomers, some prolific (and mostly men), are Sean Williams and Shane Dix (frequently writing together, and in 2003 on the *New York Times* best-seller list with a *Star Wars*-franchise trilogy, *The New Jedi Order: Force Heretic)*, Stephen Dedman, Sean Williams, Paul Voermans, Tess Williams, Simon Brown, Richard Harland, Andrew Whitmore and Russell Blackford (whose *Terminator* trilogy strove to break free of its own franchise constraints). Children's and Young Adult sf or fantasy, long ago colonized by veterans Mary Pratchett, Patricia Wrightston and Ivan Southall, is booming again and attracting awards, from such authors as John Marsden, Robin Klein, Paul Jennings, Gillian Rubinstein, Victor Kelleher, Catherine Jinks, Gary Crew, Sophie Masson, Brian Caswell, Caroline Macdonald, Dave Luckett, Sue Isle and Rory Barnes. Most of those names are just now starting to become familiar to readers in the USA, the UK and Europe, so most are still performing their impressive pyrotechnics in an off-off-off Broadway dive, south of the equator where the seasons are reversed and the local heroes are heralded more for their sporting prowess, their golden swim-suited bodies and their awesome capacity for beer than for their brilliant imagination.

iii

Sometimes this is understandable. Sf published in Australia has often been under less pressure than work submitted successfully in the great metropolitan centers. To explain what I mean, take a quick look at some examples, some modestly successful, some dire, most of them, interestingly, by immigrant writers (all but Blackford, in fact). At the nadir are works like the late stories of British-Australian Jack Wodhams, who published such tormented sentences that sometimes I was simply incapable of staying around long enough to learn if he was saying anything with them. Consider these examples from his *Future War*, published by the small press house Void:

> Trying to be as invisible as possible, Purdo slowly hastened his vehicle on as fast as he dared, his head squirming on his neck worse than he had ever previously experienced . . . Little bubbles swole to soar and burst in his brain, showering him with fever, to drench him in panic, a gross consciousness of his vulnerability . . .
>
> He'd seen *me,* and this alone mandated his prompt elimination to be the most sensibly prudent action . . . (3, 113)

By superior contrast, Wodhams' *Ryn* (Cory & Collins, 1982) was his best work to date, never published outside Australia, a funny and inventive look at reincarnation gone wrong. What do you do if you wake up in a baby's body? Wodhams offered some startling answers; annoyingly, a puncture in the last chapter let all the air out. Worse, while some of the dialogue is apt, the narrative voice leaves the impression, as usual, of being translated inexpensively from the Finnish: `Youth . . . Without its ignorance, a thought or word or deed would cease to present a challenge, a tree, a raft, a cave to no longer offer speculation to defiance and adventure' (182); `And she laughed, a pure tinkling sound that made me quite despond that I might ever see her known temper ever directed against myself' (169).

This sort of work was published with the assistance of the Literature Board of the Australia Council, a funding body whose occasional if fallible benefice provided much of the support for Antipodean sf in the last three decades or so. The Board got a rather better return on their investment with David Lake's *Ring of Truth* (1982), from the same small firm. Lake was an uneven writer who has fallen silent. This particular novel was superior to his previous fiction; it can be savaged on scientific grounds—the story of an inverted cosmos cannot be discussed without spoiling its slow revelations—but Lake's images of a genuinely strange reality function at a level of enchantment that dispels such criticism. A deconstructed sword & sorcery novel from the same publisher, Russell Blackford's *The Tempting of the Witch King* (1983), showed in a minor key that locally published work need not be unsatisfying. By then the heroic fantasy genre, after its major boost with the rediscovery of Tolkien in the late 1960s, had proliferated and run mad. Oily barbarians of the Conan variety usually vied with whimsical blue unicorns and gum-chewing sorcerer's apprentices. Not so in Blackford's somber essay into this revival of mythic realism. Fritz Leiber and Michael Moorcock defined the ground, dislocating their worlds from ours by more than time. Magic functions here, and in a curiously Aristotelian manner (if you can conceive of Aristotle as a Druid). The principal agents are gods, largely kept off stage; one of Blackford's is a delightful ego-obsessed minx who might have cavorted in pastoral garb quite happily with Marie Antoinette. War is stripped to classic terms of strategy and tactics, motives (as in archaic tales) are left as reflections of higher conflicts. This is close to the way we must see our prospects today, perhaps: entirely beyond rational reckoning.

Bertram Chandler tried something brave with his thorny, non-generic take on allohistory. After years of routine adventurer tales with his Hornblower of space, John Grimes (in one, *The Anarch Lords*, 1981, Grimes is punished for piracy by being made Governor of a world settled by anarchists; the analogy with William Bligh was deliberate), he turned to the legend of Ned Kelly, the celebrated Australian bushranger. Unlike Peter Carey's much later literary take on the doomed trajectory of working class Irish against British police and owners, *True History of the Kelly Gang* (2000), Chandler's altered history turned the Siege of Glenrowan into the start of an Australian War of Independence. If Ned Kelly had not been betrayed, captured by troopers and hanged in Melbourne in 1880, might he have gone on to become President of an Australian Republic? Granted such shifts in the fulcrum of history, how would the world a century later have turned out? Chandler's *Kelly Country* (1983) avoided standard glib adventure formats in creating his version of the parallel universe tale, at the risk of thickening his story to a yawn. Plenty happens, but in jumps and set-pieces which convince us that Kelly might have used available advanced technology in his cause (aircraft, machine-guns), without really making us care very much. Chandler's Kelly is a charismatic leader who needs plenty of pushing from behind, notably by sister Kate and by `Red Kitty', a Marxist noble who met Rosa Luxemburg in Poland (the chronology is wrong by a decade or so). Breaker Morant and Louisa Lawson do rather nicely in this version of history, and the American multinational corporations do even better in the colony they have helped liberate. Perhaps the most provocative aspect is Chandler's view of the Irish Catholic Republic of the 1980s, fighting on in Vietnam after the Kennedy-ruled USA has pulled out, ultimately vaporizing Hanoi with a borrowed nuclear weapon. His scorn is refreshing; regrettably, Chandler's style remained contaminated by pulp diction (`her almost violet eyes', `her wide scarlet slash of a mouth').

iv

These comments have conveyed only the sketchiest, impressionistic sense of sf's trajectory in Australia. Regarded from the perspective of the world stage, or at least the English-reading parts of it, the most notable absentees are Greg Egan and George Turner. I have dealt at some length with Egan in *Transrealist Fiction* (2000). Turner gained his first sf reputation as a savage technical reviewer, often with a political axe or two to grind, and only later chanced his own hand at science fiction. His impact was powerful and considerable, at least in some parts of the USA. His earlier novels had been thoroughly orthodox to the realist tradition; amusingly, *The Cupboard Under The Stairs* shared the 1962 Miles Franklin Award with Thea Astley's *The Well Dressed Explorer* (recall her dismay at suspecting that her novel *Reaching Tin River* might be turning into `sci fi').

One way to explore the secret or intractable woes of our time is by inventing and populating landscapes in centuries to come. Abused though it has been by propagandists and complacent adventure writers, there is life left in this gambit; not surprisingly, its best practitioners are, above all, astute observers of their own surroundings. In the 1960s, Turner's well-received and absolutely *non*-sf novels shared a common small-town Australian setting. His characters were driven (sometimes to madness) by psychological demons, and disabled by social constraints. Well enough received, there was always something suspiciously schematic about these `Treelake' books. Yet if the schematic is a weakness in the strictly mundane novel, it can be a positive advantage for sf, where every detail of the world must be built from scratch. And so it proved. Turner's first sf book, *Beloved Son*, was a remarkable composite of post-nuclear holocaust, the social treason of gene-mongering biologists, the moralities of politics and manipulative psychiatry, and the hazards of the religious impulse. Certainly it is significant that Turner's background as a fiction writer was in adult, naturalistic fiction rather than adolescent wish-fulfilments. What was new in this blend (at least for non-European sf) was noted by Polish-American writer George Zebrowski, who had waited almost in vain for 'imaginative developments . . . presented together with realism and truthfulness about human beings' (*F&SF*, April 1981, 56). He could name only two current successes of this kind, 'where the writer enters the hearts and minds of his characters'. One was *Beloved Son*.

In Judith Buckrich's *George Turner: A Life,* some startling claims are made about the baleful response of at least one reviewer in his own country, Australia. At any rate, I found them startling, perhaps because I was that reviewer. I 'was fast becoming Turner's literary enemy' (Buckrich, 1999, 153). Turner is quoted as calling my review of his third sf novel a 'screech'. You could easily get the impression that Turner was a victim of the well-known 'prophet in his own land' rebuff. He might have felt that, although his actual assessment of my notice of *Yesterday's Men* was 'a screech of fury'; he added that 'when opinions differ so violently about my work I must be getting *something* right. The infuriated reader is paying as much attention, though of a different kind, as the satisfied one' (*In the Heart or in the Head,* 197). In fact, as I asserted at the time of Turner's venture into the genre with *Beloved Son* in 1978, it might be argued that Australian science fiction came of age—if such a biologizing metaphor makes any sense—with that novel. Science fiction, as I have argued, has its own legitimate rules, by no means identical with those of the novel of manners, the kitchen sink drama or the poetics of existential despair, but generally its possibilities have been squandered, particularly in mass market commercial publishing. But while there is none of the regular Boys' Own precocity in Turner's sf which caused Thomas M. Disch to declare sf a branch of children's literature, still one might consider the following harsh estimate:

> He has worked hard. Every character is strongly individualized—but has no existence outside his idiosyncratic features. The dialogue is tailored craftily to character—and reads like a transcription.... Each character is carefully observed for realism—and struts his realism under the

wary control of the puppet master.

It is a demonstration of the powers of a man who plainly knows the mechanics of literature but lacks the urgency of belief or involvement to enable him to record a living experience. The characters become finally unacceptable; the intellect agrees that they could—only just could—behave as [the author] makes them do, but the emotions reject them.

This long quotation is not about Turner's work, although it could be. It is drawn from a critical article Turner himself wrote in 1971; the author in question is the notable Canadian sf writer A. E. van Vogt.[19] Curiously, the van Vogt book in question shared a central theme with *Beloved Son* and many of its successors in Turner's now substantial body of sf: the role of the immediately post-pubescent in a collapsing society. It was van Vogt's treatment of that theme which outraged Turner even more than the questionable characterization. What kinds of self-determination can the young be permitted by those in power? Who should give them guidance, and what kind? Nearly all Turner's sf novels can be seen, tangentially at least, as providing his own reply to these questions, his answer to van Vogt's rightwing libertarianism.

Most of Turner's pungent remarks about van Vogt (a fair representative of traditional sf and its mechanics) prove to return upon his own textuality. Certainly my own emotions reject almost all the characters in *Beloved Son*. Least believable is his protagonist, the Australian Albert Raft, whose descent into psychopathic megalomania was so implausible that it had to be ascribed to the misfiring application of psycho-chemical interrogation. Unlikely enough in itself, what is worse is that this fudging meant that the pivotal psychic change in the novel resulted from an accident rather than from growth, response or revelation of character.

In 1992, civilization has imploded under its own weight, but not before the first starship is launched. Forty years later, its hibernating crew of scientists returns to the new society born from the rubble. This is an unsteady society of youthful technocrats marching to the subliminal tune of reductive and totalitarian biologists. Most adults have been murdered in a monstrous pogrom. Crystals in a supersaturated solution, the 20th

---

[19] Regrettably, the source of this citation is now lost; presumably it is from an Australian fanzine review or article of that period.

century revenants precipitate Brave New World into an Elmer Gantry crusade. This major theme is heralded by Turner's epigraph, from hymnist A. C. Ainger, tagged mockingly as *The Truth About History:*

> Nearer and nearer draws the time, the time that shall surely be,
> When the earth shall be filled with the glory of God as the waters cover the sea.

Turner's apocalypse is, intentionally, just as nasty and banal as that. And yet his unsealing of the biblical scrolls is conducted with a heightened, romantic realism; none of his characters is without a feverish flush to his cheek (there are few women, all bad news). They tend, in a somewhat shocking trope common to Turner's fiction, to hiss and spit poisonously at each other, lending a peculiarly prissy tone to the confrontation of allegedly hard types. Indeed the only agreeable character in *Beloved Son* is Arthur, a sharp-tongued homosexual clone whose blatancy transcends the whiff of maiden-aunt in the rest. Arthur is an exemplar of the controlled baroque melodrama that provides the book's best scenes.

By and large, Turner worked in a realist register, which is why failures of verisimilitude became culpable flaws, errors of judgment, where in a non-mimetic register they might be permissible or even triumphant. Here is Peter, a 17-year old revolutionary. At one point he is seen `whistling and gesticulating from a window, very much the high-spirited youngster at play' (264). At another, he delivers this impromptu retort (`with heavy irony') in a voice fatally similar to the elderly Turner's own:

> `This is the era of organized rifts. Each man has his place, his assured progress and a more or less ordained end. Society runs on sets of parallel tracks, exchanging signals but not visiting crosstrack. The rifts are ethical; one just does not impress himself on what another does.' (221)

Turner's loving indulgence in set-pieces foreshadowed the rediscovery, by his innocent demagogues, of manipulatory political theatre. But finally that rediscovery seemed contrived, essentially an artifact, a *function* of Turner's auctorial dynamic. His critical writings, which first established Turner's reputation in the sf world, reveal his profound interest in the structural, formal constraints of novel-making. Still more, they show a strenuous advocate of psychological and moral integrity in the presentation of character. It was odd, then, to find these strictures abandoned so easily in his own work. None of this is to deny that *Beloved Son* and his subsequent novels deserve the close attention they have received from critics in Australia, the UK and the USA. One judges *cordon bleu* cuisine by more stringent standards than a packet of candy. Most sf remains confectionery; Turner slaved repeatedly for us over a hot stove, and his partial failures are of more value than the easy successes of market-driven entertainments. For all that, his crotchets and weaknesses need to be observed if not reproached, because his was one of the few voices attempting to speak science fiction in resolutely adult accents.

Five years after that first attempt to fuse the fictive devices of sf with his punctilious, thoughtful and sometimes savage realism, Turner's *Vaneglory* tightened the screws on his brave new world in a fresh exploration of the ultimate Faustian lure (and sf commonplace): indefinite physical longevity. One of his characters advised Akhnaton, another is at least 30,000 years old. Naturally, they are no longer very human. By re-using the same universe, thickened and clotted with the gradual revelations of its immortal residents lurking in the interstices, Turner saved himself a lot of legwork. And there are considerable pleasures for the reader in the know who can watch the working-out of implications in the earlier book. The method has its drawbacks, of course—those who have not read *Beloved Son* might be slightly unnerved, without quite knowing why, between a certain sentence of *Vaneglory* and its successor. The reason is that, strictly speaking, the whole of the former book should slip neatly into that space.

The decision makers of Turner's simplified arena are technocratic Boy Scouts who purged history's nightmare by murdering those of the old order who remained. Into this clarified social agar-agar Turner introduced his selected micro-organisms (returned star-travelers, covert immortals) and watched the Petri dish as keenly as any bacteriologist studying a lab preparation. Turner's Commissioners of Security, as supremely ethical as Richard Nixon's Mormons, must deal personally with the intolerable temptation of extended life, and do so against as background nearly as bare as myth's. One question, of course, is: Who shall guard the Guardians? Another, even more poignant, is: On what basis can the most faithful of Guardians—or anyone else for that matter—shape their decisions wisely when their options are unprecedented? The solution Turner advanced was not quite that of the archetypal peasant mob muttering with flaming brands toward Frankenstein's castle, but the resemblance was there. One of the provocative pleasures of the book is the implicit challenge for the reader to discern any alternative solution.

Finally, though, what was distinctive about Turner's use of sf as a vehicle for serious writing was not merely his determined thinking. It was his feeling, his sympathy for his characters. And that is strange enough, for one of the points he makes is that immortals are finally inhuman. The adaptation to such a singular state renders them isolate, alien. By their own standards, empathy with the mayfly humans among whom they dwell is evidence of psychosis. In much previous sf, this remote smugness of *Homo superior* was a suspicious evidence of strange compensatory fantasies in its readers (recall Heinlein's `Gulf'), giving rise to the pointed gibe that `sf' is short for `speculative fascism'. Not so here. The immortals Angus and Alastair (who speak a very pleasing Glaswegian when called on to do so), the ageless bitch Jeanie and her gang-pressed human Scots lover Donald, mercenary and inheritor of all Scotland, the starfarer James Lindley, and the Security Commissioners Beckett and Ferendija—each is arguable as fully dimensioned as any character in Turner's domestic `Treelake' sequence (an assessment Turner, interestingly, repudiated). That very fact made *Vaneglory* altogether too real for most habitual sf readers. Fifteen years earlier, before he rose to his own challenge, Turner as critic wrote of the majority of sf fans that they `have yet to learn that the real pleasure of literature begins on the day you stop using it as a drug'. All too many preferred the oozing wallow of yet another franchise volume to Turner's astringency.

Perhaps the gravest problem with his work was the sense that it was drenched in his own personality, for all its attempts upon a futurist and minatory objectivity. `A writer's self is not easily discerned in his fictions,' he declared in an interview in the Australian literary journal *Overland* (`Some unperceived wisdom', 1983, 27), but that is clearly a matter of degree. In the same issue, the critic Frank Kellaway celebrated Turner's writing career. He made it quite plain that one of the sticking points for many readers, confronted by Turner's distinctive manner, is the degree to which a conspicuous narrative voice saturates description, dialogue and interior meditation alike. Kellaway neatly turned this perception to advantage. Graham Greene and Dostoievsky, too, portrayed reality `in the distorting mirrors of their own personalities' (1983, 11). Do we decry them for not being Flauberts, Tolstoys? Of course not. But the formalisms and personal tics of such writings do strip naked, to some extent, the anonymity of the creator's private self. Doubtless no single character in a Turner novel was drawn from his own skin and bone. Yet in a general sense all were, distorted and simplified clones, rather in the manner pictured by Transactional Analysis: each self comprised of adult, child and parent. Kellaway admitted that `they are all "Turneresque" and speak a heightened, stylised dialogue' (13).

Such a method could never succeed as pure naturalism, but Turner specialized in exploring ethical and emotional problems within a schematic frame. His mainstream novels treated such topics as courage and responsibility under fire, alcoholism, madness. Following his shift from realist to science fictive narrative, his scope broadened into large-scale social and political issues ranging from the nature of ideology to the impact of drastic ecologic and technological change. True to a core sf impulse his narratives were less concerned with the morality of single personal choices (although his tales depended upon these, of course) than with those which shape histories.

It is unsurprising, therefore, that Turner availed himself of the literary armamentarium most adapted to these aims. All the more curious, then, that in this trilogy of loosely-connected sf novels the writer's presence in his work became acutely painful. No doubt this unease was focussed by the return in *Yesterday's Men* to a transformed version of the site of Turner's first mainstream novel. *Young Man of Talent* (1959), a novel of character set in the 1940s jungle war of New Guinea, is tautly structured and quite terrifyingly real when allowance is made for Turner's distancing formalism. Even more than the episodic earlier sf books, *Yesterday's Men* lurched from scene to arbitrary scene like a poorly dramatized documentary. Presumably this failure of control was the price of Turner's evident wish to prove a point at any cost. In his stinging literary criticism, he never failed to rebuke those lazy sf writers who either romanticized war or denounced soldiers as mindless thugs. In his own attempt to show what make a warrior tick, crisp delineation was spoilt by elements of rant and venom which could only have their source outside the fictive universe of the trilogy.

A notable example, echoing similar treatment of women in his earlier sf novels, is the Courtesan Anna-Lisa, a tough-minded woman referred to by virtually everyone as `a common bitch' or `that harlot'. She ends (and, one cannot help but think, appropriately, given her discursive construction) with a dislocated shoulder, half her ribs cracked, and one eye gouged out.

While Turner was here describing a social order of which he disapproved, this narrative misogyny in all three volumes grew increasingly hard to bear. It is not irrelevant or `politically correct' to complain of it, because it seems salient to Turner's ultimate revelation: `Man's basic nature doesn't change with circumstances' (117).

In short, Turner seemed to be deploying an account of the world familiar from Heinlein and his epigones. `Who seeds the universe must preserve elemental savagery. If, that is, he can harness it and not waste it on cruelty, greed and vicarious murder' (221). An admirable sergeant, repudiating any relish for killing, explains nonetheless, like any Neanderthal patriarch, that what he enjoys is `Power. Command. Challenge. Responsibility for other men's lives. . . . Being top man of the family' (217). Still, when the emotional cripples of the cast of *Yesterday's Men* do not entirely paralyze the tale with the ceaseless `sulking', `spitting with anger' and `spite', it provides a convincing portrait of warriors doing a job, and an interestingly cynical analysis of the deforming influences which make them ready to do it.

V

If these books created critical interest in Turner's sf, his *magnum opus*—eagerly awaited, heralded as Australia's finest sf novel—was *The Sea and Summer*, known in the USA as *The Drowning Towers*, runner-up for the prestigious mainstream Commonwealth Prize and the Campbell Memorial award. In fifty years' time, the Greenhouse Effect is drowning the world's coastal terrain, including Melbourne. Ninety percent of Australians are unemployable Swill, bleakly enduring Goyaesque conditions in vast tower blocks. As in *Nature's End* and other gruesome warning going back at least to Harry Harrison's *Make Room! Make Room!*, environmental ruin provokes a plan to cull the human population. In a review, the Honorable Barry Jones, founder of the now defunct Australian Commission for the Future, compared Turner to George Orwell and Margaret Atwood: the purpose of his fiction, Jones felt, `is to highlight possibilities deserving urgent thought.' Yet the novel got a puzzleheaded notice in the metropolitan Melbourne *Age* broadsheet from the late John Hanrahan, an astute reviewer evidently incapable of the squint of perspective needed to take in fiction set beyond the present day's comfortable certitudes. Hanrahan felt its inventions called for `a fairly energetic suspension of disbelief.' In Turner's future, to Hanrahan's bafflement, `the big social issues of our time, feminism and Aboriginal land rights, are not worth a mention.' Perhaps it takes a regular dose of sf to see that any future resembling a global concentration camp would not necessarily indulge the moral qualms of our age of last-ditch abundance. Of course, it is equally true that it requires sf to see that resource ruin is not inevitable in an era in which technological change is accelerating exponentially, an ameliorative proposition Turner would have laughed to scorn. Yet what is finally most impressive about *The Sea and Summer* is the portrait of two Swill brothers made good, a policeman (the sort of role Turner would use again and again) and a brilliant self-serving criminal. There is depth in these portraits, even if the environment they inhabit is not especially well-thought through (what Western government would construct, at great cost, vast termitaries on the edge of a flooding Greenhouse coast?).

Later Turner novels showed the same strengths and weaknesses, but perhaps his finest was not *The Sea and Summer* but the uncompromising *Genetic Soldier* (1994). As in *Beloved Son*, a returned time-dilated crew finds an Earth incomprehensibly changed; but now the elapsed time is a thousand years or more, and the world has been reshaped by the aftermath of Greenhouse catastrophe. Turner's blend of resurgent aboriginal culture, matriarchy, genetically engineered sexual constraints, and local power politics, together with the inevitable clash of cultures old and new, genuinely opened possibilities for Australian sf that nobody else has yet pursued.

A stickler for mainstream virtues, George Turner was Australian sf's Grand Old Man in more ways than age alone. It is frankly astonishing to realize that he was born four years earlier than Asimov, Bradbury and Frank Herbert, that he was already 23 when Heinlein's first story was published. Devoted to a belief that sf should challenge conventions, especially its own, Turner rasped away at such formulaic devices as superhuman powers, immortality, space colonies, and smote our lethargy over impending Greenhouse doom. If his dialogue was woefully mannered and his tales didactic, in a medium liable to colonization by pap merchants his soldierly gristle had its uses. Turner, like science fiction generally in Australia, was dispossessed, standing at a skeptical angle to the social verities.

vi

There are varieties of dispossession. I would like to show you some snapshots of this metaphoric sub-continent of the main, where the great world is the Future itself, as seen by those who have seized it: *America*, as H. Bruce Franklin termed it in the telling sub-title to his fine study of the sf of Robert A. Heinlein, *as science fiction*.

In 1985, in an anthology dedicated to Ursula Le Guin and Gene Wolfey—those wonderful writers and American (of course) Guests of Honor at AussieCon II, the second World Science Fiction Convention held in Australia—I tried to position that moment against local generic history:

> Here is an odd fact. I encourage you to marvel at it:
> Not until twenty years ago was the first mass-market sf collection by an Australian published in Australia.
> Why is this surprising? Well, after all, science fiction was hardly brand-new, in the world at large, twenty years ago. H. G. Wells, its major innovator, had been dead since 1946. Hiroshima and Nagasaki, by 1965, were already ash two decades past. So was the fabled American Golden Age of sf.
> Indeed, at that very moment the New Wave of rebellion against Golden Age science fiction was beginning to roll in Britain. Brian Aldiss and Cordwainer Smith and Samuel R. Delany and Tom Disch were recasting the nature of the genre. And we in Australia were . . . what? Sending out our first collection to sniff the air. (As it chanced, this novelty was a small pulpy gathering of my own small inept stories.) (*Strange Attractors*, 7)

Three years after that embarrassing collection, *A Man Returned* (1965), had appeared, nearly two generations ago, Australian sf writer and editor John Baxter compiled *The Pacific Book of Australian Science Fiction*, also the first of its kind. He was coolly ironic, as is his way (as is the Australian way, indeed):

> Nobody has ever been able adequately to define the dimension and effect of the sense of wonder; like a trace element, it is only noticeable when it is not there. One could be sure, however, that Australia did not have it. The science fiction produced here was weak stuff, feeble, deriva-

tive, lacking the spark of imagination, of wonder, which enlivened that written in Britain and the United States. Worse, there was no strong national character in what was produced. It might as well have been written by people *from* another planet as *about* them. (Baxter, 1968, unpaginated introduction)

That was a candid admission for the second paragraph of such a volume. Luckily, Baxter found, matters had improved since the late fifties:

> . . . Australian artistic life has renewed itself in a wave of innovation and experiment. Patrick White, Sidney Nolan, Richard Meale and Judith Wright have provided us for the first time with a legitimate national voice . . . The stimulus of their work has penetrated into many areas, one of the most unexpected of them being science fiction.

Even so,

> There is a colony of new and imaginative writers, a mild climate of acceptance, and a measure of support here and abroad, but that is all.

A colony within a colony, of course. Nearly a decade later, in 1977, I introduced a comparable anthology thus:

> Science fiction in Australian?
> Why, yes. It burgeons and thrives . . . in 1975—*annus mirabilis!*—the prestigious World Science Fiction Convention itself, snatched like the America's Cup from its traditional trustees, enlivened the Southern Cross Hotel . . .
> Yes indeed. Warm-blooded, clawed and billed, it hatches and suckles its young, glides daringly from tall eucalyptus trees . . . Alas, it carries a Qantas ticket in its pouch. (*The Zeitgeist Machine*, 1)

That was true then, piercingly so, as a generation and more of cultural expatriates testify. To remain in Australia's wide brown land was to be subject to that tyranny of distance cited earlier, to suffer exclusion (it was an agony) from the company of true adults, artists, wheelers and dealers. It seems hard to imagine, a mere three decades on. But that was an epoch before wide-bodied jets carried off annually a tenth of the population of the land (or whatever the staggering figure is), before the same jets, and a score or two of wretched sinking fishing boats, fetched to Australia in their hundreds of thousands the multi-Colored, many-voiced peoples of all the suffering or ambitious earth. People coming of their own free choice! Amazing! And with their arrival they made up for the departed, who themselves, of course, returned for Christmas and arts festivals to be lionized, bearing Magi word from the centers of metropolitan culture. In 1977, then, matters hung at this crux (or so it seemed to me, who had not yet left Australia's shores even on a pilgrimage, except endlessly in mediated imagination):

> Australians subsist, as everyone agrees, in a hand-me-down culture. It is of the essence of culture, admittedly, as much to be transmitted as to be renewed, but ours is curiously threadbare and ill-fitting. If a son asks for bread, the odds are high indeed that his father will give him a stone (or a lamington). It's an inevitable irony, then—and so, perhaps, no irony at all—that the world's finest science fiction to date was forged to a significant degree in the Australian experience . . .
> . . . of an American writer, `Cordwainer Smith'. (4)

I had gone in search of Cordwainer Smith in 1965, when his second collection of sf stories, *Space Lords,* revealed that he was living at the time in Canberra. It named his stockbroker. A penniless student, I flew at once to find him out, and found only that I had missed him. His last book was *Norstrilia,* about the boy Roderick Frederick Ronald Arnold William MacArthur McBann from the immensely rich world Old North Australia. Here is how he described that planet:

> Somebody once singsonged it up, like this:
> `Gray lay the land, oh. Gray grass from sky to sky. Not near the weir, dear. Not a mountain, low or high—only hills and gray gray. Watch the dappled dimpled twinkles blooming on the star bar.
> `That is Norstrilia . . .
> `Beige-brown sheep lie on blue-gray grass while the clouds rush past, low overhead, like iron pipes ceilinging the world . . .' (cited, Broderick, 1977, 5)

`It is incantatory stuff,' I commented, `taking us away from ourselves (if we allow it to) to bring us back. No Australian employing the multiple tongues of science fiction has written so well out of his native experience as Linebarger did from several visits. Nor is it sufficient to retort that the genre is after all an instrument for amplifying American accents. It *is* that, but more deeply it is a transducer of the technological experience: the myth of the man/transistor interface. Our aspirations are linked ineluctably with the machine, with what the machine has done to and for us, and our world. We all press our mouths to the grease-nipple; for us, pity and terror are newly shaped, and can benefit from new means of expression' (5-6).

vii

The colonial experience roars like a flame in my decades-old words. Not the colonialism that whites (my immigrant forebears) imposed upon those native to the gray gray land (as they saw it, blinded by the Antipodean light and memories of impossible wet green), but what we already knew poignantly as the same CocaCola-nization that was winning the East as it had won the West. My myth, as you will have noticed, was not yet the *human/chip* interface, but its parochial and unthinkingly sexist grammatical predecessor. For all that, my lament was not simply, I think, a whine of exclusion. There were indeed attempts at an Aussie sf, I noted:

They spring sometimes direct from the American vocabulary and syntax; sometimes from the electrical/chemical revival of *Fin-de-siècle* voyage into sensory derangement; sometimes from the still-fruitful exercise of surrealist confrontation with irrational realities our bureaucratic enterprise would prefer to obliterate. Our second-hand culture may be dull and anxious to remain dull, but the implosions and exhalations of radical change are seldom contained for long by the strictures of rule-book efficiency experts. (6)

In such a climate (the leftish arts-encouraging Whitlam government of 1972-1975 had been voted out resoundingly after what amounted to a constitutional *coup*, perhaps connived at by covert US interests), could sf be in any sense authentically, peculiarly Australian? I thought it might, and said so with all the dubious hauteur of a colonial factor for finer values from elsewhere:

We are, on the whole, raw, vulgar; our communal tastes lack any hint of genuine cultivation. We excuse this coarseness by appeal to 'bush mateship', a pragmatics of social accord rendered in a crucible of harsh geography, scant resources, the root-severing distance from Europe.

All this special pleading is, of course, mendacious. Last time I looked at the figures, we were the most urbanized culture on earth: 86 percent of the population in cities, suburbs, largish towns. Electronic communication grids us so uncompromisingly into the globe that in one recent notorious epiphany the Australian public was told of important US military plans before the President managed to inform his American constituency. We are, if anything, the victims of technological triumph. If the bush once spoke to our shearers and poets, its voice is now hardly audible over the crash and screech of process-line, office equipment, television commercials, overpowered motor cars and jet-lagged impresarios. (10)

Five years later, in his *Australian Science Fiction* (1982), Van Ikin found a tradition steeped in anxieties of race, of loneliness, of utopian romance and political hope. Turning his pages, it is easy to agree with the concluding words of his historical introduction:

Never afraid to tackle the topical and controversial (although sometimes unable to deal with such material effectively), Australian sf has mirrored the nation's apprehensive fascination with its own unexplored emptiness, and its fear of forfeiting its never-too-clear racial identity. If the nation's early sf reveals Australians to have been racist, sexist, and materialistic, it also reveals their more altruistic utopian aspirations, and the more recent offerings of Australian sf show that ignoble attitudes are receding. (xxxvii)

It is notable that as Australians approached the second century of Federation in 2001, there was a resurgence of bigotry and sometimes violent hatred for non-British and more broadly non-European new arrivals, which intensified following the tragedy of September 11 and the bombings in Bali. A melting pot like the USA, but in thrall to any number of overseas owners, investors, gamblers and ideologues, Australia is now the very model of a postmodern landscape. One might argue, of course, that ructions over small venomous pockets of racist ardor prove the wholesome generosity, or at least live-and-let-live, fair-go ethos, of a genuine emerging multicultural, stranded community. One might hope so, at least. Certainly that is the future which recent significant science fiction has emphasized.

viii

Yet Australian sf writers and editors cannot avoid a nagging sense of insignificance, worsened by a perennial background drone, the mocking suggestion (as Ikin and Dowling noted in their 1993 anthology *Mortal Fire*) that `It's kids' stuff really, isn't it; I mean you don't see adults reading it, do you?' (xiii). Even granting that sf is not always kids' stuff, Ikin and Dowling found recurrent misunderstandings even among enthusiasts for the genre:

> `Why do we need Australian sf when Australia is such a small-time player in technology and has no real part in the space-race?'

Dowling made the obvious rejoinder: `The central issue here is really the assumption that science fiction must always be about space or technology. That's wrong . . . ' (xiii). Ikin added, tellingly for the topic at hand:

> It's also wrong to assume that science fiction is written by and for the big players. When science fiction deals with technology, it looks at its impact upon people and society, and that involves looking at the impact of small-time player-nations like Australia. Contemporary sf in particular will frequently align itself with the underdogs, looking at whiz-bang new development from the perspective of those on the receiving end . . . (xiv)

Big time, small time, those who deal from power, those at the receiving end `Down Under' (detestable phrase): all the vivid bruises, the flinching and defiant postures, of living and writing at the edge of the world. It is inescapable, even in attempted epiphany.

I will close, though, with one final characteristic and more hopeful snapshot, from my 1988 anthology *Matilda at the Speed of Light:*

It is 200 years since whites brought the seeds of an English-speaking culture to Australia; it is a suitable time for us to burst free, at last, from the twin tyrannies of distance and difference. If the past is another country, where they do things differently, so is the future—and we shall *all* be living there. It is suitable, as we hump our blueys to the strains of `Waltzing Matilda', that the songs we sing by the hot blue light of the late twentieth century furnace should be songs in that boundary-less tongue, that voice of fecund fiction, which is framed by science. (xv)

Matilda, as I said then, is waltzing no longer. Matilda is rushing into tomorrow, embracing rather than repudiating difference, beneath the blazing sign of the Centaurus stars invisible from those shores that gave science fiction birth, and we are rushing into tomorrow with her, at the speed of light.[20]

[20] This chapter is adapted from the introduction to the anthology of Australian science fiction edited by David G. Hartwell and me, *Centaurus: The Best of Australian Science Fiction*, New York: Tor, 1999. See that volume for a selection of exemplary recent Australian sf.

BIBLIOGRAPHY

I was tempted to omit publisher details except for editions quoted at some length in the text. In the day of the Internet and on-line book buying, traditional bibliographies seem absurdly redundant. Still, such omission might have been deemed simply slipshod, if not flagrantly ... *futuristic* ... and we cannot have that when discussing science fiction. I have deviated from custom, however, in one particular: books by each author are arranged alphabetically, rather than by date of publication, since that makes the hunt for a given title rather easier.

Adams, Fred, and Greg Laughlin, *Five Ages of the Universe: Inside the Physics of Eternity*, New York: The Free Press, 1999

Aldiss, Brian W., `How to be a Dinosaur: Seven Survivors', in Aldiss and Wingrove (1986)

Aldiss, Brian W., and David Wingrove, *Trillion Year Spree: History of Science Fiction, The*, London: Gollancz, 1986

Aldiss, Brian W., `A Kind of Artistry' [1963], in Aldiss, 1965

Aldiss, Brian W., `Old Hundredth', [1960], in Aldiss, 1965

Aldiss, Brian W., *Airs of Earth, The*, London: New English Library, 1965

Aldiss, Brian W., *Hothouse*, [1962] Wendover: Goodchild, 1984

Aldiss, Brian W., *Pale Shadow of Science, The*, Seattle: Serconia Press, 1985

Allen, Roger MacBride, *Isaac Asimov's Caliban*, New York: Ace, 1993

Allen, Roger MacBride, *Isaac Asimov's Inferno*, New York: Ace, 1994

Allen, Roger MacBride, *Isaac Asimov's Utopia*, New York: Ace, 1996

Amis, Kingsley, *New Maps of Hell*, London: Four Square, 1963

Amis, Kingsley, *Old Devils, The*, London: Hutchinson, 1986

Amis, Martin, *Einstein's Monsters*, London: Cape, 1987

Amis, Martin, *Money: a Suicide Note*, London: Cape, 1984

Amis, Martin, *Rachel Papers, The*, London: Jonathan Cape, 1973

Anderson, Poul, `Final Chapter', [1954] in Broderick (2001)

Anderson, Poul, *Genesis*, New York: Tor Books, 2000

Anderson, Poul, *Enemy Stars, The*, [1959 as *We Have Fed Our Sea*] in Dann, et al, eds (1997)

Anderson, Poul, *There Will Be Time*, [1973] in Dann, et al, eds (1997)

Andre-Driussi, Michael, *Lexicon Urthus: A Dictionary of the Urth Cycle*, San Francisco: Sirius, 1994

Asimov, Isaac, `Belief', in *Alternate Asimovs, The*

Asimov, Isaac, *Alternate Asimovs, The*, London: Panther, 1987

Asimov, Isaac, *Asimov on Science Fiction*, London: Granada, 1983

Asimov, Isaac, *Caves of Steel, The*, London: Panther, 1958

Asimov, Isaac, *End of Eternity, The*, London: Panther, 1959

Asimov, Isaac, *Fantastic Voyage II: Destination Brain*, London: Granada, 1987

Asimov, Isaac, *Fantastic Voyage*, New York: Houghton Mifflin, 1966

Asimov, Isaac, *Forward the Foundation*, London: Granada, 1993

Asimov, Isaac, *Foundation and Earth*, London: Granada, 1986

Asimov, Isaac, *Foundation's Edge*, London: Granada, 1983

Asimov, Isaac, *Grow Old With Me*, in *Alternate Asimovs, The* (1987)

Asimov, Isaac, *I. Asimov*, New York: Doubleday, 1994

Asimov, Isaac, *In Memory Yet Green: The Autobiography of Isaac Asimov, 1920-1954*, New York, Doubleday, 1979

Asimov, Isaac, *Naked Sun, The*, London: Panther, 1960

Asimov, Isaac, *Pebble in the Sky*, [1950] London: Grafton, 1986

Asimov, Isaac, *Prelude to Foundation*, London: Granada, 1988

Asimov, Isaac, *Robots and Empire*, London: Granada, 1985

Asimov, Isaac, *Robots of Dawn, The*, London: Granada, 1984

Astley, Thea, *Reaching Tin River*, Port Melbourne, Vic.: William Heinemann Australia, 1990

Astley, Thea, *Well Dressed Explorer, The*, Sydney: Angus and Robertson, 1962

Ballard, J. G., `The Waiting Grounds', in *The Day of Forever*, [1960] London: Panther, 1967

Banks, Iain M., *Against a Dark Background*, New York: Bantam Spectra,

1993

   Banks, Iain M., *Consider Phlebas*, London: Macmillan, 1987

   Banks, Iain M., *Player of Games, The*, London: Macmillan, 1988

   Banks, Iain M., *Use of Weapons*, London: Orbit, 1990

   Banks, Iain, *Wasp Factory, The*, London: Macmillan, 1984

   Barclay, Glen St John, *Anatomy of Horror: Masters of Occult Fiction, The*, London: Weidenfeld and Nicolson, 1978

   Barnes, John, *Finity*, New York: Tor Books, 1999

   Barnes, John, *Mother of Storms*, London: Millennium, 1994

   Barnes, John, *Patton's Spaceship*, New York: HarperPrism, 1997

   Baxter, John, ed., *Pacific Book of Australian Science Fiction, The*, Sydney: Angus & Robertson, 1968

   Bear, Greg, *Beyond Heaven's River*, [1980] London: Gollancz, 1988

   Bear, Greg, *Blood Music*, London: Gollancz, 1986

   Bear, Greg, *Eon*, London: Gollancz, 1986

   Bear, Greg, *Eternity*, London: Gollancz, 1989

   Bear, Greg, *Queen of Angels*, London: Gollancz, 1990

   Benford, Gregory, `Real Science, Imaginary Worlds', *New York Review of Science Fiction*, 65, 1994a

   Benford, Gregory, `Stephen Baxter's *Riding the Rock* in Context', *New York Review of Science Fiction*, 175, 2003

   Benford, Gregory, *Deeper Than the Darkness*, New York: Ace, 1970

   Benford, Gregory, *Furious Gulf*, London: Gollancz, 1994

   Benford, Gregory, *Great Sky River*, London: Gollancz, 1988

   Benford, Gregory, *In the Ocean of Night*, London: Futura, 1978

   Benford, Gregory, *Sailing Bright Eternity*, London: Gollancz, 1995

   Benford, Gregory, *Stars in Shroud, The*, New York: Berkley-Putnam, 1978

   Benford, Gregory, *Tides of Light*, London: Gollancz, 1989

   Benford, Gregory and Gordon Eklund, *Find the Changeling*, New York: Dell, 1980

   Benford, Gregory and Gordon Eklund, *If the Stars are Gods*, New York: Berkley, 1978

   Beresford, J. D., *Hampdenshire Wonder, The*, London: Sidgwick & Jackson, 1911

   Bester, Alfred, `5,271,009', in *Starlight* (1976)

   Bester, Alfred, Interview with Darrell Schweitzer, *SF Voices*, Timore, Maryland: T-K Graphics, 1976

   Bester, Alfred, `Four-Hour Fugue', in *Starlight* (1976)

Bester, Alfred, `My Affair With Science Fiction', in *Starlight* (1976)

Bester, Alfred, *Computer Connection, The,* see *Extro*

Bester, Alfred, *Deceivers, The,* New York: Simon & Schuster, 1981

Bester, Alfred, *Demolished Man, The,* [1953] Harmondsworth: Penguin, 1966

Bester, Alfred, *Extro,* 1974] London: Methuen, 1975

Bester, Alfred, *Golem^{100},* New York: Simon & Schuster, 1980

Bester, Alfred, *Starlight: Great Short Fiction of Alfred Bester,* New York: Berkley, 1976

Bester, Alfred, *Stars My Destination, The,* see *Tiger! Tiger!* (1967)

Bester, Alfred, *Tiger! Tiger!* [1955] Harmondsworth: Penguin, 1967; Wendover: Goodchild, 1984

Bester, Alfred, and Roger Zelazny, *Psycho Shop,* New York: Vintage, 1998

Blackford, Russell, *Tempting of the Witch King, The,* Melbourne: Cory & Collins, 1983

Blackford, Russell, Van Ikin, and Sean McMullen, *Strange constellations: a history of Australian science fiction,* Westport, Conn.: Greenwood Press, 1999

Blanks, Harvey, *Captain Miracle,* Australian radio serial, late 1950s, n.d.

Blatty, William Peter, *Exorcist, The,* London: Blond and Briggs, 1971

Blish, James, *Cities in Flight,* [1955-62] New York: Avon, 1970

Blish, James, *Jack of Eagles* [1949] London: Arrow, 1975

Bradbury, Ray, *A Graveyard For Lunatics,* London: Grafton, 1990

Bradbury, Ray, *Dandelion Wine,* in *Novels of Ray Bradbury*

Bradbury, Ray, *Death Is A Lonely Business,* London: Grafton, 1986

Bradbury, Ray, *Fahrenheit 451,* in *Novels of Ray Bradbury*

Bradbury, Ray, *Novels of Ray Bradbury, The,* London: Granada, 1984

Bradbury, Ray, *Something Wicked This Way Comes,* in *Novels of Ray Bradbury, The*

Bradley, James, *The Deep Field,* Sydney: Sceptre, 1999

Broderick, Damien, ed. *Earth is but a Star: Excursions through Science Fiction to the Far Future,* Perth: University of Western Australia Press, 2001

Broderick, Damien, *Matilda at the Speed of Light: A New Anthology of Australian Science Fiction,* Sydney: Angus & Robertson, 1988

Broderick, Damien, *Reading by Starlight: Postmodern Science Fiction* London: Routledge, 1995

Broderick, Damien, *Spike: Accelerating into the Unimaginable Future , The* Sydney: Reed Books/New Holland, 1997; revised, New York, Tor, 2001b

Broderick, Damien, *Strange Attractors: Original Australian speculative fiction*, Hale & Iremonger, 1985

Broderick, Damien, *Transrealist Fiction: Writing in the Slipstream of Science*, Conn: Greenwood Press, 2000

Broderick, Damien, *Zeitgeist Machine, The,* Sydney: Angus & Robertson, 1977

Brunner, John, `Earth is but a Star', in Broderick (2001)

Brunner, John, Review of *The Face in the Waters,* in *Foundation* 55, Summer 1992, pp. 82-84

Brunner, John, *Stand on Zanzibar*, London: Macdonald, 1969

Buckrich, Judith Raphael, *George Turner: A Life,* Melbourne: Melbourne University Press, 1999

Bujold, Lois McMaster, *Mirror Dance*, New York: Baen Books, 1997

Card, Orson Scott, `Originist', in *Maps in a Mirror,* London: Century, 1990

Carey, Peter, *True History of the Kelly Gang, The*, St. Lucia: University of Queensland Press, 2000

Carey, Peter, *Unusual History of Tristan Smith, The*, St. Lucia: University of Queensland Press, 1994

Carter, Raphael, *Fortunate Fall, The*, New York: Tor, [1996] 1997

Chandler, A. Bertram, *Anarch Lords, The*, New York: Daw, 1981

Chandler, A. Bertram, *Kelly Country*, Melbourne: Penguin, 1983

Cherryh, C. J., *Sunfall*, New York: Daw, 1981

Chesterton, G. K., *Man Who Was Thursday, The*, [1908] http://www.bartleby.com/158/9.html

Clarke, Arthur C., `Transcience', [1949] in Broderick (2001)

Clarke, Arthur C., *2001: A Space Odyssey*, London: Hutchinson, 1968

Clarke, Arthur C., *2010: Odyssey Two*, London: Granada ,1982

Clarke, Arthur C., *2061: Odyssey Three*, London: Grafton, 1988

Clarke, Arthur C., *3001: Final Odyssey, The* London: HarperCollins, 1997

Clarke, Arthur C., *Against the Fall of Night*, [1953] in *The Lion of Comarre*, London: Gollancz, 1970

Clarke, Arthur C., *Childhood's End*, London: Sidgwick & Jackson, 1954

Clarke, Arthur C., *City and the Stars, The*, [1956] London: Corgi, 1965

Clarke, Arthur C., *Fountains of Paradise, The*, London: Gollancz, 1979

Clarke, Arthur C., *Rendezvous with Rama*, London: Gollancz, 1973

Clarke, Arthur C. and Gentry Lee, *Cradle*, London: Gollancz, 1988

Clarke, Arthur C. and Gentry Lee, *Garden of Rama, The,* London:

Gollancz, 1991

Clarke, Arthur C. and Gentry Lee, *Rama II*, London: Gollancz, 1989

Clarke, Arthur C. and Gentry Lee, *Rama Revealed*, London: Gollancz, 1993

Clavell, James, *Shogun*, London: Hodder and Stoughton, 1975

Clement, Hal, *Mission of Gravity*, New York: Doubleday, 1954

Clifton, Mark, `Star, Bright', in Donald Wollheim, ed., *Prize Stories of Space and Time*, London: Weidenfeld & Nicolson, 1953

Clute, John and Peter Nicholls, *Encyclopedia of Science Fiction, second edition*, London: Orbit, 1993

Clute, John, `Marrying Out', *New York Review of Science Fiction*, 64, 1993

Clute, John, *Appleseed*, New York: Tor, January 2002

Clute, John, *Look at the Evidence: Essays & Reviews*, Liverpool: Liverpool University Press, 1995

Compton, D. G., *Hot Wireless Sets, Aspirin Tablets, the Sandpaper Sides of Used Matchboxes, and Something that Might Have Been Castor Oil*, London: Joseph, 1971

Cook, Kenneth, *Play Little Victims*, Rushcutters Bay, N.S.W.: Pergamon Press (Australia), 1978

Corbett, Nancy, *Heartland*, Sydney: Black Swan, 1989

Crowley, John, *Little, Big*, London: Gollancz, 1982

Dann, Jack, Pamela Sargent and George Zebrowski, eds, *Three In Space: Classic Novels of Space Travel*, Clarkston, GA: White Wolf, 1997

Dann, Jack, Pamela Sargent and George Zebrowski, eds, *Three In Time*, Clarkston, GA: White Wolf, 1997

Delany, Samuel R., `"Who is John Brunner . . . ?"', Baltimore: ConStellation Program book, 1983, pp. 27-32

Delany, Samuel R., *1984: Selected Letters*, Rutherford, N.J.: Voyant Publishing, 2000

Delany, Samuel R., *Babel-17*, New York: Ace, 1966

Delany, Samuel R., *Ballad of Beta-2, The*, New York: Ace, 1965

Delany, Samuel R., *Bridge of Lost Desire, The*, New York: Arbor House, 1987

Delany, Samuel R., *Captives of the Flame*, New York: Ace, 1963

Delany, Samuel R., *Dhalgren*, New York: Bantam, 1975

Delany, Samuel R., *Driftglass*, New York: Signet, 1971

Delany, Samuel R., *Einstein Intersection, The*, New York: Ace, 1967; corrected London: Gollancz, 1968, reprinted Bantam, 1981

Delany, Samuel R., *Empire Star*, New York: Ace, 1966

Delany, Samuel R., *Empire: A Visual Novel*, illustrated by Howard V. Chaykin, New York: Berkley Windhover, 1978

Delany, Samuel R., *Fall of the Towers, The*, [New York: Ace, 1965] Bantam, 1981

Delany, Samuel R., *Flight from Neveryon*, New York: Bantam, 1985

Delany, Samuel R., *Jewel-Hinged Jaw: Notes of [sic] the Language of Science Fiction, The*, New York: Berkely Windhover, 1978

Delany, Samuel R., *Jewels of Aptor, The*, New York: Ace, 1962

Delany, Samuel R., *Mad Man, The*, [1994] New York: Rhinoseros, 1996

Delany, Samuel R., *Motion of Light in Water: Sex and Science Fiction Writing in the East Village, 1957-1965, The*, New York: Arbor House, 1988; expanded edition, Paladin, 1990,

Delany, Samuel R., *Neveryóna*, New York: Bantam, 1983

Delany, Samuel R., *Nova*, London: Gollancz, 1968

Delany, Samuel R., *Starboard Wine: More notes on the language of science fiction*, Pleasantville, New York: Dragon Press, 1984

Delany, Samuel R., *Stars in my Pocket Like Grains of Sand*, [1984] New York: Bantam Spectra, 1985

Delany, Samuel R., *Straits of Messina, The*, Seattle: Serconia Press, 1989

Delany, Samuel R., *Tales of Neveryon*, New York: Bantam, 1979

Delany, Samuel R., *Triton: An Ambiguous Heterotopia*, New York: Bantam, 1976

Delany, Samuel, *Starboard Wine,* Pleasantville, New York: Dragon Press, 1984

Derrida, Jacques, *Of Grammatology*, [1967], trans. Gayatri Chakravorty Spivak, Baltimore: Johns Hopkins University Press, 1976

Dick, Philip K., *Divine Invasion, The*, New York: Timescape/Pocket Books, 1981

Dick, Philip K., *Dr. Bloodmoney*, New York: Dell, 1980

Dick, Philip K., *Three Stigmata of Palmer Eldritch, The*, [1964] London: Cape, 1966

Dick, Philip K., *Transmigration of Timothy Archer, The*, New York: Timescape, 1982

Dick, Philip K., *Ubik*, London: Panther/Granada, 1973

Dick, Philip K., *Valis*, New York: Bantam, 1981

Disch, Thomas M., *Camp Concentration*, London: Panther, 1969

Disch, Thomas M., ed., *New Improved Sun, The*, London: Hutchinson,

1976

Doctorow, Cory, *Down and Out in the Magic Kingdom*, New York: Tor, 2003; free download: www.craphound.com/down/download.php

Doctorow, E. L., *Billy Bathgate*, New York: Random House, 1989

Doctorow, E. L., *Ragtime*, New York: Random House, 1975

Dowling, Terry, and Van Ikin, *Mortal Fire: Best Australian SF*, Sydney: Coronet, 1993

Dozois, Gardner, *Strange Days*, Framingham, MA: NESFA Press, 2001

Dozois, Gardner, ed, *Furthest Horizon: SF Adventures to the Far Future, The*, New York: St. Martins Griffin, 2000

Easton, Thomas, *Silicon Karma*, Clarkston, GA: White Wolf, 1997

Egan, Greg, 'Wang's Carpets', in Hartwell and Broderick (1999)

Egan, Greg, *Diaspora*, London: Millennium, 1997

Egan, Greg, *Permutation City*, London: Millennium, 1994

Egan, Greg, *Quarantine*, London: Millennium, 1995

Egan, Greg, *Schild's Ladder,* London: Gollancz, 2002

Eldershaw, M. Barnard (Flora Sydney Patricia Eldershaw and Marjorie Faith Barnard), *Tomorrow and Tomorrow*. Melbourne: Georgian House, 1947; as *Tomorrow and Tomorrow and Tomorrow*, London: Virago Press, 1983

Elgin, Suzette Haden, *Judas Rose, The*, London: The Women's Press, 1988

Elgin, Suzette Haden, *Native Tongue*, New York: DAW, 1984

Farmer, Philip José, *Blown or Sketches Among the Ruins of my Mind; An Exorcism: Ritual Two*, [1969] London, Quartet, 1975

Farmer, Philip José, *Dark Design, The*, New York: Putnam, 1977

Farmer, Philip José, *Fabulous Riverboat, The*, New York: Putnam, 1971

Farmer, Philip José, *Gods of Riverworld, The*, New York: Putnam, 1983

Farmer, Philip José, *Image of the Beast: An Exorcism, Ritual One, The*, [1968] London: Quartet Books, 1975

Farmer, Philip José, *Magic Labyrinth, The*, New York: Putnam, 1980

Farmer, Philip José, *Riverworld War*, London: Granada, 1982

Farmer, Philip José, *To Your Scattered Bodies Go*, New York: Putnam, 1971

Fiedler, Leslie, 'Criticism of Science Fiction', in G. E. Slusser, Eric S. Rabkin and Robert Scholes, eds., *Coordinates: Placing Science Fiction and Fantasy*, Carbondale: Southern Illinios University Press, 1983

Franklin, H. Bruce, *Robert A. Heinlein: America as Science Fiction*, Oxford and New York: Oxford University Press, 1980

Foucault, Michel, *Archaeology of Knowledge, The*, London: Tavistock, 1972

Frye, Northrop, *Anatomy of Criticism. Four Essays*, [1957] Princeton University Press, 1973

Future, Perth: University of Western Australia Press, 2001

Gawron, Jean Mark, *Dream of Glass*, New York: Harcourt, 1993

Gernsback, Hugo, *Ralph 124C41+*, [1911] University of Nebraska Press, 2000

Gibson, William, and Bruce Sterling, *Difference Engine, The*, London: Gollancz, 1990

Gibson, William, *Burning Chrome*, London: Gollancz, 1986

Gibson, William, *Count Zero*, London: Gollancz, 1986

Gibson, William, *Mona Lisa Overdrive*, London: Gollancz, 1988

Gibson, William, *Neuromancer*, London: Gollancz, 1984

Goldsworthy, Peter, *Honk if You Are Jesus,* Sydney: HarperCollins, 1992

Gotschalk, Felix, *Growing Up in Tier 3000*, New York: Ace, 1975

Graff, Gerald, *Literature Against Itself*, Chicago: University of Chicago Press, 1979

Gray, Curme, *Murder in Millennium VI*, Chicago: Shasta, 1951

Greenland, Colin, *Entropy Exhibition, The: Michael Moorcock and the British `New Wave' in science fiction*, Routledge & Kegan Paul, 1983

Greenland, Colin, *Take Back Plenty*, London: Unwin, 1990

Grossbach, Robert, *A Shortage of Engineers*, New York: St. Martin's Press, 2001

Gunn, James, ed., *Road to Science Fiction, The, Vol. 1: From Gilgamesh to Wells*, Mentor Books, 1977

Gunn, James, ed., *Road To Science Fiction, The, Vol. 5: The British Way*, Clarkston, GA: White Wolf Publishing, 1998

Gunn, James, *Isaac Asimov: The Foundations of Science Fiction*, Oxford University Press, 1982

Haldeman, Joe, *Forever Free*, New York: Ace, 1999

Haldeman, Joe, *Forever Peace*, New York: Ace, 1997

Haldeman, Joe, *Forever War, The*, New York: St. Martin's Press, 1975

Hall, Sandi, *Wingwomen of Hera: Book One of the Cosmic Botanists Trilogy*, San Francisco, Spinsters/Aunt Lute, 1987

Halperin, James L., *First Immortal, The*, New York: Del Rey, 1998

Harness, Charles, *Paradox Men, The*, [1949, 1953] New York: Crown, 1984

Harrison, Harry, *Make Room! Make Room!*, New York: Doubleday, 1966

Harrison, M. John, `The Lamia and Lord Cromis', in Michael Moorcock, ed., *New Worlds 1*, London: Sphere, 1971

Harrison, M. John, `Settling the World', in Gunn, ed., (1998)

Harrison, M. John, *Centauri Device, The*, London: Granada, 1975

Harrison, M. John, *Light*, London: Gollancz, 2002

Harrison, M. John, *In Viriconium*, London: Gollancz, 1982

Harrison, M. John, *Pastel City, The*, London: New English Library, 1971

Harrison, M. John, *Storm of Wings, A*, London: Sphere, 1980,

Harrison, M. John, *Viriconium Nights*, London: Gollancz, 1985

Hartwell, David G., *Age of Wonders: Exploring the World of Science Fiction*, [1984] McGraw-Hill, 1985

Hartwell, David G., and Damien Broderick, *Centaurus: Best of Australian Science Fiction*, New York: Tor, 1999

Heinlein, Robert A., `Gulf', *Astounding Science Fiction*, Nov-Dec, 1949; in *Assignment in Eternity*, London: New English Library, 1971

Heinlein, Robert A., `The Unpleasant Profession of Jonathan Hoag', [1942] in *The Unpleasant Profession of Jonathan Hoag*, Harmondsworth: Penguin, 1966

Heinlein, Robert A., *Cat Who Walks Through Walls, The*, New York: Putnam, 1985

Heinlein, Robert A., *Door Into Summer, The*, New York: Doubleday, 1957

Heinlein, Robert A., *Friday*, New York: Holt, Rinehart and Winston, 1982

Heinlein, Robert A., *Job: A Comedy of Justice*, New York: Del Rey, 1984

Heinlein, Robert A., *Methuselah's Children*, New York: Gnome Press, 1958

Heinlein, Robert A., *Moon is a Harsh Mistress, The*, New York: Putnam, 1966

Heinlein, Robert A., *Number of the Beast—, The*, New York: Fawcett, 1980

Heinlein, Robert A., *Puppet Masters, The*, [1951] London: Pan, 1969

Heinlein, Robert A., *Starship Troopers*, New York: Putnam, 1959

Heinlein, Robert A., *Time Enough for Love*, New York: Putnam, 1973

Heinlein, Robert A., *To Sail Beyond the Sunset*, New York: Ace/Putnam, 1987

Herbert, Frank, *Chapter House Dune*, New York: Putnam, 1985

Herbert, Frank, *Dune*, New York: Chilton, 1965

Herbert, Frank, *God-Emperor of Dune*, New York: Putnam, 1981

Herbert, Frank, *Heretics of Dune*, New York: Putnam, 1984

Herbert, Frank, *White Plague, The*, New York: Putnam, 1982

Herr, Michael, *Walter Winchell*, London: Chatto & Windus, 1990

Hofstadter, Douglas R., *Gödel Escher Bach: An Eternal Golden Braid*, New York: Basic Books, 1979

Hofstadter, Douglas R., *Metamagical Themas: Questing for the Essence of Mind and Pattern*, New York: Basic Books, 1985

Ikin, Van, *Australian Science Fiction*, St. Lucia: University of Queensland Press, 1982

Irving, John, *Hotel New Hampshire, The*, London: Cape, 1981

Jablokov, Alexander, *Nimbus*, New York: Avon, 1993

Jakubowski, Maxim and Malcolm Edwards, *Complete Book of Science Fiction and Fantasy Lists, The*, Granada, 1983

Jameson, Fredric, *Prison-House of Language: A Critical Account of Structuralism and Russian Formalism, The* Princeton University Press, 1972

Kellaway, Frank, `Visions of conflict', *Overland*, 87, May 1983, 9-13

Keyes, Daniel, *Flowers for Algernon*, [1959, 1966] Gollancz, 1987

Knight, Damon, *In Search of Wonder: Essays on Modern Science Fiction*, 2nd edition, Chicago: Advent, 1967

Lake, David, *Ring of Truth*, Melbourne: Void, 1982

Laumer, Keith, *Worlds of the Imperium*, New York: Ace, 1962

Le Guin, Ursula K., *Compass Rose, The*, London: Gollancz, 1982

Le Guin, Ursula K., *Dispossessed, The*, London: Gollancz, 1974

Le Guin, Ursula K., *Telling, The*, New York: Harcourt, 2000

Le Guin, Ursula, *Dancing at the Edge of the World. Thoughts on Words, Women, Places*, London: Gollancz, 1989

Leiber, Fritz, *The Big Time* [1961], in *Ship of Shadows*, London: Gollancz, 1979

Lessing, Doris, *Canopus in Argos: Archives*, comprising *Shikasta; The Marriages Between Zones Three, Four and Five; The Sirian Experiments; The Making of the Representative for Planet 8; The Sentimental Agents*, London: Cape, 1979-83

Levenson, Barton Paul, `The Ideology of Robert A. Heinlein', *New York Review of Science Fiction*, 116, April 1998, 1-11

Malzberg, Barry, *Galaxies*, in Dann, et al, eds (1997)

McAuley, Paul, *Books of Confluence, The*, London: Gollancz, 1998-2000

McCarthy, Wil, *Collapsium, The*, New York: Del Rey, 2000

McCarthy, Wil, *Wellstone, The*, New York: Bantam Spectra, 2003

Moorcock, Michael, *Dancers at the End of Time, The*, [1981] Clarkston, GA: White Wolf, 1998

Moorcock, Michael, *History of the Runestaff, The,* comprises *The Jewel in the Skull, The Mad God's Amulet, The Sword of the Dawn,* and *The Runestaff* (London, Mayflower, 1969)

Moore, Ward, *Bring the Jubilee,* London: Heinemann, 1955

Moravec, Hans, *Mind Children,* Cambridge: Harvard University Press, 1988

Moravec, Hans, *Robot: Mere Machine to Transcendent Mind,* Oxford University Press, 1999

Murnane, Gerald, *The Plains,* Melbourne: Norstrilia, 1982

Morrow, James, *This is the Way the World Ends,* London: Gollancz, 1987

Nasir, Jamil, *Distance Haze,* New York: Bantam Spectra, 2000

Nasir, Jamil, *Tower of Dreams,* New York: Bantam Spectra, 1999

Nicholls, Peter, ed., `Monsters and the Critics', in *Explorations of the Marvellous,* Fontana, 1978 [first in Gollancz as *Science Fiction at Large,* 1976]

Niven, Larry, and Jerry Pournelle, *Footfall,* London: Sphere, 1986

Niven, Larry, and Jerry Pournelle, *Lucifer's Hammer,* London: Future, 1978

Oliver, Chad, *Winds of Time, The,* [1957] in Dann, et al, eds (1997)

O'Reilly, Timothy, *Frank Herbert,* Frederick Ungar, 1981

Orwell, George, *Animal Farm: a fairy story,* London: Longman, 1945

Orwell, George, *Nineteen Eighty-Four,* London: Secker & Warburg, 1949

Overbye, Dennis, *Lonely Hearts of the Cosmos: Story of the Scientific Quest for the Secret of the Universe,* HarperCollins, 1991

Padgett, Lewis, *Chessboard Planet,* [1946] New York: A Galaxy Novel, 1951

Palmer, David R., *Emergence,* [1984] London: New English Library, 1987

Pangborn, Edgar, *A Mirror for Observers,* [1954] Harmondsworth: Penguin: 1966

Panshin, Alexei, *Heinlein in Dimension,* Chicago: Advent, 1968

Panshin, Alexei, *Rite of Passage,* [1968] London: Sphere, 1970

Platt, Charles, *Dream Makers: Science Fiction and Fantasy Writers at Work,* London: Xanadu, 1983

Pohl, Fred, `Gold at the Starbow's End', in *Analog,* March 1972

Pohl, Fred, *Beyond the Blue Event Horizon,* New York: Del Rey, 1980

Pohl, Fred, *Coming of the Quantum Cats, The,* London: Gollancz, 1987

Pohl, Fred, *Cool War, The,* New York: Del Rey, 1981

Pohl, Fred, *Gateway,* New York: St. Martin's, 1977

Pohl, Fred, *HeeChee Rendezvous,* New York: Ballantine Del Rey, 1984

Pohl, Fred, *Man Plus*, [1976] London: Gollancz, 1976

Pohl, Fred, *Merchants' War, The*, [1984] London: Gollancz, 1985

Pohl, Fred, *Other End of Time, The*, New York: Tor, 1996

Pohl, Fred, *Starburst*, London: Gollancz, 1982

Pohl, Fred, *Years of the City, The*, [1984] London: Gollancz, 1985

Pohl, Frederik and C. M. Kornbluth, *Space Merchants, The*, [1953] Wendover: Goodchild, 1984

Potter, Dennis, *Singing Detective, The*, London: Faber, 1986

Proust, Marcel, *Time Regained*, Book VII, Vol. III, *Remembrance of Things Past*, trans. C. K. Scott Moncrieff and Terence Kilmartin; and by Andreas Mayor, New York: Random House, 1981

Pullman, Philip, *His Dark Materials*, London: Scholastic, 2001

Roth, Philip, *Deception*, London: Cape, 1990

Roth, Philip, *The Human Stain*, London: Cape, 2000

Rottensteiner, Franz, `Mr. Budrys and the Active Life', in *exploding madonna*, ed. John Foyster, 6, April 1969

Rottensteiner, Franz, `Chewing gum for the vulgar, in the Australian fanzine *Journal of Omphalistic Epistemology*, ed. John Foyster, 1, July 1969, pp. 2-15; translated and revised by Rottensteiner from *Quarber Merker* 17, pp. 64-75, n.d.

Rousseau, Yvonne, review of Heinlein's *The Cat Who Walks . . .* , in *Australian Science Fiction Review*, vol. 1, 2, May 1986

Rucker, Rudy, `A Transrealist Manifesto', in *Seek! Selected Nonfiction*, [1983] New York: Four Walls, Eight Windows, 1999

Rucker, Rudy, *Software*, New York: Avon, 1982

Rucker, Rudy, *Wetware*, New York: Avon, 1988

Russ, Joanna, *Female Man, The*, New York: Bantam, 1975

Russell, Eric Frank, `Hobbyist', in Gunn, ed. (1998)

Sacks, Oliver, *An Anthropologist on Mars*, Sydney: Picador, 1995

Sagan, Carl, *Cosmic Connection, The*, New York: Dell, 1975

Scholes, Robert, *Structuralism in Literature*, New Haven, Yale, 1974

Shiras, Wilmar, *Children of the Atom*, New York: Doubleday, 1953

Shute, Nevil, *On the Beach*, Melbourne: Heinemann, 1957

Silverberg, `The Making of a Science-Fiction Writer', in *Worlds of Wonder*

Silverberg, Robert, *Cube Root of Uncertainty, The*, New York: Macmillan, 1970

Silverberg, Robert, *Dying Inside*, New York: Scribner, 1972

Silverberg, Robert, *Face of the Waters, The*, New York: Bantam, 1991

Silverberg, Robert, *Science Fiction 101*, see *Worlds of Wonder*

Silverberg, Robert, *Shadrach in the Furnace*, New York: Bobbs-Merrill, 1976

Silverberg, Robert, *Son of Man*, New York: Ballantine, 1971

Silverberg, Robert, *Stochastic Man, The*, New York: Harper & Row, 1975

Silverberg, Robert, *Worlds of Wonder*, London: Gollancz, 1988

Simak, Clifford, *Ring Around the Sun*, [1952] London: New English Library, 1977

Simmons, Dan, `Metastasis', in Winter (1989)

Smith, Cordwainer, `Alpha Ralpha Boulevard' [1961] , in Smith, 1963

Smith, Cordwainer, `Ballad of Lost C'Mell, The,' [1962], in Smith, 19651963

Smith, Cordwainer, `Burning of the Brain, The,' [1958] , in Smith, 1963

Smith, Cordwainer, `Game of Rat and Dragon, The,' [1955] , in Smith,

Smith, Cordwainer, *Norstrilia*, New York: Ballantine, 1975.

Smith, Cordwainer, *Space Lords*, New York: Pyramid, 1965

Smith, Cordwainer, *You Will Never Be the Same*, New York: Berkley, 1963

Smith, George O., *Fourth R, The*, New York: Lancer, 1959 (as *The Brain Machine*)

Smith, Michael Marshall, *Spares*, New York: Bantam Books, 1997

Spinrad, Norman, *The Void Captain's Tale*, New York: Timescape, 1983

Spinrad, Norman, *Child of Fortune*, New York: Bantam Spectra, 1985

Stableford, Brian, `And He not Busy Being Born,' in Gunn (1998)

Stableford, Brian, `The Final Chapter of the Sociology of Science fiction', *Foundation*, 79, Smmer 2000, 41-58

Stapledon, Olaf, *Last and First Men: A Story of the Near and Far Future*, [1930] Harmondsworth: Penguin, 1963

Stapledon, Olaf, *Odd John*, [1932] Harmondsworth: Penguin, 1972

Stapledon, Olaf, *Star Maker*, [1937] London: New English Library, 1978

Sterling, Bruce, *Crystal Express*, London: Legend, 1990

Sterling, Bruce, *Holy Fire*, London: Millennium, 1996

Sterling, Bruce, *Schismatrix*, Harmondsworth: Penguin, 1986

Strieber, Whitley, and James Kunetka, *Nature's End*, London: Grafton, 1986

Strieber, Whitley, and James Kunetka, *Warday*, London: Hodder & Stoughton, 1984

Strieber, Whitley, *Communion*, London: Century, 1987

Strieber, Whitley, *Confirmation: Hard Evidence of Aliens Among Us?* New York: St. Martins, 1998

Strieber, Whitley, *Hunger, The*, [1981] New York: Avon, 1988

Strieber, Whitley, *Lilith's Dream: A Tale of the Vampire Life*, [2002] New York: Pocket, 2003

Strieber, Whitley, *Transformation,* London: Century, 1988

Strieber, Whitley, *Wolfen, The*, New York: Bantam, 1978

Sturgeon, Theodore, `The Other Man', [1956], in Sturgeon, 1972

Sturgeon, Theodore, `Skills of Xanadu', [1956], in Sturgeon, 1972

Sturgeon, Theodore, `Touch of Your Hand', [1953] in Sturgeon, 1978

Sturgeon, Theodore, *More than Human*, [1954] London: Gollancz, 1986

Sturgeon, Theodore, *Touch of Strange, A*, [1958] Feltham, Middlesex: Hamlyn, 1978

Sturgeon, Theodore, *Worlds of Theodore Sturgeon, The*, New York: Ace, 1972

Swanwick, Michael, *Stations of the Tide*, New York: Ace, 1991

Swanwick, Michael, *Vacuum Flowers*, New York: Ace, 1988

Thompson, E. P., *Making of the English Working Class, The*, London: Gollancz, 1963

Thompson, E. P., *Poverty of Theory, & other essays, The*, London: Merlin Press, 1978

Thompson, E. P., *Sykaos Papers, The*, London: Bloomsbury, 1988

Tiedemann, Mark W., *Asimov's Aurora*, New York: ibooks, 2002

Tiedemann, Mark W., *Asimov's Chimera*, New York: ibooks, 2001

Tiedemann, Mark W., *Asimov's Mirage*, New York: ibooks, 2000

Tucker, Wilson, *Year of the Quiet Sun, The*, [1970] in Dann, et al, eds (1997)

Turner, George, `Some unperceived wisdom', *Overland*, 87, May 1983, 14-19

Turner, George, *Beloved Son*, London: Faber and Faber, 1978

Turner, George, *Cupboard Under The Stairs, The*, London: Cassell, 1962

Turner, George, *Drowning Towers, The*, New York: William Morrow, 1988

Turner, George, *Genetic Soldier*, New York: Morrow/AvoNova, 1994

Turner, George, *In the Heart or in the Head*, Melbourne: Norstrilia, 1984

Turner, George, *Sea and Summer, The*, London: Faber, 1987

Turner, George, *Vaneglory*, London: Faber and Faber, 1981.

Turner, George, *Yesterday's Men*, London: Faber and Faber, 1983.

Turner, George, *Young Man of Talent*, London: Cassell, 1959

van Vogt, A. E., *Slan*, [1953] London: Panther, 1960

van Vogt, A. E., *Voyage of the Space Beagle, The*, in Dann, et al., (1998)

Vance, Jack, *Dying Earth, The*, [1950] London, Grenada, 1972

Vance, Jack, *Emphyrio*, New York: Doubleday, 1969

Vance, Jack, *To Live Forever*, [1956] London: Grafton, 1987

Varley, John, *Golden Globe, The*, New York: Ace, 1998

Varley, John, *Steel Beach*, New York: AcePutnam, 1992

Vidal, Gore, *Kalki*, New York: Random House, 1978

Vidal, Gore, *Messiah*, New York: Dutton, 1954

Vinge, Joan, *Snow Queen, The*, London: Sidgwick and Jackson, 1980

Vinge, Vernor, *A Deepness in the Sky*, New York: Tor, 1999

Vinge, Vernor, *A Fire Upon the Deep*, New York: Tor, 1991

Vinge, Vernor, *Marooned in Real-Time*, New York: Bluejay, 1986

Vonnegut, Kurt, *Mother Night*, New York: Gold Medal, 1962

Wallace, Ian, *Croyd*, New York: Berkley, 1967

Wallace, Ian, *Dr. Orpheus*, New York: Berkley, 1968

Watson, Ian, *Book of Being, The*, London: Gollancz, 1985

Watson, Ian, *Book of the River, The*, London: Gollancz, 1984

Watson, Ian, *Book of the Stars, The*, London: Gollancz, 1984

Watson, Ian, *Chekhov's Journey*, London: Gollancz, 1983

Watson, Ian, *Converts*, London: Panther, 1984

Watson, Ian, *Embedding, The*, London: Gollancz, 1973

Watson, Ian, *God's World*, London: Gollancz, 1979

Watson, Ian, *Jonah Kit, The*, New York: Scribner, 1975

Watson, Ian, *Martian Inca, The*, London: Gollancz, 1977

Watson, Ian, *Miracle Visitors*, London: Gollancz, 1978

Watson, Ian, *Sunstroke*, London: Gollancz, 1982

Wells, Earl, `Robert A. Heinlein: EPIC Crusader,' *New York Review of Science Fiction,* 56, April 1993

Wells, H. G., *Time Machine, The*, [1895] London: Chancellor Press, 1983

Wheatley, Dennis, *Star of Ill-Omen*, London: Hutchinson, 1952

Williams, Walter Jon, *Aristoi*, London: Grafton, 1993

Winter, Douglas E., ed, *Dark Visions*, London: Gollancz, 1989

Wodhams, Jack, *Future War*, Melbourne: Cory and Collins, 1982

Wodhams, Jack, *Ryn*, Melbourne: Cory and Collins, 1982

Wolfe, Gene, `Hero as Werwolf', in *The Island of Doctor Death and Other Stories and Other Stories, The*, New York: Pocket Books, 1980

Wolfe, Gene, *Book of the New Sun*, New York: Timescape/Pocket Books, 1980-83

Wolfe, Gene, *Castle of the Otter, The,* Shingletown, CA: Ziesing, 1982

Wolfe, Gene, *Fifth Head of Cerberus, The*, London: Gollancz, 1973

Wolfe, Gene, *Free Live Free: A Fantasy*, London: Gollancz, 1985

Wolfe, Gene, *Peace*, [1975] New York: Berkley, 1982

Wolfe, Gene, *There Are Doors*, New York: Tor, 1988

Wolfe, Gene, *Urth of the New Sun, The* London: Gollancz, 1987

Womack, Jack, *Ambient*, London: Unwin Hyman, 1988

Wright, John C., *Golden Age: A Romance of the Far Future, The*, New York: Tor, 2002

Zebrowski, George, *Brute Orbits*, New York: HarperPrism, 1998

Zebrowski, George, *Cave of Stars*, New York: HarperPrism, 1999

Zebrowski, George, *Macrolife*, New York: Harper, 1979

Zebrowski, George, *Swift Thoughts*, Urbana, Il.: Golden Gryphon Press, April 2002

Zelazny, `For a Breath I Tarry', in *Last Defender of Camelot, The*, New York: Pocket Books, 1980

Zindell, David, *Broken God, The,* London: 1994

Zindell, David, *Neverness,* London: Grafton, HarperCollins, 1989

Zindell, David, *War in Heaven,* New York: Bantam Spectra, 1998

Zindell, David, *Wild, The,* New York: Bantam Spectra, 1996

Zoline, Pamela, `The Heat Death of the Universe', 1967, in Broderick (2001)

Index, x, y, z, t:
Dimensions of Science Fiction

www.ingramcontent.com/pod-product-compliance
Lightning Source LLC
Chambersburg PA
CBHW030714110426
42739CB00029B/115